Why You Can Have Confidence in the Bible:
A Helpful, Trustworthy Resource

"Harold J. Sala has dedicated his entire li[...] ble 'build themselves up in their holy faith' b[...] [...]ving that God
means what He says. Thi[...] ok—I heartily
recommend it!"

Tim LaHaye
[...]nd coauthor of LEFT BEHIND

"Dr. Sala...makes the most profound ideas very simple to grasp—and even
very difficult truth is irresistibly sweet...he explains why Scripture is trustworthy and why it is important to embrace—and obey—the truth of the
Bible. I love his infectious joy and confidence in God's Word. This book is
a real treasure."

John MacArthur
President, Master's College and Seminary; pastor and Bible teacher

"If you are looking for a life-changing confidence-lifter on the Word of God,
this is a book for you. I know of no more helpful bridge to confidence in
the Christian life than the truth expressed in this book, linking apologetic
evidence and practical Christian living."

Norman L. Geisler, Ph.D.
Author; apologist; Dean, Southern Evangelical Seminary

"A thorough resource that will answer your questions and renew your faith
in the Holy Bible and give you the confidence you need to stand up to the
challenges against biblical truth and authenticity. ...Clearly explained, comprehensive and helpful; this book is a must-read."

Greg Laurie
Pastor and evangelist, Harvest Christian Fellowship

"Sala combines scholarly research with fascinating historical illustrations to
uncover a book that has shaped the lives of countless over the centuries and
one that has life-changing relevance for today. I commend his work to you
with much appreciation for his insight."

Ravi Zacharias
Author and speaker

Why You Can Have
Confidence
in the BIBLE

Harold J. Sala

HARVEST HOUSE PUBLISHERS

EUGENE, OREGON

Cover by Left Coast Design, Portland, Oregon

Cover photo © Alloy Photography / Veer; Back cover author photo © vasquezstudios.com

WHY YOU CAN HAVE CONFIDENCE IN THE BIBLE
Copyright © 2008 by Harold J. Sala
Published by Harvest House Publishers
Eugene, Oregon 97402
www.harvesthousepublishers.com

Library of Congress Cataloging-in-Publication Data

Sala, Harold J.
Why you can have confidence in the Bible / Harold J. Sala.
    p. cm.
Includes bibliographical references.
ISBN-13: 978-0-7369-2343-9 (pbk.)
ISBN-10: 0-7369-2343-8 (pbk.)
1. Bible—Evidences, authority, etc. 2. Apologetics. 3. Bible—Inspiration. I. Title.
BS480.S243 2008
220.1'3—dc22

2007028656

Lovingly I dedicate this book to my seven grandsons—
William and Andrew Craddick; Ryan, Cole,
and Carson Deushane; Christian and Corey Sala—
and my sole granddaughter, Taylor Deushane
(whom I call "Princess").

May the Book I have written about encourage your hearts,
guide your steps, and give you a staunch faith
in a sovereign God who sent His Son to redeem us,
just as it has for your parents, your grandparents,
and your great-grandparents.

And may confidence in God's Word be your heritage,
one that you pass on to your children, and they
in turn, pass on to their children after them.

Acknowledgments

Like most authors, I have written this book standing on the shoulders of a significant number of individuals who gave of themselves in helping me develop a love for the Bible and understand its true greatness and uniqueness. I am indebted to them not only because of the knowledge they conveyed in a classroom, but also because of the manner in which they shared their hearts and lives one-on-one and lived out the message they espoused.

Three professors deeply influenced me—Daniel Krusich, whose rich knowledge of biblical text helped me realize this was no ordinary book and transmitted an awe and love for the Bible that has never dimmed; Marshall Neal, a no-nonsense scholar whose academic excellence was balanced with a measure of humor, common sense, and wisdom; and Timothy Lin, whose life brought together scholarship and piety and gave me a lifelong role model that has served me well.

I also want to acknowledge the contributions of Bonnie Sala Craddick, who edited and critiqued the manuscript, along with Dorothy Jean Furlong, who proofed the manuscript and made valuable suggestions. Beng Alba has also greatly contributed to this book by smoothing rough spots and clarifying what seemed unclear. My thanks goes to Ray Vigneault for his suggestions on the chapter on science and God. I am also grateful to Thurman Wisdom, who carefully evaluated the chapter on manuscripts, as well as Elizabeth Trever, the wife of the first American to see the very important Isaiah manuscript found in Qumran. She graciously met with me, giving me personal insights about the intriguing drama that unfolded when God allowed centuries-old manuscripts to escape their dark hiding places to emerge in a twentieth-century world dominated by scientific skepticism.

My thanks also goes to the men who graciously endorsed this book, and the publisher, whose faith in the subject I've written about cements a common bond of understanding.

Contents

Coming to Grips
with the Bible

It has been called the most beautiful book ever written. Its name: *The Book of Kells*. And who was Kells? More properly the question should be, "Where was Kells?" Kells was a village in Ireland where dedicated scribes living in its monasteries in County Meath painstakingly copied the pages of the first four books of the New Testament. They decorated the pages with the most exquisite calligraphy ever done, with pictures rivaling those in the finest museums of the world. And this was done by nameless monks between the seventh to ninth centuries using dyes made from local products, long before the advancements of the modern era.

Eventually this magnificent work made its way to Trinity College Library in Dublin, Ireland, where it is on public display today. When I stopped in Dublin on my way back from Ukraine, this old book was number one on my must-see list.

As I stood in line with people from various nations, I thought, *This is remarkable. Here we are standing in line on a chilly morning, waiting to see a book that was written and decorated almost 1,200 years ago.* Then I began thinking of the dedicated scribes who painstakingly copied

Jerome's Vulgate translation into Latin, cutting the sheets of animal skin, known as vellum, into pieces (we would call them pages) about 9 by 13 inches, preparing the covers of wood overlaid with leather.

Long before Stephen Langton, the Archbishop of Canterbury, put divisions of chapters into the text of the Bible in the late thirteenth century, these monks made notations by inserting slight pin marks in the text. The colors are remarkably well preserved, and how these gifted men ever conceived something so intricate and yet so beautiful is part of the mystery that surrounds it today. Never putting their names to their work, they emphasized the importance of what they were writing and drawing.

Then I also thought of the centuries-old religious battles that have racked Ireland, along with the rest of the world, as the advice of Jesus to love your neighbor and your enemy was pushed aside. It was as if the Book had been placed in a library under glass, well preserved but not easily accessible, and certainly not taken to heart or obeyed.

The pages of *The Book of Kells* are replete with artists' renditions that illustrate the text—creation, angels, beasts and demons, saints and sinners, and, of course, Jesus and the disciples.

It is little wonder that even H.L. Mencken, an American critic sometimes described as "the American Nietzsche," called the Bible "probably the most beautiful piece of writing in all the literature of the world."[1]

❦

If I were to ask you, "What is the most important book in the world?" you would probably say "the Bible." After all, it's the bestseller in all history. But if I asked you if you read the Bible, more than likely you'd tell me, "Yeah, I read it once," or, "My wife reads it sometimes," or a similar answer. And if I asked you what impact the Bible has had on your life, you might be at a loss to tell me.

You might point out, "Hey, I know a lot of people who claim to be Christians, but their lives aren't any different than mine. They fight with their wives, get divorced, drink too much on weekends, use drugs, get depressed—well, they're no different from me. So why read the Bible?"

You're right! It's true that, even among those who own a Bible and attend church with some regularity, there are many whose lives are about the same as those who never dust off the cover of the Book. Buddhists burn incense and Muslims pray five times daily and some Christians only keep a Bible as a kind of good-luck charm. There is little difference in the private lives of many who claim to be Christians and those who don't. Why?

In my experience, the chief reason, in practical terms, that the Bible seems "irrelevant" in people's lives today is that they have never come to grips with whether or not God is truly the author—whether the Bible is inspired by God or is at best simply a book of religious teachings that good men have put together over the years or, at worst, a religious book based on myths and legends. But if there is a compelling case for the authenticity of the Book, demonstrating that it *is* inspired by God Himself, we can hardly afford to ignore what it says.

Though you may have never actually said the words, you may be thinking while reading the Bible, *Can I really trust this Book?* This is a legitimate question. In fact, it may be the most important question you have ever asked in your life.

Would you take just a couple of hours to walk with me across some bridges that can answer your question? More than 3,000 years ago the writer of Proverbs said that to answer a matter before you hear the facts is folly and shame (Proverbs 18:13). It's still true!

With an open mind, take a look at some of the evidence and then decide for yourself as to whether or not God has spoken. Once you have rationally considered the evidence, it is quite likely, when you read what God has said in the Bible, you will never again want to respond, "So what?"

Harold J Sala

CHAPTER ONE

Can This Book Be Trusted?

"The truth is that the light which shines in this incredible Book simply cannot be put out."

—MALCOLM MUGGERIDGE

Gilbert Keith Chesterton was someone I would like to have met. He was a giant of a man, a brilliant intellectual, writer, and critic. This larger-than-life British journalist had a voracious appetite, smoked cigars, and weighed nearly 300 pounds. He was also a heavyweight in the literary world. He had a keen grasp of human nature and a sharp tongue that often cut to the bone. People either loved him or hated him. No one was indifferent towards him.

On one occasion he was asked, "What book would you like if you were to be cast adrift on a lonely island in the Pacific and were permitted to have only one book?" A friend, knowing him to be a religious man, volunteered, "I suppose you would choose the Bible."

"No, not this time," he smiled.

Another friend ventured, "I'd wager you would take a copy of Shakespeare."

"You are wrong," said Chesterton.

"What would you choose then?" they pressed.

"If I were stranded on a lonely island in the Pacific, the book I would choose of all the books in the world would be one entitled *A Manual on How to Build a Ship.*"

Yet Chesterton, an intensely practical and devout Christian, would no doubt have agreed that when it comes to navigating the turbulent, dark waters of life in the twenty-first century nothing compares with the *Bible.* The Bible is the only book in the world that shows us how to escape the gravitational pull of our old natures which drags us into a quagmire of human failure.

In his book *Alone,* first published in 1938, Admiral Richard E. Byrd tells of spending a long arctic winter at Latitude 80° 08' south—on the Ross Ice Barrier, on a line between Little America and the South Pole. Spending three months there in a nether twilight wasn't an exciting thought. Byrd's original plan was to have three men do the scientific experiments while living near the South Pole in a small hut. Two men, he thought, could argue, "leaving the mark of Cain in the heart," as he described it. When logistics prevented the execution of the original plan, Byrd took it upon himself to be the sole person who would man the small base.

No one was ever more alone than Richard Byrd during that grueling four-and-a-half months, with temperatures hovering 50 to 60 below zero and ferocious storms with strong winds threatening his very survival.

On one occasion Byrd had been cooped up in the small hut through a terrible storm, and having "cabin fever," he felt he would go crazy if he didn't go outside for a breath of air. Little did he realize at the time that a vent pipe from a stove that was malfunctioning was producing carbon dioxide that left him with delusions and mental fatigue.

Bundling up against the cold, he dressed as warmly as possible, took his walking stick and began briskly striding across the snow-crusted ice. Snow was falling, covering his tracks almost as quickly as his boot marked the footprint. Suddenly Byrd realized he had gone far enough that the hut could no longer be seen and there were no tracks in the snow to retrace.

He quickly realized that, should he fail to find the hut, he would wander aimlessly for a few hours at most and then fall to the ice in the perpetual sleep of death. No one was within hundreds of miles to come looking for him. He had instructed the last of his team, "I give you a hard-and-fast order not to come for me until a month after the sun returns."[1]

The true measure of the man was that he did not panic. Using the heel of his boot, he chipped away shards of pack ice, known as *sastrugi*. Then he stacked them one on top of the other, making a tower that could be a reference point. Using his flashlight as a stick, he scratched an arrow in the snow pointing the way he had come. Only then did he do an about-face and begin walking in the direction from which he had come (or thought he had). Byrd knew that without a fixed point of reference, he could miss the tiny shack and he would be lost.

He would walk until the ice tower was about to fade from his sight. Then he'd stop, retrace his steps, and change directions ever so slightly. He did this several times, each time with anxiety growing in his heart. "That miserable pile of snow was nothing to rejoice over," he wrote, "but at least it kept me from feeling that I was stabbing blindfolded."[2] He tried again—nothing! "You're lost now," he told himself. He made another pile, then took 30 steps more. Finally, faintly in the distance, he saw the hut. Never did a king's palace look as good as the little hut where there was food and warmth.

For centuries the Bible has been a fixed point of reference, and no matter how far society and individuals have strayed, the Bible has yet served as a guide for human conduct, a moral framework producing a sense of right and wrong, a source of truth, an inspiration for the world's great art, music, and literature, and has provided guidelines for personal behavior. Whether or not its directives were followed or ignored, it was still there—a kind of Rock-of-Gibraltar bulwark of truth against which almost everything is measured.

The Book has been translated into literally thousands of languages. A knowledge of this book has been an integral part of the erudition of Western education and has played a prominent part in society and civilization. A portion of the book of Psalms was the first work to be printed with movable type by the German inventor Johann Gutenberg in Mainz, Germany, around the year 1450.

In 1971 when Astronaut Ed Mitchell went into space as part of the crew of *Apollo 14,* he took with him the first book to go into space—a Bible. A King James version of the Bible—a small piece of micro-film about two-and-a-half inches square, having been reduced 62,000 times, containing 773,746 words, could be easily read, provided the reader wore glasses with the ability to magnify the text 100 times.

American presidents take the oath of office swearing to uphold the constitution as they place one hand on the Bible and raise the other hand affirming, "So help me God."

In the Nazi Holocaust thousands of men and women went to their deaths quoting the words of Psalm 23, "The Lord is my shepherd," or Psalm 91, "He who dwells in the secret place of the most high shall abide under the shadow of the Almighty." Untold millions of people pray, "Our Father who art in heaven, hallowed be thy name…" or quote the great chapter on love found in 1 Corinthians 13.

In 1968 an American naval vessel strayed into territorial waters claimed by North Korea, and a handful of North Korean soldiers took the vessel. Aboard were 70 crew members and seven officers. What followed was described by some of the men as 11 months of hell. After a few weeks of captivity, the men began to put together a

Bible of sorts—pieces of toilet paper with as many verses of Scripture written on them as could be cited from memory. The toilet-paper Bible was then circulated among the men for comfort and strength. I suspect that there were some pretty strange omissions and revisions of the text, but the words brought comfort and hope to the men.

In January 1979 Chinese leader Deng Xiaoping went on a fishing expedition—no, not off the coast of China but to the U.S. Among other things he was fishing for were military hardware, computer technology, and industrialization, and his quest took him to the office of the President of the United States, Jimmy Carter.

Carter, a professed Christian as well as a Baptist Sunday-school teacher, kept a well-marked Bible on his desk. Surprised to find a Bible on the desk of one of the most powerful men in the world, Deng commented about the book. Seizing the moment, President Carter told Deng that this was the Book that had made America great. Then, as American presidents seem empowered to do, he lectured Deng *ex cathedra* about letting missionaries back into China.

Deng didn't exactly get the message. Upon his return home, however, he allowed the Bamboo Curtain, which had been firmly in place since Communists took over, to gradually lift—a kind of trade-off for what he wanted. In 1979 I was among the first 10,000 foreigners allowed into China. At that time only two churches were open in all of China—one in Beijing and one in Shanghai. No Chinese would dare enter those churches. I remember peering into the church at Shanghai then, with its polished pews almost empty, save for a few foreigners who were attending.

At that time, "watchers" with their red armbands as badges of authority observed neighborhoods to ensure there was no contact between the foreigners and locals. Only the bravest would approach a foreigner for conversation. Such was the young man who stopped one of the members of our group and after a few hesitant phrases in English softly asked, "Do you have a Bible with you?" (At the time, Bibles, having been banned by the Communist government, were extremely scarce.)

The English tourist replied, "Yes, I have one." And the dialogue went on like this:

"Do you have it with you?"

"No; it's at home where I live in England."

"Do you read your Bible?"

"No, not really; it's simply part of my library."

Puzzled, the young man asked, "If you have a Bible, why don't you read it?"

A Book taken seriously?

The young man's question is one that many of us today need to confront. For years the Bible has been and still is the bestselling book in the world, yet there is little evidence to indicate it is among the world's best-read books. To the contrary, researcher George Barna contends that 93 percent of us own Bibles, yet less than half of those who own one ever read it. Another researcher, George Gallup Jr., agrees with him. As the result of his research, he says, "People revere the Bible, but they don't read it—that's what it comes down to."

How seriously do people take the counsel and advice found in this book? Consider this:

- There are slightly more divorces in the Christian community than in the secular world in spite of the fact that many churches strive to dissuade congregants from divorcing, according to pollster George Barna. The rationale is, "God doesn't want me unhappy and, besides, if I'm doing wrong, He'll forgive me."

- Statistics indicate that Christian singles are about as sexually active as non-Christians.

- Ignoring what is clearly taught in Scripture accounts for the fact that there is very little difference in business ethics and morals whether you are an atheist, a Buddhist, a Muslim, or a Christian.

• Christians compartmentalize their faith, separating it from their behavior when they rationalize that it's OK to use bootlegged software or download "free" songs—ignoring the fact that they are being stolen and justifying the whole thing by saying, "Of course, I knew it was illegal, *but I didn't think it was wrong.*" Following the examples of their parents' generation, teens reason, "If everybody is doing it, then I might as well get on the bandwagon too." Says Geoff Boucher, a *Los Angeles Times* staff writer, "Surveys show that born-again Christian teens are just as active in stealing and swapping music as their secular peers who pinch the latest Eminem rap hit or Kelly Clarkson power ballad."[3]

The problem with ignorance

You can be ignorant about many things and get along quite nicely. You can hire technicians to fix your computer, ask specialists to diagnose and cure your medical problems, hire consultants and marketing experts, tap think tanks, and find someone who knows what you don't; but when you have an ignorance of the Bible you become vulnerable to a host of doubts, conjectures, and uncertainty regarding some of the great issues of life.

Take for example the shock waves created by the dropping of a literary bomb: *The Da Vinci Code* by author Dan Brown. Before you discount the vast number of people who have bought into this strange mixture of falsehood, conjecture, and warped history, consider the following facts:

• Since its release in 2003 *The Da Vinci Code* has been translated into 44 languages and has sold more than 40 million copies—nearly twice the number of Rick Warren's life-changing, bestselling *Purpose-Driven Life.*

- One year after its release, the book was declared a bestseller in 100 countries, while Doubleday, the publisher, called it "the all-time bestselling adult novel."[4]

- In late 2005 Brown was named as one of The World's 100 Most Influential People by *Time* magazine. Brown, as the bestselling fiction author in history, has made appearances on CNN, *The Today Show,* National Public Radio, and the Voice of America, as well as being featured or castigated on occasion in every major newspaper and publication in the world.

- The rights to the book were bought by Columbia Pictures and Imagine Entertainment. In 2006, the film *The Da Vinci Code*, starring Tom Hanks, was shown worldwide. In spite of the debunking of the film as neither factual nor historical, the number of visitors to the Louvre in Paris, where the book situates the scene of the crime, skyrocketed.

- Gary M. Burge, writing in *Christianity Today,* says,

> Though the general public is fascinated with the book's conjectures, *The Da Vinci Code* has merely brought into the open a heated discussion among scholars that is at least 50 years old. Among Dan Brown's more controversial claims are these:
>
> - Jesus had an intimate relationship with Mary Magdalene.
> - Jesus and Mary Magdalene were husband and wife.
> - Jesus and Mary Magdalene had children.
> - Church leaders (some mysterious Catholic order) hid the secret.

- Long-suppressed gospels—such as the Gospel of Mary, the Gospel of Thomas, and the Gospel of Philip—now are finally telling us the truth.[5]

While evangelical Christians and Catholics complained vociferously that the basic plots of the story were cleverly woven fabrications, many individuals bought into Brown's allegation that he had produced (in his own words) "scientific evidence that the New Testament is false testimony."[6]

Is the plot truth or fiction? *USA Today* said the book consists of historical facts with a contemporary storyline.[7] That, of course, is Brown's contention. He begins the book with the caption "FACT," alleging the following: "All descriptions of artwork, architecture, documents, and secret rituals in this novel are accurate."[8]

Are people convinced that the book is historically accurate, that they have been misled and deceived by organized religion, which purposely chose to put a spin on the truth to suit its purposes?

One out of every three Canadians who has read the book is now convinced there are descendants of Jesus and Mary Magdalene presently walking on planet Earth as the result of their sexual liaison, according to a survey by Decima Research, Inc.[9] Researcher George Barna says that 53 percent of Americans who have read the book have been helped in their "personal growth and understanding."[10]

Is the faith of some individuals shaken by what they have read or seen? Consider a letter addressed by a listener to the Radio Bible Class, an evangelical radio ministry:

> I don't know where else to turn. I pray to God that you can help me. I began to read the book by Dan Brown called *The Da Vinci Code.* It was an interesting book until I got to the part where he's talking about how Christianity began, how it's all false, and that Christianity is basically a lie and stolen from pagan religions. The secret societies, the Holy

Grail, the church changing facts, removing parts of the Bible. Is it all true?

So much of it makes sense. There were things that I had heard before and ignored. But now I have to know. Is the last 25+ years I've been a Christian all a lie? Was Jesus just a man? Did it all really happen? Was he married to Mary Magdalene? Is everything I was raised to believe just made up for the sake of money? I have to know...

Now I am doubting if there is a heaven, a God, and Jesus. Please help me! Please, in God's name, help me.[11]

If you confront what the Bible says, with the understanding that what God said is to be taken at face value and embraced, then neutrality about some issues is not an option. In simple terms the truth of this Book touches my life, my conduct, my attitudes, my money and how I spend it, as well as my thinking.

Many, of course, never get to that point. While vast numbers of people say they are Christians—and yes, own and carry Bibles to church with them—in reality they never fully confront what this Book says. They dance around it, spiritualize it, and consider it a benchmark or a lofty ideal, but impractical in the world in which we live. But most simply ignore the Bible, thus embracing situational ethics and weaving through the minefields of life hoping that they will not be discovered and embarrassed when society condemns their behavior.

So how do you know whether or not this Book should be taken at face value, whether or not it is the living Word of God, and whether or not its truth should serve as moral and spiritual guidelines for living? Answering those questions is what this book is about. Jesus made a promise. He said, "If anyone chooses to do God's will, he will find out whether my teaching comes from God or whether I speak on my own" (John 7:17).

Why is this Book important?

Consider the fact that no other book in the entire world...

1. introduces you to a God who is a loving Father—not an angry deity—who loves you, will forgive you, and will embrace you as His child in spite of your failures.

2. gives you a history of humankind from the time of creation.

3. contains hundreds of fleshed-out prophecies telling how the great drama of the ages will be played out, articulating the flow of nations, armies, and history.

4. makes claims to uniqueness and authority as does no other book ever written.

5. answers the most important questions that arise from the human heart:

    Who am I?
    Where did I come from?
    For what purpose was I created?
    Where do I go after I die?
    What should I value?

6. provides a basis and foundation for your faith.

7. brings you comfort in times of sorrow and encouragement in times of difficulty.

8. gives you hope that there is life beyond the grave and that heaven is a reality.

9. shows you God's purpose and will for your life.

10. produces benevolence and charity in the lives of those who practice its teaching.

There is one more issue—a bottom line confrontation that goes beyond the question of whether or not there is truth in this Book: "Is what this Book says compelling in my life? If I am God's child, if I am serious about Him who sent His Son to redeem me and has a better plan and purpose for my life than I would ever discover on my own, what impact or effect or compelling influence should the Bible have on my life?"

I have been broadcasting since 1963 and over the years I have received literally thousands of letters and e-mails and talked with hundreds of people who have come for counseling and personal help. They have poured out their hearts, telling of personal difficulties. The following are typical:

- "Six months ago my husband of 32 years left for a much younger woman. He told me that it was 'everything that he has always wanted.' Prior to this time he was president of the Sunday school class, head usher and never planned anything that would interfere with going to church on Sunday. For the past ten years I have taught a Bible seminar class. We are now divorced, and my husband believes the world is where it is at. I would appreciate your prayers."

- "My husband has left me and is pushing for a divorce. We've been married for five years and have three boys, 4, 3, and 1. Jim and I are both born-again Christians. We used to be very active in our church and close to our families."

- "I have just made the biggest mistake of my life. I cannot explain why I did what I did apart from the fact that I had too much to drink and didn't think about what I was doing. After I was at a business conference for three days, the department heads all met for a final dinner. First there were cocktails, then dinner, then after-dinner drinks. Bob and several of us then went for a walk. I ended up in his room and the next morning I could not believe that I did what I would have condemned in others. My husband John and I have been married for five years, have two boys, go to church together every Sunday. And besides that, we love each other. I don't know how to explain what happened."

- "For several years I have been in a committed relationship with a woman. Both of us care deeply about each other and feel offended that members of our church refuse to accept us, saying 'we are living in sin.' If God made us the way we are, and we both are Christians, why should not our church fellowship accept us as equals when God accepts us as we are?"

All of these heart cries come from people who claim to be believers in Jesus Christ. Yet they were willing to disregard everything they grew up with and what they say they believe, and were willing to trade their integrity for a feel-good-for-the-moment relationship, no matter what the Bible says about their actions.

An authority for life

Many people today, if asked whether or not they believe the Bible, would quickly say, "Yes, of course, I believe the Bible." But acknowledging it as authoritative with regard to their conduct is another matter.

In the realm of faith, the matter of authority is a red-hot issue. Who says that you should believe this or disbelieve that? By whose authority do you challenge long-held beliefs and practices? It seems to me that a lot of people today lack any real authority for what they believe. For example, why are you a Christian and not a Buddhist, or a Muslim, or an animist? Why do you believe what you do?

Some appeal to their experience, saying, "I feel it down in my heart!"

Josh McDowell, a onetime agnostic turned apologist, has asked over 1,400 young people whether or not they believe the Bible, and when they respond that they do, he asks, *"Why?"* While Josh says there are more than 50 legitimate answers to that question, only one person has ever given him an adequate answer.

Speaking to a group of 250 high-school seniors, Josh walked into the audience and singled out a 17-year-old young man who seemed to be a leader. The conversation went like this:

Josh: "Do you believe this [holding his Bible] is the Word of God?"

Student: "Yes."

Josh: "Do you believe it is true?"

Student: "Yes."

Josh: "Do you believe it is historically accurate? Can you trust it?"

Student: "Yes."

Then dropping his voice Josh asked, *"Why?"*

The student had no response.

The following day Josh was outside an auditorium talking with a group of people when the same youth walked up and blurted out, "I know the answer to that question!"

"What question?" asked Josh, having forgotten the conversation that had taken place some 14 hours earlier.

The young man held up a Bible saying, "Why the Bible is true."

Josh got excited, thinking, *This kid has really thought through the issue.*

Everybody was listening.

"Why?" he asked.

"Because I believe it!" exclaimed the young man.

"Come again?" said Josh.

"Well, it's true because I believe it," the youth answered.

Josh: "Is it true for your friends at school?"

Reply: "No, not unless they believe it."

Josh countered with another question: "Do you know the difference between you and me?" Continuing without waiting for an answer, he said, "To you it is true because you believe it; for me I believe it because it is true."[12]

In recent years, the belief that the Bible is true and should be accepted as authoritative has been widely challenged by a skeptical, unbelieving mind-set.

When Western Reserve University sent out 10,000 questionnaires asking, "Do you believe the Bible to be the Word of God?" 7,442 people responded; and 82 percent of the Methodists, 89 percent of the Episcopalians, 81 percent of the United Presbyterians, and 57 percent of Baptists and Lutherans said, *"No!"* The majority of those who responded challenged the authority of the Bible.

In the 1960s 65 percent of Americans said they believed the Bible is true, yet some 35 years later, the number had dropped to 35 percent. But even more shocking, 67 percent deny there is such a thing as truth, and 70 percent hold to the position there are no moral absolutes.[13] Within barely a generation we have moved from a position that there are clearly defined moral issues—situations and deeds that are right or wrong—to one of moral relativism and uncertainty. While a previous generation failed to live up to what they consider right or wrong, there were, at least, standards of morality and decency that were generally acknowledged.

The heart is a rebel that resists authority

I was fortunate enough to have come to a personal relationship with Jesus Christ at the age of 12, and shortly thereafter I felt an inexplicable call to prepare myself for Christian ministry. I began to study the Bible; and though I cannot explain just how, I acquired both a love for God and a fear of Him at the same time. Some theologians call it "a reverential trust." It's part and parcel of the same thing. It's the balance between knowing that God is real and personal yet is the Sovereign of the universe who doesn't simply wave His hand and say,

"It's okay, you poor child! It's your biology—your DNA—that causes you to sin."

You walk down a dark alley, taking a shortcut to your car from a late night at the movies, and suddenly a man with a ski mask pulled down over his face and with a Smith and Wesson .357 in his hand stops you and says, "Give me your money." You quickly become cooperative. Swiftly, with no argument, you give him everything you have.

On payday, however, when your wife says, "Honey, I need some money to get shoes for the kids," you immediately open your wallet and say, "Here, dear, take what you need."

What's the difference? You respond to one in fear, to the other in love. And that's the way it is when it comes to desiring to do the will of God from your heart. You settle the issue that God's direction is not a yoke and burden but the path to greatest happiness and joy.

The heart, though, is a rebel. Seven centuries before Christ, Isaiah wrote, "We all, like sheep, have gone astray, each of us has turned to his own way; and the LORD has laid on him the iniquity of us all" (Isaiah 53:6). The only way that your rebellious heart can be tamed into submission to the purpose and plan of God is through an understanding of His great love, and the only way you will find a love worth knowing and having is through His Word.

❧❧

Once you respond to His great love, a romance follows that makes the issue of authority a nonissue. If, however, you are uncertain of the trustworthiness and integrity of the Bible, or you have unresolved questions about God and a relationship with Him because you do not have a working knowledge of the Bible, you will be uncertain when you come to the fork in the road.

In this book I am giving you six solid bridges that you can walk on in your quest to validate what the Bible says about your personal life. In His ministry Jesus was never taken aback by individuals who came with sincere questions. Nor do I believe God is offended when we sincerely come to Him and ask Him to show us whether or not He is the Truth.

I once had a conversation with a young woman, a science major at a university, who having grown up in a Christian home, left "all of that" behind when she went away to the university. "I don't believe the Bible," she told me.

"You're a science major, right?" I countered. She nodded her head as I continued: "I am sure that before you made the decision to pronounce the Bible obsolete and untrustworthy you studied the book carefully because the scientific method embraces research and analysis before reaching a conclusion, right?" "Well, not really," she said, adding, "Actually, I've never even read the Bible."

Making a decision *a priori,* having never considered the evidence, is prejudice of the worst kind. Large numbers of individuals have even approached the study of this Book with hostility and extreme prejudice and, having been confronted with the evidence, did an about-face and embraced the very Book they had scorned and mocked.

Find out for yourself what makes the Bible worthy of your belief and trust! Don't take what you have grown up with and, whatever you do, don't take the opinion of a professor who may know a great deal about DNA and recombinant enzymes but knows nothing—as in *zero*—about the Bible. (As one of my professors once said, "It isn't that they are ignorant; it is simply that they know so many things that are not true!")

Let's get started.

- When famous explorer Richard Byrd got lost in a snow-storm on the Ross Ice Barrier, he used a fixed point of reference to find his way back to safety. How could the Bible serve as a reference point for your life?

- Many people say they revere the Bible. They have at least one copy in their home, but seldom take the time to actually read it. If you have a Bible, how often do you read it? What are some steps you could take to make time in God's Word a healthy habit?

- When everyone is a "law unto himself," where does that lead in society?

- If I believe God's plan and purpose for my life is better than I could discover on my own, what compelling influence could the Bible have on my life?

CHAPTER TWO

The Bridge of Uniqueness

*"The highest proof of Scripture is derived in general
from the fact that God in person speaks in it."*

—JOHN CALVIN

Charles Haddon Spurgeon, the British expositor of bygone days, told the story of a poor woman who was confronted by an agnostic who asked, "What are you reading?" She replied, "The Bible, the Word of God." He countered, "Who told you that is the Word of God?" She said, "He told me so, Himself." "Told you so!" he scornfully retorted, "Can you prove that?" Looking skyward the old lady replied, "Can you prove to me there is a sun up there in that sky?" He answered, "Why, of course! The best proof is that it warms me and I can see its light." "That's it!" was her joyous reply. "The proof that I have that this is the Word of God is that it warms my heart and lights my soul!"

You would probably agree that the Bible does this, but is it enough to simply appeal to the subjective element of experience? I've had people tell me the same thing in response to reading modern gurus, or Eastern prophets who sit draped in white hallucinating on drugs. Upon what does the authority of the Word rest? Is it based upon what you were taught in parochial school or you grew up believing? Is its source your experience, a warm feeling in your heart (for example, *"I just know it is true!"*)—or certain pragmatic facts that form the bedrock for your faith? Of the countless millions of books in print that fill the shelves of libraries all over the world, no rival exists when it comes to the uniqueness of the Bible (defining the word *unique* as "only one of its kind," or "without duplication"). How is this book unique?

1. The Bible is unique in its authorship

James Henry Breasted, an authority on ancient civilizations, authored one of the few high-school textbooks that made a lasting impression on me, a thick textbook titled *Ancient Near Eastern Civilization*. Breasted was the first American to ever earn a Ph.D. in Egyptology and the one credited with coining the oft-used term "fertile crescent" to describe the span of civilization reaching from Egypt to Mesopotamia.

Breasted, whose picture appeared on the cover of *Time* magazine on December 14, 1931,[1] was a scholarly, forerunner of the Indiana Jones-type who wrote factually, yet with such exuberance and excitement that I devoured his book. It made me want to take a shovel and personally go exploring myself. Visiting the museum of Egyptology in Cairo years later, I recall the artifacts were exactly as the pictures I had seen in vivid black and white in the textbook.

I remember with fascination how Breasted described the first written documents ever found, originally written in the Tigris-Euphrates River valley near the Sumerian states of Kish and Ur. Those first documents were pretty common, garden-variety sort of writings—deeds to property, inventory lists, marriage covenants. Breasted contended, as do most scholars today, that writing began about 4000 BC, though no one knows exactly how it developed. Quite certainly no one ever sat down and said, "I think I'll invent something that will allow written communication." At first pictures or marks represented words, and gradually these were accepted in a given geographic area and became standardized. Carbon ink was used to inscribe broken pieces of pottery or stones, and by the year 3000 BC writing was common.

Writing on stone

Preceding the production of papyri in Egypt, a method of pictorial writing had been developed in Egypt known as hieroglyphs. Tombs and monuments record the exploits of Pharaohs with this picture writing "based on a complicated system of consonants."[2] People were communicating then just as much as we do today.

Babylonians did the same thing. About 1750 BC—some 300 years before Moses felt compelled to write "In the beginning God created the heavens and the earth"—Hammurabi, the Babylonian king, appointed stone masons to produce a *stele* (an upright stone monument) with 250 laws. It was massive—about seven-and-a-half feet in height and six feet in width, with the laws carefully inscribed. Visit the Louvre Museum in Paris and you can see it for yourself, with its rules, and its punishments if those rules were broken.

Hammurabi's law code included provisions for all kinds of injustices—repayment of thefts, agricultural rights, the rights of slaves, children, women, individuals who had been injured, compensation for murder.

Papyrus: paper of ancient Egypt

About 3000 BC (and perhaps even a long while before that—nobody knows for sure) Egyptians discovered a use for papyrus, a reed which grew along the banks of the Nile. It could be cut and placed in strips, with a secondary layer of strips being placed on top perpendicular to the first layer, then rolled firmly and dried.

From this they made such diverse products as boats (the basket in which baby Moses was placed along the Nile was probably made of papyrus), sandals, fuel, tables and chairs and, far more important in relationship to the Bible, writing materials. The Egyptians thus gave the world the substance that would eventually be used in the libraries of the world, with papyrus sheets being joined into scrolls.[3]

The book of Job speaks of papyrus asking, "Can papyrus grow

tall where there is no marsh? Can reeds thrive without water? While still growing and uncut, they wither more quickly than grass" (Job 8:11-12).

Each year the banks of the Nile overflowed, flooding surrounding marshes where papyrus grew in abundance; but without the marshes, there would be no papyrus, reasoned the writer. He also points out the weakness of the substance—it is organic and in its natural environment, without water the reed quickly withers and dies. It was this writing material that was used to record much of the original manuscripts of Scripture. Because it lacks the durability of a piece of clay or the hide of an animal, papyrus is subject to disintegration and decay and thus eventually becomes unreadable.

Moses wrote the Ten Commandments on tablets of stone, but in all probability the Bible as we know it was first written on papyri. This also explains why those original documents have long since disintegrated but fortunately, not before they were accurately copied and preserved for us today.

Should you have an opportunity to visit Cairo, you will find numerous museums where you will see what was used for the centuries-old process of making writing materials from papyrus.

The birth of the Bible

Surprising as it may be to some, the Bible was obviously not the first document to be written, although it is the oldest surviving book in print. But it is the first book ever written that comprehensively began with creation and provided a history of God, man, and the devil, with implications on how these truths relate to present-day living. It also contains clearly outlined prophecies extending to the time when God says, "Enough!" and calls a halt to life as we know it.

Who wrote the Book and how were they qualified?

The simple answer is that about 40 individuals wrote the manuscripts and documents we now call the Bible (from the Greek word *biblia,* meaning "books" or "scrolls").[4]

What were these writers' qualifications and backgrounds? A study of their biodata shows vast differences in education levels, backgrounds, places in society, and even abilities.

- Some were simple laborers such as Amos, who tended sycamore trees, and Peter, James, and John, who were fishermen.

- Some were priests who had studied the Scriptures and had received a theological education.

- Some were men with either direct or indirect connections to royalty. Moses was the adopted son of an Egyptian princess and without question received the finest tutoring and education that ancient Egypt could provide.[5] David and Solomon were kings. Isaiah, possibly a cousin to the king, had access to the royal court.

- One was a physician from Syria, probably the only Gentile who contributed to the Bible. As the author of the Gospel that bears his name and the book of Acts, Luke was the largest single contributor (in volume of what he wrote) to the New Testament.

- Then there was the rabbi turned evangelist. Saul, whose name was changed to Paul, wrote 13 letters to various groups and persons. He was the theologian of the New Testament, a man destined to greatness even if he had never been converted on the road to Damascus.

- Another was a tax collector, Matthew, who was sitting at his table in the customs house when Jesus called him. He eventually wrote the first Gospel.

How does one account for the fact that so many different individuals could write about God, history, and religious beliefs and yet their writings reflect essential harmony, unless they had been guided by an unseen Hand and Power? That is exactly what the Bible contends. That influence was the Holy Spirit, according to Peter, who states that "men spoke from God as they were carried along by the Holy Spirit" (2 Peter 1:21).

To understand the implications of the complexity and enormity of this, visualize the following: Suppose that 40 individuals from all over the world were summoned by the director of the Hermitage Museum in St. Petersburg, Russia. Their assignment was to find a piece of marble in any shape or color and to bring the same to the Hermitage on a specific date. Generally, there could be no communication between these individuals. Most of them had no idea that someone else was involved in this project. Then upon the given day the various pieces of marble were unveiled. Some were quite small. Others were very large and had to be transported by trucks or flown in by cargo jet. A few of the pieces were brilliantly colored. Others were opaque and lighter in shades and colors, yet—and think through the monstrous odds against this—when the individual pieces of marble were put together in a kind of jigsaw puzzle, a beautiful mosaic took shape revealing a beautiful scene. Talk about a miracle! Such would be added to the Seven Wonders of the World and people would come from far and wide to see this phenomenon.

Here's the analogy: Some portions of the Bible are short—Philemon and the second and third letters of John are only a few verses in length. Others are lengthy (have you ever wondered when you would get through the "so and so begat so and so's" in the Old Testament genealogies?). Yet the documents comprising the Bible fuse together in a marvelous pattern of God's love for humankind, and His refusal to let them turn and walk away from Him.

But even more significant is that what they wrote blends in literary harmony. Going back to the analogy of 40 individuals who are summoned to bring a piece of marble to a great museum, let's suppose that on this piece of marble they are to write their thoughts about God, humankind, where civilization is headed and, perhaps, write a brief history of the world. Can you conceive of anything as I have described having a sense of meaning or continuity unless what was written was supernaturally directed? It is at this point you are forced to recognize that the odds are preposterously stacked against this having just happened, and you are confronted with the supernatural character of the book.

Speaking specifically of the Old Testament Scriptures, Paul says, "All Scripture is God-breathed and is useful for teaching, rebuking, correcting and training in righteousness" (2 Timothy 3:16). Another version puts it: "All Scripture is inspired by God." It should be noted, though, observes Norman Geisler, that the "single time the New Testament used the word *inspiration*, it is applied only to the writings and not the writers."[6]

How did this inspiration affect the outcome of what was written? Were the men who wrote simply scribes who mechanically recorded what God dictated, or did their personalities and individuality come through? A careful study of the biblical books shows their individuality in the way they wrote and expressed thoughts and ideas. Even though their literary styles differed, there was a mystical supersedence that rendered their words as the words of God Himself. Their writings bore His stamp. Erwin Lutzer explains,

> Inspiration does not just mean that God approved of their writings, but that men actually wrote His words. His ideas became their ideas, and they accurately recorded what He wanted us to know.[7]

The record of what the Bible teaches is inspired and authoritative. However, Scripture contains the factual recording of many kinds of evil and violent deeds—certainly the equivalent of an "R" (restricted) film rating. But it truthfully and accurately conveys what happened so we can benefit and learn from the mistakes of others.

When was the Bible written?

The Bible came together over a period of 14 centuries—a fact so enormous that it almost defies belief. How so? Over the centuries ideologies and accepted popular wisdom changed from generation to generation and from century to century. Yet no one revised what had previously been written in Scripture in order to make it harmonize with the latest documents.

Starting at the beginning of the Bible, Moses wrote the first five books of the Old Testament, known as the Pentateuch (from two Greek words, *penta* meaning "five," and *teuchos* meaning "tool[s]," hence, the five books of the law). Jews refer to the same thing as the *Torah*. Historians date the giving of the law at about 1400 BC.

These five books were not God's first revelation of Himself and His plan for humankind but they were, however, the first written record of this. Undoubtedly God revealed much about His plan and purpose for humanity to the descendants of Adam and Eve, and these stories were passed from generation to generation—an oral history. Some stories, such as the account of the Flood, were duly related in different cultures and geographic localities.

What about oral history? Can people accurately remember lengthy dialogue without written documentation as we think of it today? Should you have grown up with a traditional Western education using textbooks—line upon line, precept upon precept—you might be surprised.

I remember the first time I was in Africa speaking to a large group of people, many of whom were illiterate. "I would like to teach you a new song," I said, adding, "I'll sing it for you, and then we'll try to sing it together." I sang the song once, and then to my great surprise, the audience all sang it—full voice and with volume, not missing a single word. No repeating of the lines was necessary. Even today many people groups learn what they know by rote and quickly memorize what they hear with an amazing exactness—a skill lost in the Western world.

The Bible itself bears witness to its distinctive and unusual authorship. When the books of the Old Testament were written, they were immediately recognized as the Word of God and placed in the Ark of the Covenant in the tabernacle. More than 3,000 times the prophets rang out the words, "Thus says the Word of the LORD." More than 90 times the New Testament asserts, "It is written!" That was their source of unquestioned authority. They knew what had given these documents validity—the voice of God on the mountain accompanied by the bolts of lightning and the clap of thunder. Isaiah wrote, "The grass withers, the flower fades, but the word of our God stands forever" (Isaiah 40:8 NKJV).

There is little evidence that anyone in ancient days questioned the authority of the Hebrew Old Testament. Men may have ignored it, spurned it, and violated its teaching, but they knew it was the Word of God. When Jesus was here, He fully accepted the authority of these books we call the Old Testament. He said, "One jot or one tittle shall in no wise pass from the law, till all be fulfilled" (Matthew 5:18 KJV). Those somewhat strange English words *jot* and *tittle* refer to the smallest strokes of a pen in writing two Hebrew letters. The NIV translates these words as, "Not the least stroke of a pen, will by any means disappear from the Law until everything is accomplished." Jesus had no intention of taking the smorgasbord approach of sifting out what He liked and rejecting the rest.

The New Testament church fully accepted the authority of the books that came from the pens of the Old Testament writers of Scripture. Both Jesus and Paul quoted Moses, recognizing his authorship as the writer of the first five books of the Bible.

Following the recording of the first book of the Bible, other books were added. Some were history and some were poetry. Other books were largely prophetic in nature. But all had the ring of genuineness. Those scrolls were placed in the Ark of the Covenant or collected by scribes and considered to be sacred.

God gave humankind this Book because He wanted to communicate His love to the world, and it could only follow that He would do so in languages that were widely used and understood at the time. This meant that Hebrew was the primary language of the Old Testament, and a type of Greek known as *Koine* (a street version of the language used in the marketplace and by literally millions of people throughout the then-known world) became the language of the New Testament.[8]

When a need arose for the Bible to be translated because groups of people no longer knew Hebrew or Greek, translations were undertaken, now numbering in the thousands. It is fair to say that the Bible has been translated into more languages than any other book in all of history and continues to be the world's most widely distributed book.

2. The Bible is unique in its structure

One of football's greatest coaches, Vince Lombardi, would begin every season by holding a football in his hands. He would then address his players, many of whom were seasoned veterans, and say, "*This is a football!*" Yes, of course, they knew it was a football. They had been kicking and tossing one since they were kids. Why state something so obvious? He was stressing that fundamentals need to be re-emphasized.

Open a Bible and you will immediately recognize it is a single book, but divided into two parts, which we call the Old Testament and the New Testament. While the two are separated by some 400 years, they are as integrally connected as the two hemispheres of your brain. Both function together. St. Augustine said the Old Testament is unveiled in the New Testament. Or as others have put it, "The new is in the Old concealed, and the Old is in the new revealed."[9]

The late pastor of First Baptist Church in Dallas, Texas, W.A.

Criswell, used to tell the story of a lad with a car that would hardly run. To drive up a particular hill, the boy had to go as fast as possible down one hill in order to gain speed. Then the poorly running car would usually make it up the next hill. One time, as he was gaining speed going down the hill, he noticed two cars coming from his right. Quickly he decided that he could slow down a bit to let the first car cross the intersection, then accelerate and dash in front of the second car. What he did not know, however, was that the first car was towing the second car with a steel cable. "When the young fellow got out of the hospital and finished paying the bill, he had learned this great theological lesson," said Criswell. "That it is very difficult to divide things that are bound together."[10] So it is with the Old and New Testaments.

The Bible is an anthology of books

In the Old Testament you will find the law that God gave through Moses, historical books, beautiful poetry, and prophecy (some call them major prophets and minor prophets because the major prophets were longer books, not necessarily more important).

In the New Testament you find biographies of the life of Jesus, the continuation of the infant church established on the Day of Pentecost, the teaching of Paul and others, which explains how to apply the truth of the Gospels to our lives and world, and finally, a thrilling book of prophecy culminating with Armageddon and the return of Jesus Christ to establish His kingdom forever.

In spite of the popular terminology referring to the Old and New Testaments, it would have been more descriptive to have called them the Old and New Covenants. (The word covenant, *diatheka* in Greek, notes an agreement between two individuals or parties.) The first described the agreement, or covenant, God made with the patriarchs: Abraham, Isaac, and Jacob, and their descendants. But the New represents the covenant that God made with humankind based upon the sacrifice of God's Son, Jesus Christ, who paid the price for the redemption of humanity. The New Covenant is about God's relationship with His people following the coming of Jesus Christ.

It is comforting to know that the Sovereign God who created the universe cares enough about His subjects to enter into an agreement that He is bound by His character to honor and that His Word will not be broken. As the Puritan scholar Perry Miller put it,

> When you have a covenant with God, you no longer have an ineffable, remote, unapproachable Deity; you have a God you can count on.[11]

The following is an overview of most English Bibles.[12]

OLD TESTAMENT		NEW TESTAMENT	
Law	Law—5	Gospels—4	Narration
Writings	History—12	History—1	Continuation
Prophets	Poetry—5	Letters—21 (13+8)*	Explanation
Former	Major Prophets—5	Prophecy—1	Consummation
Latter	Minor Prophets—12		
	39 BOOKS	**27 BOOKS**	
Here's how to remember	3 x 9 = 27	39 + 27 = 66	The traditional Bible

*13 by Paul; 8 by others

3. The Bible is unique in its claims

We have already considered two unique claims that are made by Peter and Paul. Peter says that the Bible did not originate with men; rather men wrote as they were "carried along" by the Holy Spirit. Paul affirms the same thing categorically saying, "All Scripture is God-breathed." The word "all" is inclusive.

To suggest as some do that some portions of Scripture are inspired and others are not leaves us in a quandary: Who is to determine what is inspired and what is not? Are we to presume that the parts we like are "inspired" and when something bothers us, we relegate that to the trash heap?

I'm thinking of the time I was looking for an apartment for missionaries who were returning from Colombia. Knowing that a certain woman owned an apartment complex near the church I then pastored, I knocked on her door and explained my mission. Thinking she might respond with kindness because missionaries were to occupy the apartment, I explained who they were and what they were doing— translating the Bible into the language of the people they served.

But she immediately retorted, "I don't believe in missions!" Somewhat taken aback, I countered, "Surely you believe in the words of Jesus." Hesitantly she said, "Yes, to the extent that they are translated correctly."

"Do you know that one of the last things that Jesus told the disciples was to go into all the world and proclaim the Good News to all the world?" I asked.

"I don't believe that Jesus ever said that!" she retorted, adding, "I think that someone added those words after His death."

Many approach the Scriptures as a kind of religious smorgasbord, picking and choosing what they want, making excuses for not saying, "If this is what God said, regardless of whether or not I like it, I accept the truth of His word. Issue settled!"

Consider some of the additional statements the Bible makes of itself:

"The grass withers and the flowers fall, but the word of our God stands forever" (Isaiah 40:8). Forever is a long, long time! When you are a kid, "forever" is the length of a church service, or the duration of the school term, or the length of time that it takes for the dentist to drill out your cavity, but the concept is time without end. The Hebrew word translated "forever," which incidentally is the same word translated "eternal" in the following entry, means "to veil from sight" or "to conceal." Isaiah used the word to contrast the fragility of a rose or a flower that fades with the certainty that the Word will endure the unrelenting assaults of its detractors and have no end.

"Your word, O LORD, is eternal; it stands firm in the heavens" (Psalm 119:89). The psalmist suggests that God's directions and counsel recorded in Scripture originated in His presence and will stand the test of time. The word the psalmist used that is translated "stands firm," *natsab,* means "established" or "fixed." The same word was used of a monument that had been firmly planted in the ground—one firmly established. *Smith's Bible Dictionary* says the same word was used of a well-fortified army garrison. It was also used of a "column erected in an enemy's country as a token of conquest" (1 Samuel 13:3).

"I tell you the truth, until heaven and earth disappear, not the smallest letter, not the least stroke of a pen, will by any means disappear from the Law until everything is accomplished" (Matthew 5:18). An illustration from the Hebrew text to which Jesus was referring gives meaning to what He said. The phrase translated "the smallest letter" (Hebrew *yod*) was the tenth letter of the Hebrew alphabet. It was the equivalent of the Greek *iota* (again the smallest letter of the Greek alphabet—the equivalent of an apostrophe). And the second phrase, "least stroke of a pen" or "tittle" (as translated in the King James Version), can be illustrated as follows using the Hebrew letter *daleth*.

The slight extension of the horizontal line crossing the vertical one is known as the *keraia.* It was the omission that Jesus was speaking of. Was Jesus speaking in hyperbolic terms, exaggerating to make a point? No. He was making a strong argument—one they understood much better than we do today. He was saying, "Scripture will be fulfilled exactly as it is written!" English translation cannot demonstrate how the slightest stroke of a copyist's pen can completely change the meaning of a word. For example, compare the following Hebrew words and how they are translated.

ה ל ל   ח ל ל

to praise   to profane

The only visual difference in how they are formed is the slightest stroke of pen closing the left-hand leg of the radical on the right. But the two words stand in apposition when it comes to their meaning.

Passages such as that written by Peter about the heavens and the earth passing away with a great noise and the earth melting with fervent heat didn't mean much until the atomic era was ushered in on the gleaming wings of science. What appeared to be hyperbole during Peter's time comes within the range of possibility every time the doors to the nuclear silos are rattled and a nation threatens to start the nuclear chain reaction. What Peter wrote could easily play out in the context of today's nuclear world. Did Peter understand the scope of what he was writing? Probably not, but God did.

"Heaven and earth will pass away, but my words will never pass away" (Matthew 24:35). Both of the two previous statements were made by Jesus Christ. Scholars are in agreement: No other religious document in the entire world makes such claims. "What about the Koran?" you may ask. Are such dogmatic claims made by its founder? An English translation of the Koran tells you what it says in direct terms. (Incidentally, Islamic scholars say that unless you read and understand Arabic, you cannot appreciate the beauty of the Koran.) But even an Internet concordance of the book shows no claims such as that made by Jesus Christ, recorded in the New Testament.

"If you risk asking the hard questions of the Koran," says Ravi Zacharias, "you risk being branded, and, in some cases, you even risk your life. The Christian, however, has always been willing to subject the Bible to the severest analysis and is able to come out, knowing that it can survive the blade of the skeptic."[13]

"The word of God is living and active. Sharper than any double-edged sword, it penetrates even to dividing soul and spirit, joints and marrow; it judges the thoughts and attitudes of the heart" (Hebrews 4:12). The contention of the writer of Hebrews is that *the Bible is alive!* How so? It has a way of penetrating our hearts and minds, quickening us to the truth of what God says and orders for our lives. It convicts, reproves, guides, and comforts.

That was the position of Professor J.B. Phillips, a scholar of the classics at Cambridge University, who had a pretty disparaging view of the Bible. In his own words, he had a "rather snobbish disdain for the book." In spite of his expertise in the classics, he had never taken time to give serious consideration to this Book, but that changed when he began to study it—thinking about the task of a modern translation. What happened as he confronted the issues I am writing about? He said, "I found myself provoked, challenged, stimulated, comforted and generally convicted by my previous shallow knowledge of the Scripture." He said it was "strangely alive" and "it spoke to my condition in the most uncanny way." His deduction? "It is my serious conclusion," he said, "that we have in the New Testament words that bear the hallmark of reality and the ring of truth."[14]

How assess it then? Accepting the fact that the Bible is given by God gives it uniqueness and, far more important than this, it gives authority to the words you read on the pages of your Bible.

4. The Bible is unique in its formation

From the moment ink dried on a papyrus scroll until the text of what was written saw printer's ink on the Bible that you read, three steps or progressions over a long period of time can be observed in relation to the Bible's creation.

Step 1: Revelation by God

God, not wanting humankind to walk in darkness, revealed something of Himself to His spokesmen (known as prophets), who then recorded the revelation. Sixty-one times in the Old Testament you will find the phrase, "The Word of the LORD came to me..." Ten times the prophet Jeremiah writes, "The Word of the LORD came to me..." He specifies "the second time," and so forth. At times he was a reluctant recipient of the Word. He made excuses, pleading that he was just a youth, but when God revealed something or spoke through him, it was immediately recognized as the Word of the Lord by those who heard or read it.

When Moses came down from Mount Sinai, his face so glowed with the glory of God that he had to cover it. There was no question in anyone's mind. They knew God had spoken and what Moses had brought down, written with the finger of God on those stone tablets, was His Word. Moses was God's spokesman. When his sister, Miriam, challenged his authority, she was struck with leprosy—an evident token of God's displeasure with her not-to-be-repeated challenge.

Forty-eight times in 30 chapters Ezekiel, a prophet in exile in Babylon used the same term—"the Word of the LORD came to me..." It was a powerful connection with heaven, and men listened.

Step 2: Reception by men

The second part of this transaction is that God's Word was received by men. And how did people know whether or not God, in fact, spoke through the prophet? Moses gave them a very simple test: Did what the prophet say that God revealed take place? If it didn't, then what should happen to the prophet? "A prophet who presumes to speak in my name anything I have not commanded him to say, or a prophet who speaks in the name of other gods, must be put to death" (Deuteronomy 18:20). Strong penalties for those who faked revelations from God!

There were times, though, when the message was rejected. When Jeremiah wrote of impending doom, King Jehoiakim took a penknife (probably a sharp knife that was used to shape the tip of a quill pen used for writing) and cut up the scroll, throwing it in the fire. But Jeremiah again wrote the words of the prophecy, which long survived the king.

Revelation from God resulted in reception by men, accompanied by the recognition that God had indeed spoken through the prophet, priest, psalmist, or writer. But one more step follows.

Step 3: The collection and preservation of the text of Scripture

Focusing specifically on the writings of the Old Testament we recognize the following:

- The writings of Moses were preserved by being placed in the Ark of the Covenant in the tabernacle in the wilderness (Deuteronomy 31:26).

- The words of Samuel (the prophet who anointed David as king) were written "on a scroll and deposited...before the Lord" (1 Samuel 10:25).

- The law of Moses was eventually preserved in the temple in Josiah's day (2 Kings 23:24).

- Daniel had a collection of "the books" in which were found "the law of Moses" and "the prophets" (Daniel 9:2,6,13).

- Ezra, the scribe, possessed copies of the law of Moses and the prophets (Nehemiah 9:14,26-30).

By 400 BC, the Old Testament in the form we presently know it had come together. It is nothing less than astounding that it has endured the test of time without corruption and loss.

The collection of New Testament documents is a story that is both complex and less clearly defined as that of the Old Testament. Open a New Testament and the first four books you find are known as Gospels. But actually there is but one gospel—that is, the good news of what Jesus said and did,[15] but it is recorded by four individuals. We know them as Matthew, Mark, Luke, and John. (The Civil War general Stonewall Jackson, a dedicated Christian, named four of his cannons "Matthew, Mark, Luke, and John" because, he said, "They spoke the Gospel.")

These four, however, were not written in the order they appear in your Bible. In all probability Matthew was the first to write an account of the life of Christ, followed by Luke, then Mark, and finally John.[16] Why the order in which they appear in your New Testament? Because of the common themes or subject matter.

The first three—Matthew, Mark, and Luke—are known as *synoptics*—a term that simply means they told the same story from three different viewpoints. Matthew (the tax-collector Jesus called as he sat at the revenue table) is the most Jewish of the three, and his account is considered generally as the most chronological. Writing from a Jewish standpoint, he pictures Jesus as the long-awaited Messiah.

Mark, on the other hand, is writing from a Roman viewpoint. His book, which is marked with a staccato speed, is sometimes called "the Businessman's Gospel." Throughout the book, he liberally sprinkles a Greek word *euthus* meaning, "straight-way, immediately, or forthwith." The 16 chapters in this book are filled with exciting events. What happened in the ministry of Jesus was what he focused on in his writing. It is quite likely that Peter dictated much of what Mark recorded.

Luke, a Syrian physician, writes with a tenderness that reflects his personal training and compassion. He specifically mentions the place women had in the ministry of Jesus and paints the passion of Christ very vividly. In his book, Jesus is the perfect man, appealing to the Greek mentality.

John—unlike the first three—singles out 21 days in the life of our Lord and focuses on the events that take place at that time. Chapter 13 through the end of the book focuses on the last seven days in the life of Jesus Christ.

After the Gospels comes the book of Acts. It details the continuation of the life of the early church, recording the three great missionary journeys of Paul, stopping quite abruptly with Paul under house arrest in Rome, leaving the impression that originally more was written which has not survived.

Twenty-one letters (13 by Paul) and eight others known as general letters or *epistles* (an old term that simply means *letters*) provide instruction and guidance for the lives of men and women who were struggling with what it means to be a Christian in a non-Christian world. Most of Paul's letters were written specifically to deal with problems in the lives of believers, something that should not be ignored by those who think that Christians ought not to have problems.

It is probable that Matthew wrote a version of his book in Aramaic at about AD 37.[17] Then he wrote the equivalent of this in Greek about AD 45 to 50. Luke is generally dated about AD 58, Mark AD 67 to 68 and John between AD 85 and 90.

Then James, the half-brother of Jesus, wrote the book that bears his name—the first of the letters—about the same time as Matthew's Greek account of Jesus' life, about AD 45 to 58.

Paul's letters can be grouped as follows:

	Letter	Date	From
Group 1	1 Thessalonians	AD 50 or 51	Corinth
	2 Thessalonians	AD 51 (6 months later)	Macedonia (Acts 20:1)
Group 2 On second missionary journey, AD 50 to 53	1 Corinthians	AD 54 to 55	Ephesus
	2 Corinthians	AD 54 to 55	Macedonia (Acts 20:1)
	Galatians	AD 55 to 56	Corinth (Acts 20:2)
	Romans	AD 56	Corinth
Group 3 Under house arrest— known as Prison Epistles	Ephesians	AD 60 to 61	Rome
	Philippians		
	Colossians		
	Philemon		
Group 4 During final imprisonment	1 Timothy	AD 65 to 66	Rome
	Titus	AD 65 to 66	Rome
	2 Timothy	AD 65 to 66	Rome

The rest of the New Testament books, often known as general letters, including Hebrews, Peter's letters, the three letters by John, and Jude, were written between AD 67 and 96. Then John, writing from the Isle of Patmos in exile, penned the book we know as Revelation, bringing to a close the 27 books that were eventually recognized as the New Testament.

A final disclaimer: When John put down his quill pen, he didn't breathe with a sigh of relief and say, "Whew! That's it, now let's rush this to the printer." It took quite a long period of time for these 27 documents to be recognized as being those bearing the stamp of authenticity and genuineness. The process of how these books gained universal acceptance is a story I'll tell in chapter 3.

5. The Bible is unique in its endurance and preservation

No other book in all history has been so revered, so cherished, and so copied as the book we know as the Bible. More than 20,000 ancient manuscripts of various parts of the Bible exist today[18]—a vast number including over 5,300 ancient Greek manuscripts, 8,000 manuscripts of a Latin translation of the Bible, over 1,000 manuscripts of various translations, and thousands of biblical quotations found in the writings of the early Church Fathers.

Compare what I have just written with the fact that the world over, there are only 13 manuscripts of Plato, the great Greek philosopher. Only eight manuscripts containing the history of Thucydides, written about 400 BC, are in existence. Edward Gibbon, the British historian, considered the Roman historian Tacitus to have been one of the finest and most accurate of ancient historians, yet only two of his manuscripts have survived in spite of the fact his *Annals* consisted of 16 major works and he later wrote three more, considered minor works.

In the libraries and museums of the world there are only a few manuscripts containing the writings of Sophocles, Euripides, Virgil, and Cicero. According to John Warwick Montgomery, there are but four manuscripts containing references to Tiberius Caesar, and all four are in sharp conflict with each other, yet no one denies that he lived and walked on planet Earth.

How then can anyone make so preposterous an assertion that the one who is the primary figure of the thousands of ancient manuscripts, Jesus Christ, never lived or walked the shores of Galilee?

Keeping in mind that movable type wasn't put into widespread use until the 1450s by Johann Gutenberg, remember that Scriptures (both Old and New Testaments) were copied by hand. It was a painstaking, laborious job. Often scrolls were made in a kind of classroom, known as a scriptorium. The teacher or leader would sit at the front of desks where scribes would carefully, word for word, write down what was read or dictated by the teacher. It was serious business.

Should a mistake be made, scrolls were often given ceremonial burial—something that has provided rich resources for subsequent generations when they were later discovered. When a scroll became too old to be of use, it was also buried or burned.

Ancient rabbis have related that when Scripture was being copied, even if a king should walk into the room, the scribe would not rise until he had completed the portion he was copying, reasoning that the king was mortal—he would eventually die, but God's Word was sacred and would endure forever.

Down through the centuries the Bible has been held in high esteem as the Word of God and been afforded a veneration that has waned only in the past few decades. In 1933 the British government bought from the Russian government for a relatively small amount of money a manuscript known as Codex Sinaiticus, or the Sinai Manuscript. It was transported by train; then the train was met by a British delegation, who brought this very important manuscript by taxi to the British Museum, where it was kept for a period of years. As the taxi passed through the streets of London, men stood quietly and *removed their hats* in respect for the document.[19] But today we've come a long way from giving the Bible that kind of respect.

The contribution of Jewish scribes known as Masoretes in preserving the Old Testament

The Hebrew word for "tradition" is *masorah;* hence the term *Masoretes*—a group to whom a debt of gratitude is owed by all who love the Bible. Here is why. As the church gained power and influence especially during the third and fourth centuries, Jewish rabbis began to become concerned that the focus of attention was upon the "Christian" documents that were being widely distributed and copied.

Fearful that the Old Testament Scriptures would become corrupted or fall into disarray, pushed aside by the proliferating New Testament documents, two Jewish rabbinical schools were established, one in Caesarea on the Mediterranean and the other in Tiberias on Galilee.

Their objective was to collect and organize the Old Testament documents, codify them, and preserve them. Little did they realize what a great service they were doing to the very church they feared, in that the Old Testament is the cradle of the New, and though believers are under grace, not law, the Old Testament provides the foundation that brings understanding to the New.

Their contributions included...

- adding vowels and accents to the text.
- developing a standard for pronunciation.
- collecting and classifying thousands of scrolls and documents.
- elevating respect for the Old Testament Scriptures.
- preserving authentic texts that became the standard for the 1,500 years following.

The fascination, though, with the Masoretes is in how they kept their copying so accurate. Neil Lightfoot explains that through an intricate and complex procedure of counting,

> they numbered the verses, words, and letters of each book. They counted the number of times each letter was used in each book. They noted verses that contained all the letters of the alphabet, or a certain number of them. They calculated the middle letter, the middle word, and the middle verse of the Pentateuch; the middle verse of Psalms, the middle verse of the entire Hebrew Bible, and so forth. In fact, they counted almost everything that could be counted. With these safeguards, and others, when a scribe finished making a copy of a book, he could then check the accuracy of his work before using it.[20]

On the margin of the text, the Masoretes would make annotations about which readings were verifiable. Short of being able to access the entire text by a computer, it is inconceivable how a finer system could be put in place to ensure the accuracy of the transmission of Scripture.

You might be wondering, *Were there errors of omissions or additions to the text for clarification?* Yes, all of these were done, and actually there are many. So does this create confusion and uncertainty for us, wondering whether something important was left out or something strangely got reinterpreted by someone?

The contribution of modern science

Starting in the nineteenth century, scholars developed an approach to resolving the differences in manuscript readings known as textual criticism. "The function of the textual critic is plain," says Neil Lightfoot. "He seeks by comparison and study of the available evidence to recover the exact words of the author's original composition." His task is "to weed out the chaff of bad readings from the genuine Greek text."[21] Paul D. Wegner defines textual criticism as "the science and art that seeks to determine the most reliable wording of a text"[22]—in other words it is to determine what is the closest possibility to the original text.

After the persecution of the church (as detailed in Acts 7), believers began to scatter. Some went down into Egypt and settled in Alexandria. Some went to Caesarea, a Roman city, where persecution by Jews was less severe. Some went to the north, to the great city of Constantinople, and some went to the west and settled in Rome, where a church was well established. And wherever they went, they took with them the precious letters and copies of the Gospels they treasured.

Eventually these cities became centers of manuscript production and manuscripts from them were referred to as families.

- *Alexandrian:* from Alexandria, Egypt
- *Western:* from Rome
- *Byzantine:* from Constantinople
- *Palestinian:* from Tiberias

Then in modern times, as manuscripts were both discovered and made accessible to scholars, it became apparent that many of the differences in manuscript readings could be explained on the basis of their origin.

Obviously if an error was made—say a copyist in Alexandria had inadvertently misspelled a word, repeated a phrase, or dropped a line as he transcribed a passage—that reading would then be transmitted in successive copies of the same passage. Therefore, if something that was missing in an Alexandrian manuscript was in manuscripts coming from another area or family, the reading was suspect. Each time a successive manuscript reproduced the omission or error, it was considered a variant, which means the actual number of variants is far, far greater than the actual differences in the text. This means, bottom-line, that about one word in a thousand is questioned, said the brilliant scholar and textual critic F.J.A. Hort of Oxford.[23]

How serious are these variants? Inconsequential. No important doctrine, teaching, or historical fact is jeopardized in the slightest—an amazing fact that gives you confidence as you pick up your Bible and read.

Over a period of time several general rules of procedure were adopted by textual critics:

- The older manuscript is usually considered better. It's closer to the date when the originals were written and this means there was less time for anything to become altered or corrupted.

- The shorter reading was adopted (based on the assumption that when someone wanted to clarify something that was difficult, he added a few thoughts of his own).

- The more difficult reading is preferred. Why? Scribes, wanting to be helpful, often tried to simplify and clarify the text.

- The reading that best suits the style and character of the writer is preferred.

- The reading that has no doctrinal preference is considered less likely to have been altered.

- Readings that best fit the context are considered more likely to reflect the original text.

How the Scripture survived attempts to discredit it during times of threats

From the day that Matthew took it upon himself to write a narrative of Jesus' life, death, and resurrection, there have been enemies who would destroy Scripture if they could. One of my professors, Dr. Bernard Ramm, commented tongue-in-cheek, "The death knell has sounded a hundred times for the Bible, but the corpse never stays put."[24]

One of the first was a Roman emperor whose full name was Gaius Aurelius Valerius Diocletianus—otherwise shortened to Diocletian. He was an egomaniac of a ruler who pronounced himself a "deity" and demanded worship (not the first nor the last to be seeking a vacancy in the Trinity!). He gilded his nails and sprinkled gold dust in his hair, so historians have told us. But far more damning was the fact he issued an edict in AD 303 with the intent of destroying all Christian churches and Bibles (both Old and New Testament scrolls).

In the year preceding the edict a council was held at Nicomedia, and a political decision was made—Christianity had to be destroyed. Both churches and Bibles were targeted. According to Eusebius, one of the day's respected Christian leaders (known as a Church Father), an edict was issued "to tear down the churches to the foundations and to destroy the Sacred Scriptures by fire; and commanding also that those who were in honourable stations should be degraded if they persevered in their adherence to Christianity."[25]

Churches were demolished and thousands of manuscripts (then

rolled as scrolls) were surrendered to Roman soldiers, who burned them publicly in the streets and markets of Rome.

So convinced was Diocletian that he had put an end to this book that he erected a monument inscribed with these words: *Extincto nomine Christianorum* ("The name of Christian is extinguished"). But only ten years later, according to historians, Diocletian died an agonizing death—of what we are uncertain—but there is agreement that his internal organs were affected (perhaps by parasites or ulcers).

A postscript: Following Diocletian, Constantine became emperor, and under his watch the church made significant gains and the persecution subsided. About the year AD 332, Constantine ordered that fifty Bibles be produced for the churches he was erecting in Constantinople. These books were "to be written on fine parchment, in legible manner, and in a convenient portable form, by professional scribes thoroughly accomplished in their art."[26] Two magnificent Bibles from Constantine's era have survived, known as the Sinai Manuscript and the Vatican Manuscript, though these two are probably not among the ones ordered by the emperor.

François-Marie Arouet de Voltaire, who died on May 30, 1778, said that in "another century...there will not be a Bible on earth."[27] He missed that one for sure. Should he be aware of what is happening in the twenty-first century, he would learn, to his great surprise, that the British Foreign Bible Society alone publishes one copy of the Bible every three seconds, and worldwide, a very conservative estimate is that a Bible is printed every second of every day, to say nothing of concordances, Bible study guides, and related materials. To his chagrin Voltaire would learn that when he died the Geneva Bible Society purchased his press and upon this published an entire edition of the Bible.

Time or space doesn't allow an exhaustive treatment of how from time to time the Bible has been targeted by evil sovereigns and governments such as England's Henry V, who considered Bible reading to be a crime and passed a law to punish those who owned Bibles.[28] Meanwhile, in these more recent times, Communism, as an atheist form of government, has philosophically opposed the unmonitored distribution of Scripture.

Challenges of the twentieth century haven't destroyed the Book

I vividly recall one exchange I had with customs officials in China. In the early 1980s, I brought a group of about 25 people up the Pearl River with each of us carrying Bibles for Christians in China. During that time, we estimated that there was only about one printed text of the Bible for every 250,000 believers in China.

When Bibles were found in the hand-carrys of those in our group, as the leader I was quickly singled out and taken into a small room where several customs officials were gathered.

"What seems to be the problem?" I asked, about the way you would if a policeman pulled you over for speeding.

"You have Bibles, and Bibles are not allowed in China."

"You have nothing to fear from this book; it will only make people honest, trustworthy, and good law-abiding citizens," I replied.

Despite my sound reasoning explaining the merits of the Bible, I lost the argument. The government of China, however, finally capitulated and relaxed its position of being "anti-Bible." It is a kind of "if you can't beat 'em, join 'em" story that is well worth telling.

6. The Bible is unique in its being the official biography of the world's most influential Person

Larry King is a popular talk-show host who has interviewed many of the world's greats. There is no question he hesitates to ask, but on one occasion a guest turned the tables and asked him who he would most like to interview from a historical perspective. One of those he named was Jesus Christ.

"What would you have asked him?" the guest challenged him. The implications for Larry King, of course, were very weighty.

He replied, "I would like to ask Him if He was indeed virgin-born because the answer to that question would define history."[29] King, Jewish by ethnic background, went to the very heart of the issue—was Jesus' birth supernatural? If He was not born of a virgin, He was not whom Scriptures represent Him to be, and He then would have been an imposter. Because the writers of the Gospels present Him as "born of a virgin" in fulfillment of prophecies, should He not have been virgin-born, everything else they wrote would be suspect. Was He the unique fulfillment of passages such as Isaiah 7:14, prophesying that the "virgin will be with child and will bring forth a son"? The New Testament says He was, in clear and certain terms, with full understanding of the implications.

The central figure of the New Testament is Jesus Christ, and apart from the Bible, there is little to either instruct or inform us regarding His person, His mission, His life, death, and resurrection.

The New Testament is the official biography of this Man, the most influential Person in all history, the One whose coming became the Continental Divide of all history.

While Jesus is mentioned by Josephus, the Jewish historian who became pro-Roman, and Roman historians Tacitus and Suetonius, it is the 27 books of the New Testament that flesh out the story.

Simply put the New Testament documents demonstrate that Jesus was

- unique in His birth and childhood.
- unique in His youth.
- unique in His ministry, starting about age 30: He said things no other person dared to say; He did things that cannot be explained apart from divinity.
- unique in suffering, death, and resurrection.

The often quoted passage from C.S. Lewis sums it up:

> Either this man was, and is, the Son of God: or else a
> madman or something worse. You can shut Him up for a
> fool, you can spit at Him and kill Him as a demon; or you
> can fall at His feet and call Him Lord and God. But let us
> not come with any patronizing nonsense about His being
> a great human teacher. He has not left that open to us. He
> did not intend to.[30]

7. The Bible is unique in its message

The tremendous acceptance of Rick Warren's book *The Purpose-Driven Life*—now with over tens of millions of copies in print, having been on the New York Times Bestseller List for more than 42 consecutive months—is a reflection of the desire of people to know what life is about. The question of existence, what makes life meaningful, is one of the paramount issues of our day.

Prior to the publication of Warren's book, I was presented with a draft of the manuscript. Like other reviewers, I read the book and thought, *This is good and it will be helpful to a lot of people,* but to my surprise and—I think it is fair to say, even that of the author's—the book has been successful beyond anything that could be imagined. The phenomenal success of the book (even Pope John Paul II, it is reported, had a Polish copy of the book by his bedside at his death) is a reflection of the desire of people to fill the void and emptiness in their hearts.

Without elaboration I want to propose that this book, the Bible, alone answers the deep questions of life:

- Who am I? (personality)
- Where did I come from? (existence)
- Where do I go after I die? (meaning)

- What is life about? (purpose)
- Where is the world headed? (prophecy)

Those answers are found in no other book, no other source, or no other person, and that's what makes the Bible unique.

The bottom line: The Bible is unique

The planks of uniqueness are among the first you traverse as you cross the bridge of confidence to what the Bible says. You glimpse the fingerprints of the mighty hand of God in the timing, the manner, and the distinctive character of the Book. And all of this leads to the next issue: the authenticity of the documents that comprise the Bible. That's why so much rests upon the primary evidence—the manuscripts and the stories they tell—the subject of the next chapter.

• How could so many different individuals from different backgrounds contribute to the Bible over hundreds of years, and yet have their writings reflect essential harmony?

• Undoubtedly God revealed much about His plan and purpose for humanity to the descendants of Adam and Eve, and these stories were passed along as oral history. Describe ways your family passes along its history from generation to generation.

• What is a covenant? Describe the difference between the Old and New Covenants.

• J.B. Phillips, a scholar of Classics at Cambridge University, once held a disparaging view of the Bible. Then he actually studied it. He said it was "strangely alive" and "spoke to my condition in the most uncanny way." What do you think he meant by that?

CHAPTER THREE

෨෨

The Bridge of Manuscript Evidence

"More than 5,750 manuscripts of the New Testament exist today, making the New Testament the best-attested document in all ancient writing." [1]

—NORMAN L. GEISLER

You are reading a respected periodical—not the cheap pulp kind you find at the checkout counter of your grocery store with screaming headlines about babies being fathered by aliens from outer space—and you notice an article on the Bible. With your interest piqued, you turn to the article. As you read you find statements such as, "The Bible has been through countless translations from the time its chapters were originally penned to the present. Along the way there have been changes and alterations that have diminished the purity of the doctrine." The writer charges that the purity of the Bible has been "tampered with by religious philosophers, councils, panels, and kings." [2]

Immediately you think, *Isn't that what Dan Brown charged in* The Da Vinci Code? *It can't all be smoke and mirrors!* You reason that if it is in print then surely there must be some truth in what is written. Besides, you notice there is a Ph.D. following the author's name. *Can't be a fool,* you think, *and have* his *education and experience.* You reason, *If it isn't true, wouldn't the magazine get sued?*

Then what about the cover stories you periodically find on news magazines such as *Time, U.S. News and World Report,* and *The Economist?* A few of the more blatant ones I have filed are these:

- HOW TRUE IS THE BIBLE?—*Time*[3]

- IS THE BIBLE FACT OR FICTION? Archaeologists in the Holy Land are shedding new light on what did—and didn't—occur in the greatest stories ever told—*Time*[4]

- IS THE BIBLE TRUE? New discoveries offer surprising support for key moments in the Scriptures—*U.S. News and World Report*[5]

How can you be sure with cover stories such as these? Each time I pick up such a magazine or read a similar account in a newspaper, I fully expect a smattering of facts and a great deal of conjecture along with inaccuracies—all concocted to sell magazines. Of course, for every conservative scholar that is quoted an opposing view has to be presented. That's the stuff that creates magazine sales. The result: The average person who is not well-grounded in Scripture closes the magazine saying, "You know, I'm confused. I really don't know what to believe."

Individuals who have never made a thorough study of the manuscripts or have a strong prejudice against the Bible and, subsequently, have an agenda to discredit the Bible, are not valid sources of authority. Most of what is acclaimed today as "new discoveries" have actually been around for a long time. It was not by coincidence that news stories broke touting the discovery of the "Gospel of Judas" at the time *The Da Vinci Code* movie was being released. That document, which is neither "new" nor a "gospel," as we will see later in this chapter, had been available to scholars who had rejected it as being authentic for at least 50 years.

You may be thinking, *What do a few old manuscripts have to do with my life today?* If you are concerned with the integrity of the Bible, they are of great importance. When manuscripts that are very, very old, are discovered and their substance is the same as the text of the Bible you have in your home or office, you are assured that the text has not been changed or altered; your confidence in what God tells you in the Bible increases.

The story told by old pieces of papyrus and the skins of animals

God has providentially allowed the preservation of biblical manuscripts that have been passed from generation to generation. Realize also what a great contribution the science of biblical criticism has made to verifying and preserving the accuracy of the biblical text. This knowledge and understanding can carry you across the chasm of doubt or question.

It is more than coincidental that at the very time when science and technology seemed to eclipse spiritual values, God has seen it fit to allow manuscripts to be discovered that are at least 1,000 years older than anything of the same portion of Scripture in existence at the time of the discovery. Popular wisdom tells us that truth is always stranger than fiction. If you don't believe that, perhaps you will after you've read the following section.

The discoveries at Qumran

Should you visit my office, you will see a reproduction of the first few chapters of the Isaiah scroll found in Cave 1 in Qumran, a short distance from the Dead Sea in Israel. The story behind the important discovery of the scroll is a good starting point.

It was spring of 1947 and hostilities were accelerating between Israel (not yet an independent nation) and her Arab neighbors. A young man,

Jum'a Muhammad from the Ta'amireh Bedouin tribe, had lost some of the goats he was tending.[6] Muhammad began searching for them. Wandering up a wadi, or desolate valley, he saw a cave—something relatively common, caused by erosion when the rains gushed down the ravines towards the Dead Sea far below. *Is it possible that the goats may have wandered into the cave?* he thought.

He picked up a rock and threw it into the opening of the cave. The strange noise he heard though wasn't the bleating of a goat. *It's a spirit!* he thought, and fearful of what might be there, he tucked tail like a scared puppy and headed towards the warmth and security of the goat-skin tent which was the family home.

That evening as the family sat around the fire recounting the events of the day, Muhammad told them how he had encountered an evil spirit. His cousins scoffed at him. "There's no such thing," they said, and to prove that, the next morning they accompanied their cousin to the cave to find out what had made the noise.

Reaching the cave high above the ravine was not easy. But they got there and when they did, they discovered that the noise from the rock was the result of the stone's shattering an old earthenware vessel that originally was about 36 inches tall. Among the broken pieces of pottery they found an old scroll that centuries before had been placed in the jar and sealed with a kind of bituminous pitch—hardened by the hot, arid weather. The cousins were illiterate so the writing on the scrolls meant nothing to them. Eight or nine other scrolls were in the cave, which came to be identified as Cave 1.

The story I've just related is the popular one that I would like to believe, but may be a public-relations sort of tale that makes good copy but embellishes what actually happened.[7]

Two days after the cave was initially discovered, one of the cousins (not Jum'a Muhammad, who originally located the cave but did not explore it) arose early in the morning while the others were sleeping and scaled the 350 or so feet to the cave's entrance, lowering himself feet first into the cave to see what treasure he might find.

Harry Thomas Frank describes what in all probability actually happened.

> At dawn of the next morning Muhammad Ahmed-el-Hamed, who was nicknamed "The Wolf" (edh-Dhib), woke first. Leaving his two cousins sleeping on the ground he scaled the 350 or so feet up to the cave... With effort the slender young man was able to lower himself feet first into the cave. The floor was covered with debris including broken pottery. But along the wall stood a number of narrow jars, some with their bowl-shaped covers still in place. Edh-Dhib scrambled over the floor of the cave and plunged his hand into one of the jars. Nothing. Frantically he tore the cover from another, eagerly exploring the smooth inside of the empty container. Another and yet another with the same result. The ninth was full of dirt. The increasingly desperate young Bedouin at last closed his hand around something wrapped in cloth. He extracted two such bundles and then a third, which had a leather covering but no cloth wrapping. The cloth and the leather were greenish with age. These were all edh-Dhib took from the cave that morning.[8]

How the manuscript was discovered, however, is not germane to the importance of what was found! Says Frank summarizing what happened: "Scholars who later interviewed edh-Dhib think that this boy had in his hands on that winter morning nothing less than the great Isaiah Scroll, the Habakkuk commentary, and the Manual of Discipline!"[9]

The cousins took the scrolls back to base camp. The Isaiah Scroll was placed in a bag and hung on a tent pole for a period of time. Since Bedouins are nomadic, wandering from place to place searching for grass and water for their flocks, it was several weeks before they went to

Bethlehem, where they often traded with Khalil Iskander, a merchant who went by the name of Kando, and bartered the scroll for provisions and a small amount of money.

Did Kando know what he really had? Probably not at first, but he did have the savvy to realize any ancient scroll was worth some money (after all, he made his living hawking antiques and artifacts). Yes, he knew they were valuable but how valuable they actually were never crossed his mind. When Kando first saw them, he thought they might be Syrian. He also knew he had hot merchandise. Though Bethlehem was then in Jordanian hands, he knew that if authorities found out about the scrolls, they would immediately confiscate them and give him trouble. Big trouble. It is reported that to safeguard his cache for a period of time he buried the priceless 2,000-year-old scrolls behind his little shop.

By most accounts Kando originally bought three—possibly four—manuscripts from the Bedouins. Then whether Kando persuaded the Bedouins to return to the caves and search for more manuscripts or else engaged in his own illicit excavations will never be known for certain. But the "battle for the scrolls" was on as Bedouins and archaeologists both searched the caves for contraband manuscripts.

Kando tried to determine what he really had and how valuable the scrolls were. He contacted a trusted friend, an Armenian, who like himself dabbled in artifacts and antiques. This Armenian dealer, who lived in the walled Old City of Jerusalem, made contact with Professor Eleazer Sukenik, who held the chair of Archaeology at Jerusalem's Hebrew University. The Armenian thought that this man might buy the scrolls for the university.

By then it was almost a year later, and the 1948 War of Liberation had sealed Bethlehem from Israel proper. British authorities, then concerned with security issues, had erected barriers in the Old City, and to be allowed passage from one to the other required a military pass. Professor Sukenik agreed to meet the Armenian dealer the next morning. They had to see each other at the security terrace because the professor wanted to avoid being asked why he needed a pass. A no-man's land of looped barbed wire separated the two men, and Sukenik watched with keen interest as enough of the scroll was unrolled for him to read some of the text.

I can only imagine his eyes focusing intently on the old Hebrew text as he recognized this was the book of Isaiah—and the oldest text he had ever seen. He later wrote in his journal that he had been "privileged by destiny to gaze upon a Hebrew scroll that had not been read for more than two thousand years."[10] Professor Sukenik, realizing the tremendous value of what he saw, arranged for the clandestine purchase of three of the scrolls. The remaining four scrolls were acquired by the Orthodox Archbishop Athanasius Yeshua Samuel, Metropolitan of the Syrian Jacobite Monastery of St. Mark in Jerusalem who paid Kando £24 or about $97 US dollars. The archbishop then sought to find out exactly what he had and how valuable they were—a search that was about to end.

It is at this point in the drama, which is stranger than fiction, that a 33-year-old American, John Cecil Trever, became involved in the story. Trever graduated with honors from the University of Southern California with a degree in religion in 1937. The following year he married his sweetheart Elizabeth and then went to Yale, where he took another undergraduate degree, then took two graduate degrees, including a Ph.D. in Old Testament with an emphasis on ancient Semitic languages and paleography (the study and analysis of ancient handwriting). Trever wrote his doctoral dissertation on the book of Isaiah, never thinking how important this research would ultimately become in his life.

Trever was also an amateur photographer who had an intense interest in microphotography and botany. In 1947 Trever was one of three men to receive a fellowship at the American School of Oriental Research in Jerusalem (now known as the Albright Institute of Archaeological Research). Before leaving for Israel, Trever took a crash course in developing color film, and Ansco (the film company that rivaled Eastman-Kodak at the time) gave Trever a trunk full of the latest equipment needed to develop the film. Packed with his gear was a new professional camera, one that he never thought would be used to show the world what had come out of the dark cave at Qumran.

Along with his equipment Trever brought a newly acquired set of 35 mm slides of the Nash Papyri[11] and had become sufficiently familiar with them to recognize the similarities in style and structure with the Isaiah manuscript which he first saw on February 20, 1948, when Archbishop Samuel and two of his fellow monks came to the institute bearing the scrolls they had acquired.

Trever, with his colleague William Brownlee, immediately identified the text from Isaiah—the Old Testament book that had been the subject of his doctoral research. Convincing the archbishop that he was trustworthy, not a small accomplishment as he related in correspondence to his wife, the archbishop agreed to leave the scrolls with him overnight. According to his wife, Trever immediately began photographing the manuscript, working all night because of the uncertainty as to how long he would be allowed to keep them.[12]

With the archbishop's permission, Trever sent the prints to Professor William Foxwell Albright, his friend and mentor at the American School of Oriental Research at Johns Hopkins, who was recognized as the dean of biblical paleographic and archaeological research. Albright, probably the most widely recognized authority of manuscript dating, established the accepted date that the scroll was produced at around 100 BC. "The quality of his photographs often exceeded that of the scrolls themselves over the years, as the texts quickly eroded once removed from their linen wraps," says an observer.[13]

Consider this: Was John Trever in Jerusalem by chance or was he part of God's greater plan? Did God prepare him to be at the right spot at the exact time with him having unusual qualifications, including a doctoral dissertation that allowed him to recognize the importance of what he saw? That was the question I put to Trever's wife, Elizabeth, now in her 90s. She affirmed the latter in no uncertain terms. Almost daily Trever wrote to her as he shared his excitement and joy at being able to help identify these documents that had been buried for some 1,900 years in a dark cave.

The following year Archbishop Samuel took the scrolls to New York seeking to sell them for the greatest possible amount. Thereafter, the scrolls seemed to fade from the radar screen.

Now fast-forward some five years. On June 1, 1954, an advertisement appeared in the *Wall Street Journal* captioned, "Four Dead Sea Scrolls for Sale." Here is the rest of the story:

> The advertisement was brought to the attention of Yigael Yadin, Professor Sukenik's son, who had just retired as chief of staff of the Israel Defense Forces and had reverted to his primary vocation, archaeology. With the aid of intermediaries, the four scrolls were purchased from Mar Samuel for $250,000. Thus, the scrolls that had eluded Yadin's father because of the war were now at his disposal. Part of the purchase price was contributed by D.S. Gottesman, a New York philanthropist. His heirs sponsored construction of the Shrine of the Book in Jerusalem's Israel Museum, in which these unique manuscripts are exhibited to the public.[14]

Until the discovery of the Isaiah manuscript, the oldest Hebrew text of Isaiah was a manuscript in book form known as a *codex*. Since it was found near Cairo, Egypt, it was dubbed the Cairo Codex. It contains the Old Testament prophetic books and is dated AD 895 so the newly discovered text of Isaiah pushes back by about 1,000 years the date for an extant manuscript of the book of Isaiah.

If the text of Scripture has been altered, amended, or tampered with as some claim (such as the publications whose featured titles I quoted at the beginning of the chapter allege and many mistakenly accept), it would readily become apparent as the Isaiah manuscript found at Qumran is laid side by side and compared with the manuscript dated AD 895.

What has changed in the Isaiah text? Nothing of substance, say scholars. The variations are slight—obvious slips of the pen and mis-spelling, differences in structure—but nothing that is significant—a remarkable testimony to the integrity of the Scriptures. Two of the Isaiah scrolls found in the Qumran trove are "word for word identical" with the traditional Masoretic text.[15]

The scrolls that came out of Cave 1 were the first to attract fame; however, since 1947 there has been no stone unturned. Some 40 caves have given up over 800 documents, including portions of every Old Testament book in the Bible, with the exception of the book of Esther. Consistently those important manuscripts and documents have only substantiated the text of our Bible; several of those manuscripts, how-ever, add additional light to the history of biblical times and the structure of the New Testament books.

Sir Frederic Kenyon, former director of the British Museum and author of *The Palaeography of Greek Papyri,* writes, "In no other case is the interval of time between the composition of the book and the date of the earliest manuscript so short as in that of the New Testament."[16] In his book *The Bible and Archaeology* he says, "The last foundation for any doubt that the scriptures have come down to us substantially as they were written has now been removed."[17] The following is part of the evidence supporting Kenyon's position.

The remarkable journey of an old scroll from St. Catherine's to the British Library

Around AD 550 the Emperor Justinian built a fortress on a narrow gorge in the Sinai Peninsula to protect monks from the raiding Saracen tribes. It was believed that this was where God spoke to Moses through the burning bush. (Visitors are easily convinced that it well may have been here, because the heat is intense.)

Reaching St. Catherine's today is quite difficult, but in the 1840s when a 29-year-old man came to the world's oldest monastery, it was far more challenging. His name: Constantin von Tischendorf. One of the nineteenth century's most brilliant and colorful scholars, Tischendorf in all probability is owed a greater debt than any other person when it comes to preserving and illuminating biblical manuscripts. During his lifetime this German-born son of a physician logged more miles on the back of horses, camels, and in carriages (and some by ship) than a lot of platinum-club world travelers today.

In his book *How We Got the Bible,* Neil Lightfoot tells how young, brash Tischendorf arrived by camel caravan at St. Catherine's in 1844. After he presented his credentials, he was hoisted by monks over the door—a 30-foot-high barricade that remained closed for security purposes—on a crossbar. His was not a religious pilgrimage but a scholar's search for biblical documents. Throughout his life, Tischendorf remained committed to the premise that he was seeking neither fame nor financial rewards but sought to eliminate questions regarding the text of the Bible.

Several years earlier, Tischendorf earned hash-marks of academic credentials with the publication of a critical edition of the Greek Testament. He was serious, brilliant, motivated, and daring. And all of those factors came together in this young scholar who was given a small apartment and undoubtedly scrutinized by the aged monks, who were not quite certain what to do with this young man so highly acclaimed.

One morning Tischendorf was astonished to see that the librarian was lighting a fire using old sheets of parchment. He noticed that among them were "a considerable number of sheets of a copy of the Old Testament in Greek" that, according to Tischendorf, were "the most ancient that I had ever seen."[18]

Several basketsful of these ancient pieces of parchment had already been fed to the fire; however, he was able to acquire about 43 of these pages—one-third of the pile—and upon his return to his home in Leipzig published them, telling no one where he had found them.

Wanting to get the rest of them, he returned to St. Catherine's in 1853, and to his great disappointment no one seemed to know anything about the remaining sheets of parchment. *Had they been burned? Were they holding out on him? Had someone else visited there, paid a king's ransom for the lot, and packed them off somewhere else?* He wasn't sure. He did, however, observe that part of one was being used for a bookmark. He recognized it as coming from Genesis 24, leading him to be relatively certain that the original scroll had to include the entire Old Testament in Greek (known as the Septuagint).

Months turned into years. Tischendorf was getting older, yet still determined to make one more trip to St. Catherine's. Thus in 1859 under the sponsorship of Alexander II, the Czar of Russia, he made the long, weary trip down into the Negev to the monastery.

Again, nothing! No one talked. No one seemed to know anything. Disappointed, he gave up and advised his Bedouin couriers to prepare to leave within three days. In the afternoon, however, the steward of the monastery invited him to have tea with him in his cloister that evening. Upon arriving at his room, the steward said, "And I, too, have read a Septuagint," and produced what Tischendorf later described as "a bulky kind of volume, wrapped in a red cloth."

Although he was ecstatic, this time he masked his excitement, fearing that the youthful exuberance he had displayed fifteen years earlier had left the impression that they had something extremely valuable that like gold should be kept in a safe-deposit vault. He asked permission, however, to take the scroll to his room overnight.

He described his elation saying,

> I knew that I held in my hand the most precious biblical treasure in existence—a document whose age and importance exceeded that of all the manuscripts which I had ever examined during twenty years' study of the subject. I cannot now, I confess, recall all the emotions which I felt in that exciting moment with such a diamond in my possession.[19]

"The first thing he did when he reached his room," writes Dr. Ludwig Schneller, in a biography of his famous father-in-law, "was to go down on his knees and thank God for the nearly miraculous find."[20]

Tischendorf convinced the monks that the manuscript could better be studied in Cairo and arranged to take it there, intending to return it at a later time. The manuscript, known today as the Sinai Manuscript, never found its way back to the old monastery. It was taken to Russia and shown to the Czar, who, if you remember, had financed the expedition. After much haggling and disagreement among the monks, the manuscript was officially given to the Russian Czar in exchange for 9,000 Russian rubles and medals given to the monks. It remained in St. Petersburg long after the Czar died, but in 1933 when the nearly bankrupt Communist government needed money, it was sold to the British museum for the sum of £100,000 (then about the sum of $500,000).

An interesting sidebar regarding the sum of money that was paid, which in 1933 represented a considerable fortune, is the fact that the same day the transaction took place a first edition of the works by

François-Marie Arouet de Voltaire was sold in a flea market in Paris for the equivalent sum of 11 cents in U.S. currency. And who was Voltaire? An eighteenth-century intellectual and philosopher who, as we noted earlier, is most remembered by Christians as the man who said Christianity would not survive him by 100 years.[21]

I shall never forget my first visit to the British Museum, walking through the corridor where the Sinai Manuscript was prominently displayed. (It has since been moved and is now housed at the British Library.) When I saw the manuscript for the first time, I was filled with awe and wonder—not the same kind I experience when I see a sunset over the ocean or hold a newborn infant in my arms, but the kind that is the result of knowing that over the centuries God providentially allowed something to survive the ravages of time and decay.

Apart from the sentiment, how is the Sinai Manuscript important and what does it contribute to our confidence that the Bible is the Word of God?

First, with the exception of missing fragments of the text, this document is generally considered to be the oldest complete manuscript of the entire Bible.[22] Dated by scholars at about AD 350, the Sinai Manuscript establishes a benchmark of comparison and contributes to our knowledge and understanding of what has happened in the intervening centuries.[23] Along with the Vatican Codex, the Sinai Manuscript is recognized as one of the two finest manuscripts of the Bible in existence.

Another hidden pearl of great price

It is both ironic and chagrining that the most important biblical manuscript, both in completeness and accuracy, lay hidden in a nondescript repository in the Vatican for years before the world of scholarship had access to it.

Dated about AD 325, the important Vatican Codex found its way to Rome and the Vatican sometime in the fifteenth century. It lay there, preserved and silent until—you probably guessed it—Constantin von

Tischendorf appeared on the scene. Having learned of its strategic importance, Tischendorf petitioned the Vatican to see it. The Vatican reluctantly gave him permission to examine the text with one caveat—he was not allowed to copy a single line of the text.

Undeterred, this bold and brilliant scholar, whose IQ must have pushed genius level, would memorize the text each brief period he was permitted to view the manuscript. At night in the privacy of his room he would painstakingly write down verbatim what he had seen, letter by letter, sentence by sentence.

Then the crisis came. Not being able to restrain himself, one day he jotted down a few sentences on paper so he could compare it with the text found at Mt. Sinai. He was caught in the act of scribbling by an observant librarian and denied any further access to this precious document.

An additional contribution to the cause by Alexandrian Jews

The third most important biblical manuscript of both testaments originated in Alexandria, Egypt, hence its name: The Alexandrian Manuscript. Today it is part of the collection of documents found in the British Library. Written on vellum in large script (known as uncials), the manuscript made its way to Constantinople and eventually on to England. Dated from the fifth century, the manuscript is in a good state of preservation and lacks only a few portions of Scripture.

The contribution of thousands of papyri long buried in the sands of Egypt

Beneath the sands of Egypt have been found literally thousands of fragments of the Old Testament—some of which had been given ceremonial burial as they wore out or were damaged in one way or another. The hot, dry air has been kind to the papyri, which would have deteriorated and disintegrated in a more humid climate.

Synagogues had storerooms attached—known as a *genizah*—where scrolls were kept in a depository awaiting ceremonial burial as Jewish law forbade destroying anything containing the name of God, including personal letters and legal contracts. These worn-out manuscripts were periodically buried in the sand outside the storerooms, eventually providing a treasure trove.

The two men primarily responsible for the tremendous number of papyri found at Oxyrhynchus, Egypt, were two Oxford graduates, B.P. Grenfell and A.S. Hunt, a very colorful pair with their proper manners, handlebar mustaches and a love for discovery.

Between 1886 and 1906 these two young scholars, both in their mid 20s, unearthed literally tons of papyri that had long been buried in the dry Egyptian sands. And what did they find? Mundane things such as grocery lists (yes, written by wives to remind their husbands of what was needed in the kitchen), business invoices, personal letters—correspondence—and of far greater importance, hundreds of manuscripts containing both the text of Scripture and quotations—all of these in a number of different languages. About 170 of these contain New Testament texts, including one said to be the oldest fragment of the New Testament dating to the early second century. Known as P^{52}, this piece of papyrus was dated about AD 125, less than a generation after the last New Testament book was written. Today it is in the archives of the University of Manchester (where it was first known as John Rylands P^{457}).[24] Eventually earlier fragments of the New Testament were discovered, but before I discuss this, another question needs to be addressed: How important are all of these papyri manuscripts?

Most of the papyri discoveries date to the second and third centuries, when Christianity was being established; however, some date back to even the first century AD. As the result of the many papyri discoveries, scholars have been able to identify basic Greek grammar and date other Scripture documents. They provide insights to how New Testament words were used, and what those same words really mean. One of the most important contributions, says Howard Vos, is that "these manuscripts help to confirm the text found in the uncials [earlier manuscripts written in block letters] and to bridge the gap between the original and the uncials."[25]

Elsewhere in the world papyri also speak

One first-century papyrus fragment in particular that has drawn a great deal of interest is a fragment of a manuscript which, if it is valid, appears to be the oldest writing of the New Testament ever discovered. The Pontifical Biblical Institute, which is a part of the Roman Catholic Church, announced that the Reverend Jose O'Callaghan discovered fragments of chapters 4, 5, and 12 of Mark's Gospel dating from the year AD 50. This is at least 75 years older than any other portion of the New Testament ever discovered, even older than the Rylands papyrus previously discussed. And who was Professor O'Callaghan? A Jesuit scholar at the University of Barcelona and a recognized authority on papyrus documents.

Professor O'Callaghan made the remarkable discovery at Cave 7 at Qumran. Here seven papyri fragments were found, all containing Greek scripts, which indicate that the desolate caves behind the Essene settlement were used as a repository for Christian manuscripts and writings—probably after the destruction of the Qumran community in AD 73. The fragments of this important manuscript are very tiny—the largest of which measures only 2.7 by 1.3 inches and contain only five complete words—none of which is positively distinctive and identifiable.[26]

The date of AD 50 attached to the fragment of the gospel of Mark takes us back to about 17 years from the time when Jesus walked the shores of Galilee. This, of course, created no small stir among Bible scholars. It also closes the gap between when Mark was written and when this document was made to only a few years.

Additionally, fragments of New Testament documents include a portion of Acts 27 (dated about AD 50), Romans 5, 1 Timothy 3,

2 Peter 1, and James 1 (dated AD 70 plus). And why are these important? R.C. Sproul answers that question: "They add a powerful argument that these writings originated with the generation that knew Jesus personally."[27]

The story a document tells

Without question every manuscript has a story to tell. A scholar doesn't need to have a background in criminal investigation to know what it is, but there are markers that are important. One such marker is the kind of material the scroll is written on. Largely because of the expense and the unavailability of more durable writing substances, most biblical manuscripts were written on papyrus, the forerunner of paper as we know it. The problem with papyrus is that it doesn't hold up indefinitely since it is made of organic matter. And that is precisely why we don't have the original manuscripts—the ones written by the writers of the various books themselves.

Better is parchment or vellum (a high-grade quality of parchment made of the skins of young animals) because this endures indefinitely. The best-quality writing material was calfskin, coming from an unborn or a stillborn calf. But the problem here was that each page required a piece of hide that had been scraped and prepared to take ink. It was both expensive and time-consuming, to say nothing of the fact it was not nearly as readily available as papyrus sheets.[28]

Generally the following guidelines are noted:

- papyri: first to the fourth century
- parchment: fourth to eighth century
- vellum: eighth to fourteenth century

Another detail that was important was the kind of ink used. Why is this important? Because the kind of ink, the handwriting style, and the composition of the same often were markers revealing when and where the manuscript was written.

When I was living in Manila, Philippines, my secretary would often pick up a letter and say, "This was written by a graduate of..." and she would tell me what university the person had attended.

"How can you tell that?" I inquired. A former nun, she explained that in certain schools the sisters required students to develop a style of penmanship that was unique to that school.

In my father's day, letters were stylistically decorated with swirls known as Spencerian penmanship—something that has long since disappeared. Likewise, the styles of penmanship found on those ancient biblical manuscripts have a story to tell—often indicating the approximate period of time when they were written; and, at times, provide clues as to where they were written as well.

The Greek Old Testament Alexandrian Jews gave the world

Millions of people today are indebted to a missionary by the name of William Cameron Townsend. He was laboring in Guatemala in 1917 when he was asked, "Why, if your God is so smart, hasn't He learned our language?" Challenged, Townsend devoted the rest of his life to translating the Bible into the vernacular of thousands of people.

The situation was not really that much different in the third century BC. Many Jews lived in Alexandria, Egypt, and spoke Greek better than Hebrew—the language of the Scripture. Yes, rabbis knew Hebrew, but when the Law was read in synagogues it was often incomprehensible to the average person. In a Hellenistic culture the average Jew spoke a somewhat corrupted variation of Hebrew.

That is what motivated a prominent Alexandrian Jew by the name of Aristeas to write a rather lengthy letter to his brother Philocrates in Jerusalem telling him about the Pharaoh's request of the royal librarian, Demetrius, to have the Law translated and added to the royal library.

History tells us that this letter is consistent with the fact that Ptolemy II (285–247 BC) expanded the library in Alexandria and would surely have included the Scriptures in the library.

Eventually this letter was sent to the Jewish high priest in Jerusalem, Eleazar, asking his help in translating the Law. If we can believe Aristeas' letter, he was one of those asked to carry out the request of Eleazar.

In response, some 72 scholars (six from each of the 12 tribes) were sent to Alexandria, where the Pharaoh provided them luxurious accommodations. They translated the Law in—are you ready for this?—exactly 72 days.

While the details of what was written in the letter of Aristeas may reflect a large measure of poetic license, there is one thing for certain—the Hebrew text of the Old Testament was translated into Greek during the second and third centuries BC in or near Alexandria—likely the island of Pharos.

A wide-ranging variety of Septuagint readings indicates that, long before the Christian era, the Septuagint was widely read and used by Jews throughout the Mediterranean world. In all probability there were multiple translations that eventually were codified and included in an accepted version.[29]

The Septuagint (literally meaning *seventy*) became the Bible of Jesus and the disciples. Most of the New Testament quotations of the Old are from the Septuagint. Eventually the Septuagint became so identified with early Christianity that reactionary Jews produced another translation that they felt was less "Christian" and more Jewish.[30]

How did we end up with what we call "the Bible" today?

The following discussion is not a definitive answer to that question; however, it gives you a brief summary of how the 66 books you find in your Bible came to be recognized as authoritative.

In most English Bibles, you will find 39 books in the Old Testament and 27 in the New Testament. But how do we know these are "the only ones" that are authoritative and belong in the Bible? What about more recent discoveries including some of the scrolls and writings found in the Caves of Qumran?

Let's start with the 39 Old Testament books, which were written over a period of about 1,000 years. The selection of the books forming the Old Testament, according to the knowledge we have today, was never problematical—questioned and challenged, yes, but never in jeopardy. Over 3,000 times writers invoked the Almighty as their source of authority saying, "Thus says the Lord"—a powerful, almost indisputable certification to uniqueness.

Moses wrote the books of the law, known as the Pentateuch, which were immediately placed in the Ark of the Covenant. They remained there during the 40 years the Israelites wandered in the wilderness. Following the conquest of Canaan, Joshua's book telling of the conquest was added to the collection, which stayed intact until there was a final home for them in Jerusalem.

From Joshua's day to the time of Solomon, prophets, priests, and poets recorded history and wisdom literature. When the temple built under Solomon was completed, these books along with some prophetic writings were considered to be sacred and authoritative and preserved. Daniel referred to this collection as "the books" (Daniel 9:2), and Isaiah as "the books of the LORD" (Isaiah 29:18, 34:16). The writings of Isaiah, Jeremiah, Ezekiel and Daniel (considered to be major prophetic books because of their length) were then added to this collection along with 12 final prophetic books, Hosea through Malachi (referred to as minor prophetic books because of their shorter length).

During the days of Ezra and Nehemiah, following the Babylonian Captivity, the Old Testament books as we know them today were essentially codified and recognized by all Jews, bringing the Old Testament canon to completion about 432 BC.

Were there other religious books in existence? Yes, there were—probably many of them, now lost to posterity. Joshua 10:13 and

2 Samuel 1:18 both refer to the Book of Jashar. But there was a consensus as to what was God-given and to be accepted and revered and what was interesting but lacked the sense of divine urgency and stamp of the Almighty.

It was the church, however, that was confronted with the task of determining what books are unquestionably inspired by the Holy Spirit and should be included in the New Testament, and what books are interesting, perhaps factual and even offer spiritual comfort and encouragement, but lack the same ring of authority as do other books. Now, let's go to the issues surrounding the New Testament starting with the first four books.

Today we commonly refer to those first four books in the New Testament as the Gospels; however, the early church referred to these four simply as "the gospel," not considering each one "a gospel."

The Gospels, it is generally agreed, came together very quickly and were accepted as Scripture after John wrote the book that bears his name.

The New Testament letters, however, were another matter. Of the 21 letters in the New Testament, 13 came from the pen of the apostle Paul, who without question wrote far more than this number of letters. They were arranged by length with the longest book, Romans, being placed first in the group with Philemon, the shortest, concluding the group of letters.

Paul, however, wrote far more letters than these included in the New Testament. For instance, we know for a fact he wrote at least four letters to the church at Corinth. In his first letter he tells them that in his previous letter he told them not to associate with sexually immoral people (1 Corinthians 5:9), and in 2 Corinthians 10 Paul alludes to previous letters addressing problems in the church. Today, we have only two of Paul's letters to Corinth. It is only logical that Paul, following the pattern of ministering to a church, then addressing the needs of that group by letter after he left them, would have written many more letters than we have now in the Bible. Of note is the fact that Paul asserted that what he wrote had been inspired or directed by God Himself.[31]

We also know that individual letters to specific churches were read in other churches, someone removing the name of the recipient and replacing it with the name of the secondary church. "After this letter has been read to you," Paul wrote to the Colossians, "see that it is also read in the church of the Laodiceans and that you in turn read the letter from Laodicea" (Colossians 4:16).

Peter acknowledged Paul's unique authority saying he wrote with "the wisdom that God gave him," recognizing that some things written by Paul "are hard to understand," yet put them in the same category as "other Scriptures" (2 Peter 3:15-16).

The other eight letters known as general letters include Hebrews, James, 1 and 2 Peter, the three letters of John, and Jude. A number of these letters were somewhat controversial, with differing opinions as to whether they were, in fact, inspired by the Holy Spirit and should be universally accepted by believers everywhere. Why the controversy? Part of the answer is the lack of communication between individuals who were separated by geography and lacked the facility of dialogue as we know today. Neil Lightfoot explains:

> Because these collections were made at different times and places, the contents of the various collections were not always the same. This helps to explain why not all of the New Testament books were at first received without hesitation; while in other instances uncertainty of a book's authorship, as in the case of Hebrews, presented temporary obstacles to universal acceptance.[32]

The contribution of a heretic

It was actually a radical who brought the issue to a head. At around AD 140, a pastor's son by the name of Marcion drew up a list of New

Testament books. Marcion took a blue pencil and deleted both sections and books that were widely accepted by churches. He entirely rejected the Old Testament, and penciled out part of Luke, accepting the rest, including ten of Paul's letters (rejecting 1 and 2 Timothy, and Titus). "You have gone way too far," cried the church. But their objection didn't greatly disturb Marcion, who had gathered a cultlike group of people who followed him as a great spiritual teacher with insights others lacked (not any different from modern cult figures today).

Of course, the wrath of the church descended upon him. He was excommunicated and treated as a heretic. His unexpected yet greatest contribution, however, was that he forced the church to determine which books should be accepted and which ones rejected.

By the Council of Nicaea in 325, there was general agreement regarding the New Testament books, yet some books were disputed, including Hebrews, 2 and 3 John, James, and Jude. In 357 a pastor and teacher by the name Athanasius listed the 27 books of our New Testament as being authentic or canonical.[33] By 397 at the Council of Carthage both the Eastern and Western church agreed—this was it! Twenty-seven were recognized and no more.

An observation of great importance is due at this point. It was not the church who decided what books were and what were not to be included. It was the sovereign work of God's Holy Spirit, and the church merely recognized that. F.F. Bruce, one of the twentieth century's most widely acclaimed scholars, puts it like this:

> One thing must be emphatically stated. The New Testament books did not become authoritative for the Church because they were formally included in a canonical list; on the contrary, the Church included them in her canon because she already regarded them as divinely inspired, recognizing their innate worth and general apostolic authority, direct or indirect. The first ecclesiastical councils to classify the canonical books were both held in North Africa—at

Hippo Regius in 393 and at Carthage in 397—but what these councils did was not to impose something new upon the Christian communities but to codify what was already the general practice of those communities.[34]

The 66 books comprising the Bible are referred to as a canon, coming from the Greek word *kainon*. That word was first used to describe the length of an Egyptian Pharaoh's bent arm from his elbow to the extended middle finger, and, so we are told, that length was precisely recorded on a piece of black marble. That was the official measurement against which everything else was assessed. Pieces of papyrus were then marked as we would a ruler, and that became the national or kingdom standard—or canon.

Were there principles that guided in the selection of these books, which means many were excluded? Yes, four criteria are generally recognized which follow:

1. *Was the book written by an apostle (one of the twelve Jesus called) or someone associated with Jesus?* Luke, of course, was not an apostle, but he traveled with Paul. Mark, again not one of the 12, was like a nephew to Peter, who may have dictated the gospel that bears Mark's name.

2. *What of the contents of the book?* Did they reflect the character of the other books—morally, doctrinally, and generally?

3. *Was the document in question universally accepted?* It took a longer period of time for some books to meet this criterion.

4. *Is there evidence of inspiration?* Paintings bear the signature of the artist. Silver has the hallmark of the craftsman, and evidence of inspiration means the manuscript bears the indisputable mark that God spoke through the writers.

Bibles containing 14 additional books between the two testaments

The *Apocrypha* (from a word meaning *hidden*) is the word generally applied to additional books found in Catholic or Orthodox editions of Scripture and omitted in most other versions. Most of these books were written between 200 BC and AD 200, often assuming the character (speaking in the first person) of someone long deceased. These books were never accepted by Jews or included with the Old Testament (They were written after the Old Testament had drawn to a close).

While there are many Old Testament quotations in the New Testament, especially in Matthew and the book of Acts, there are none directly from the Apocrypha. Most of the early church leaders (including Origen and Jerome) rejected these books.

But why were they written? While we will never completely know the motives of the authors, it is apparent, believed F.F. Bruce, that some were written to fill in the blank spots, providing additional information about "the 'hidden years' of our Lord's life before His entry upon public ministry" and provide information that they considered essential to an understanding of the Epistles.[35] A few were written to promulgate beliefs that reflected Gnostic or heretical views and were immediately rejected by the Church. Most of the Apocryphal books, however, quote what we call today the New Testament documents.

Did Jesus and the apostles ever quote from these books? Some scholars believe that they alluded to them, just as they also did to secular writers; however, it is evident that these books were never directly quoted as sources of authority as were other Old Testament writers. Even the nature of these writings seems to fail the "evidence of inspiration" test. "The trouble with so many of the books of the Apocrypha," says Neil Lightfoot, "is that they abound with exaggerated plots, fanciful stories, and just plain fiction."[36]

In 1546, at the Council of Trent, the Roman Catholic Church pronounced 11 of these 14 books authoritative and canonical, in spite of the fact that respected priests for centuries had written and spoken against these books. Many believe that their action was a response to Martin Luther's attacks on the Roman Church, especially denouncing practices or beliefs such as prayer for the dead and purgatory as unscriptural, practices taught or implied in the Apocrypha.

Is it possible that there are more "undiscovered" gospels out there somewhere?

The answer to the question about the existence of other gospels all depends on who you believe and by what standard you accept or reject something. Take, for example, the notoriety over a manuscript that was purported to be lost for 1,700 years then discovered, known as the "Gospel of Judas."

Why the name? The document's final words read, "Gospel of Judas," and the content of the same is fashioned to lead the reader to conclude that the writer is the disciple of Jesus, the one who betrayed Him in the garden for 30 pieces of silver, and then hanged himself in contrition for the dark deed. It seems to be more than a mere coincidence that *National Geographic* magazine released a special on this manuscript during Holy Week, as though it was something just discovered, when, in effect, scholars have known about the document discovered in the sands of Egypt for a long, long time.[37]

"Just one more confusing old manuscript," say some, not quite sure what to believe and what not to believe. There is one thing for certain: Nobody counterfeits brown wrapping paper. And what does that mean? For everything in the world that is valuable, and authentic, there is a counterfeit, a cheap imitation, a piece that is fraudulent no matter how colorful or interesting it may be. So is the "Gospel of Judas" real or counterfeit?

Here are the facts:

Fact 1: Judas never put his hand to this document. While the

New Testament was written in Greek, this document was written in Coptic, an Egyptian language, in all likelihood unknown to Judas. Furthermore it was probably written at around AD 400, though some scholars, based upon the scribe's handwriting, the ink that was used, and the linguistic styles commonly used in the second and third centuries, say that it was written earlier in Greek, perhaps about AD 200. Yet two centuries after the whole event is completely out of sync with the dates for the other New Testament documents. Consider that in existence today is a portion of John 18 dated AD 125. An unknown author, with an axe to grind, a point to prove, asserted that Judas was the writer of the "Gospel of Judas," when the disciple who betrayed Jesus had actually been dead for a long, long time.

Fact 2: The whole message of the document flies in the face of the New Testament books. It reflects a Gnostic message that the flesh is evil and we need to escape from it—which is why Judas, who betrayed Jesus, looks like the hero, not the villain. Paul condemned this teaching in his letter to the Colossians.

Fact 3: Church fathers consistently denounced Gnostic teaching, and to suggest that this fits into the New Testament framework reflects a bias that is better known as heresy. No wonder Paul wrote, "Even if we or an angel from heaven should preach a gospel other than the one we preached to you, let him be eternally condemned!" (Galatians 1:8).

Fact 4: The suggestion that this is a "gospel" is a misnomer—a fraud designed to glean support through confusion. It pictures Judas as being obedient to the command of Jesus to deliver Him to the Romans—that Judas was a good guy who has just been given a lot of bad press. The Greek word uniformly used in the New Testament for "gospel" means "good news," a "good message." The first record of the word's use, pointed out the Greek scholar Adolf Deissmann, was on a Greek inscription when one army triumphed over another and a runner carried the "good news" of the victory. This document neither focuses on a salvation message nor on "good news" of deliverance from the penalty and power of sin.

Fact 5: This is but one of many manuscripts or documents written in the aftermath of the spread of Christianity where "wannabes"—people who wanted to be significant—wrote using an assumed name.

When anthropologist and missionary Don Richardson told the story of the gospels to the Sawis of Papua New Guinea, he was appalled that they cheered for Judas. *No,* he thought, *they got it wrong.* He retold the story and then realized that they, indeed, liked Judas. Then Richardson learned that the Sawis valued treachery above integrity, and so they cheered for the bad guy. But, thank God, as the result of Richardson's ministry there, the changed Sawis no longer cheer for the traitor. They know the truth, and the truth has set them free.

The reality (which, however, doesn't sell magazines or newspapers) is that the early church was well aware of some of the manuscripts that recently have been portrayed as "new" or as Gospels—and rejected them because of their failure to meet the qualifications generally accepted that determine whether something is authentic or a fraud.

But will we find more "lost letters" with claims of authenticity? Yes, and that should be expected. Long before the "Gospel of Judas" came to light, a Gnostic writing identified as the "Gospel of Thomas," containing 114 "sayings" of Jesus, was roundly rejected by the church. Other writings, also identified as "gospels," were written in the second century and likewise rejected by the early Church.[38]

The bottom line

The Bible is the best preserved and best documented book in the world. In the 1950s, Dr. Charles Ryrie, one of the day's foremost biblical scholars, said, "More than 5,000 manuscripts of the New Testament exist today, which makes the New Testament the best-attested document in all ancient writing." Today, however, that number has increased to over 5,750 manuscripts—the result of archaeological finds throughout the Middle East.

Taking the Bible as a whole that number swells, including not only the text itself, but more than 86,000 quotes of the New Testament that we find in the sermons and writings of the early Church Fathers, along with translations into Latin, Aramaic, and other languages of the first to the fifth centuries.

Compare the vast number of biblical source documents with the scarcity of support for the texts of secular writers. For example, Homer's *Iliad* is preserved in a total of 647 manuscripts; Euripides in 330; and the writings of the Roman historian Tacitus are preserved in a single document dating from the ninth century.

Equally significant is the huge time gap between the deaths of secular writers and the date of the earliest manuscript containing their writings. Some 350 years separate the death of Virgil from the earliest manuscript of his writings; 500 years separate Pliny and the earliest written record of his life; an unbelievable 900-year gap exists between Horace and what he wrote; 1,400 years span the gap between Plato's death and the earliest document written by him.[39] In his book *Can Man Live Without God?* Ravi Zacharias so aptly summarizes,

> In real terms, the New Testament is easily the best attested ancient writing in terms of the sheer number of documents, the time span between the event and the document, and the variety of documents available to sustain or contradict it. There is nothing in ancient manuscript evidence to match such textual availability and integrity.[40]

A century ago two of the most respected Greek scholars of all times, B.F. Westcott and F.J.A. Hort, were convinced that only one word in a hundred was even questioned, and today, with so many recently discovered manuscripts, we can be confident that about 99.9 percent of the words in the original text have been recovered, contended Dr. Kenneth Kantzer, the late editor of *Christianity Today* and dean of Trinity Seminary.

Church historian Dr. Edward Panosian says that all of the passages or words about which there is even the slightest question would make up no more than a half page of a 500-page book. That doesn't leave much room for conjecture. And I have to add that no single doctrinal issue is questioned—none.

Totally without foundation is the myth that the Bible has been copied and recopied, translated and retranslated, so that today what we have doesn't even resemble the original written by Moses, the prophets, Matthew, Mark, Luke, and John along with the apostle Paul and other writers. Those who allege this demonstrate their ignorance of the facts.

Whether or not you use the Book as a measure of truth, a guide for your life, and a blueprint for living, the evidence supporting its veracity and integrity is overwhelming. It cannot be ignored.

- What do a few old manuscripts discovered in the desert have to do with my life today?

- At a dinner with friends, someone mentions they just rented *The Da Vinci Code* movie, which leads them to believe Jesus was married to Mary Magdalene. How would you respond to them?

- Professor José O'Callaghan, a scholar at the University of Barcelona, discovered fragments of Mark's Gospel believed to date from the year ad 50, about 75 years older than any other previously discovered manuscripts. Why is this discovery important?

- When the Sawis of Papua New Guinea heard the story of the Gospels for the first time, they cheered for Judas because their culture valued treachery above integrity. In what ways has modern culture affected the value system of you or your friends so that wrong appears to be right?

๛

CHAPTER FOUR

The Bridge of Archaeology

*"No archaeological discovery has ever
controverted a biblical reference."* [1]

—ARCHAEOLOGIST NELSON GLUECK

In 1979, the National Aeronautical and Space Administration (NASA) launched two space probes known as *Voyager I* and *Voyager II*. Among the various items on board the spacecrafts was a notebook containing 118 photographs of people on earth, cassette tapes of music that was popular at the time (no doubt today they would have simply included an I-Pod), triangulated directions on how to get to planet Earth, and greetings written in 60 languages, including Latin and Hittite. *Voyager I* spun out of the solar system in 1986, and its next stop is 40,000 years away when it reaches the nearest star, Alpha Centauri.

It is interesting to me that Hittite was one of the languages chosen by NASA to represent the cultures and people who have inhabited our planet. For many centuries the only reference to the once mighty nation of the Hittites was found in the Bible, and historians uniformly denied they ever existed. [2]

Then in December 1915, Professor Bedrich Hrozny, a Bohemian linguist and professor at the University of Prague, announced to the world that he had discovered the key to the Hittite language and that it related to Indo-European languages. The Hittites were then duly acknowledged and certified as a legitimate people, and gradually their great importance in relationship to Middle Eastern culture and their historic interaction were recognized.

The attitude, however, that something historically recorded in Scripture should be considered mythical or untrustworthy unless archaeology provides support for it is widely entrenched in academic circles.

Dr. James Hoffmeier, professor of Old Testament and Ancient Near Eastern History and Archaeology at Trinity Evangelical Divinity School, contends that a growing number of secular scholars hold the Bible to an unreasonable standard, arguing that it "has to be substantiated by archaeological evidence" in order to be considered true.

They are known as "minimalists," and are essentially doing the same thing that some revisionist historians are doing who deny that the Nazi Holocaust ever took place, and interpret world history with a national bias, presenting their fictional version as factual.

Furthermore, denying that the Bible is factual and historical also has a political twist to it as well. For example, Israel believes that the Scriptures contain a historical record of how God called Abraham and promised that his descendents would be as numerous as the stars of the heavens, that they would be given the land from the Mediterranean on the west to the Euphrates on the east, and from Egypt on the south to Lebanon on the north (note that part of the land once occupied by the Hittites is included in this promise). In other words, what Moses wrote is considered by many in Israel as a title deed to the property, something highly disputed by the Palestinians who say, "Hey, we've lived here for centuries. This land belongs to us."

So at first, it seems simple enough. Discredit the documents that are used to support a claim to the land, and you have disenfranchised those who think they have a right to it. Understanding how important archaeology is in validating a claim to the land, the Palestinian Authority has encouraged archaeological exploration done by those who interpret their finds favorable to their claim that Palestinians were here as Canaanites, long before the Jews migrated from Egypt.

The Israelis, however, are convinced that archaeology, which is far from being a pure science,[3] still weighs heavily in their favor. So convinced are they that they proposed a "horizontal division" in a peace settlement that would give Israel control of everything beneath the surface of the ground, and the Palestinians control of everything above ground.

The conflict intensified as Palestinians used bulldozers to excavate new openings to the al-Aqsa Mosque and Dome of the Rock in Jerusalem. This infuriated Israeli archaeologists. Jeffrey Sheler explains, "Sifting through the earth the Palestinians dumped out, they found ceramics, glass, and other artifacts they say date from between the First Temple period (850–586 BC) through the fifteenth century AD."[4] There's one thing which is indisputable: Once an area has been bulldozed, there is no reconstructing the evidence of what took place there over the centuries. It's gone forever.

Going back to my premise that secularists consider the Bible to be myth or fiction until it is proven accurate by archaeology and history, the vast findings of archaeology are either ignored or minimized by some scholars who refuse to accept any kind of evidence.

I'm reminded of an acquaintance who was talking with a friend who rejected the authenticity and historicity of the Bible. "And what kind of evidence would you accept to prove that the Bible is historical and factual?" he asked. The detractor, caught off guard, answered, "I don't know. I'd have to think about that."

Vast numbers of archaeological findings corroborate the context of the Bible historically in matters of data, names, places, customs, and practices. So archaeology proves that the Bible is true, right? Not necessarily because it is impossible to prove anything to someone who rejects the evidence; nonetheless, the development of scientific technology and methods that are superior to the "start digging for hidden treasure Indiana Jones–style"—have done much to confirm the biblical record, adding strength to the bridge of confidence that gives you assurance the Bible is to be trusted.

What is modern archaeology about?

Let's begin with a working definition of archaeology as "the scientific study of the remains of the past." The English word *archaeology* comes from two Greek words: *archios* and *logos,* and means "the study of ancient things." In a broad sense it can be considered the scientific study of people, cultures, and civilizations that have been lost and evidence of which is recovered through a variety of disciplines and means.

Naturally the question arises, "How did cities as well as nations such as the Hittites get 'lost' anyway?" Some cities, such as Nineveh, had so completely disappeared that the army of Alexander the Great marched by and didn't even know that they were passing the ruins of a once great city. Much later Napoléon Bonaparte and his army passed by the ancient city of Babylon and never knew it was there either.

Yet obviously some landmarks have not disappeared. The pyramids built as much as 1,000 years before Moses are relatively permanent. They have stood the test of time and are expected to continue standing for a long, long time. Geographic landmarks—such as Galilee, the Valley of Esdralon where Armageddon will be fought, Elisha's fountain at Jericho, the vast fortress of Masada where 960 Jewish patriots took their lives rather than surrender to the Romans in AD 73, Mt. Hermon, the Kidron Valley, and the Mount of Olives—will remain very much as they are at the present time. But other landmarks, nations, and significant structures had all but vanished until they were resurrected by modern archaeology. Questions such as "Why did they disappear and what happened?" are valid.

Modern archaeology takes away the conjecture and offers explanations as to what happened to nations and people as well as cities and places. It shows how a city may have been built in a certain location because it had an accessible water supply, or the site was readily defensible, or was located on a trade route or harbor insuring economic viability. Then hostility with a neighboring nation or people resulted in its destruction. After the war the buildings, having been constructed mostly of mud brick with little reinforcement, were leveled, and a new city was built on the ruins of the old, thus burying the previous level and everything in it.

At times the vagaries of famine or drought drove people away. A harbor silted over in a period of several centuries and eventually the livelihood from shipping became diminished to the point that people moved away. Such happened to the great city of Ephesus, where the Cayster River flowed into the Aegean Sea. Today the old coastline is some five miles inland, whereas in Paul's day Ephesus was a harbor.

Earthquakes also took their toll on cities. Locals, thinking that the quake was the judgment of a god, would not rebuild on the same site. And so the rubble and sand began to pile up—about a foot a century, and eventually the place was marked by a mound known as a tell. Nobody, of course, bothered to put up a sign saying, *Here lie the ruins of ancient [whatever],* and with the passing of generations, details about these places were replaced by legends.

Other cities were destroyed and not rebuilt because of the judgment of God. The great city of Tyre, for example, was destroyed and not reconstructed just as the prophet Ezekiel foretold because of the manner in which they had mocked Israel (see Ezekiel 26:2-3). Likewise, according to the eighth century prophet Obadiah, the Edomites were driven out of the red city of Petra for the same reason.

It is little wonder that archaeology has always been cloaked with a fascination as well as a mystique as to what hidden treasure could be found—whether it was gold in an Egyptian tomb that had been sealed for 3,000 years or an ossuary (stone box) with an inscription on the side of it bearing a secret code.

"Biblical archaeology has changed drastically from 100 years ago, when its focus was on treasure hunting and finding artifacts to 'prove the Bible true,'" says writer Jeffery Sheler.[5] He's right. The days of the simple dig-and-discover method are long gone. Scientific knowledge and the tools of technology have greatly changed the way archaeologists ply their skills.

While archaeology is not an exact science such as chemistry or mathematics with formulas and precepts, it has developed into a fairly complex discipline involving many different facets of exploration and analysis. Today an archaeologist is now like a general practitioner in medicine who, as necessity dictates, calls in specialists to deal with areas where he lacks expertise. He may call upon chemists, hematologists, geologists, climatologists, anthropologists, DNA experts, computer specialists, and forensic experts. Today even satellite imaging and radar get into the act.

You've come a long way

History tells us that the first archaeologist may have been Nabonidus, the son of Nebuchadnezzar of Babylon and the father of Belshazzar, with whom Nabonidus was co-regent during the last chaotic days of the Babylonian Empire. While he was restoring some buildings in northern Babylon, he uncovered a temple platform at Sippur which had been built by Nrim Sin, the son of Sargon I. A clay cylinder records his comments, and if we can believe the veracity of what is written on the cylinder, then 3,200 years had elapsed between the burial and his discovery.

Modern archaeology began in 1799 when the forces of Napoléon Bonaparte discovered the Rosetta Stone during Napoléon's incursion into Egypt. Soldiers were digging the foundation of an addition to a fort near the town of el-Rashid (Rosetta) and one of the soldiers in the expedition by the name of Boussard found a huge slab of black granite. When the spade struck the rock, little did he know or even imagine what a vast treasure he was about to uncover. The black slab measured 45 inches by 28½ inches, 11 inches thick.

Written on this stele are three languages—14 lines of Egyptian hieroglyphics, 32 lines of demotic, and 54 lines of Greek in large letters known as uncials. It was nearly a century later (1882) that a French scholar, Jean François Champollion, deciphered the writing.

When the French lost the war, the English graciously expropriated the treasure and carted it off to the British Museum in 1802, where it has remained except for two years when it was securely ensconced in a London subway 50 feet below ground so that it would be safe from the devastation of German bombs in World War 2.

How is an expedition actually done?

Anyone who has ever seen the movie *Raiders of the Lost Ark* knows the answer—get a shovel and start digging, right? Hardly! Though thousands of tremendously important archaeology sites have been ransacked and desecrated (if not destroyed) by amateurs and treasure seekers, serious archaeologists take a totally different approach.

Until the stratigraphic method was pioneered by Sir Mortimer Wheeler and Kathleen Kenyon, archaeologists would often dig a hole in a mound known as a tell, make a trench, or sink a shaft, sifting the rubble for valuable artifacts. While the method often did produce pieces of pottery, bones, jewelry, gold or precious stones, manuscripts, and a variety of household objects, what was removed was of value primarily to museums or collectors. The manner in which things were removed destroyed the possibility of evaluating the items in relationship to the culture and learning something of their relationship to a lost culture and civilization. Once an item is removed from an excavation site there is no second chance to see its relationship to its environment. Furthermore, the item may immediately begin to degrade, having been removed from the airtight environment that preserved it.

Modern archaeologists go about the task in a different manner. The stratigraphic method initially entails photographing terrain, geography, and anything that may relate to the site to be excavated. Once the topographical data has been recorded, a vast grid is superimposed on the area with sections of about 10 square meters being denoted. A ridge between sections known as a balk, allows them to be numbered, then carefully each grid is removed, about one square meter at a time. Whenever something is found, before it is removed or even touched by human hands, it is photographed and analyzed by senior staff members.

But I'm getting ahead of myself. Long before the first shovelful of anything is excavated, an often complicated series of hurdles have to be circumvented as summarized by the following steps:

1. *Locating an archaeological site with valid reason to consider excavation.* While no more than 5 percent of ancient sites in the Middle East have been excavated, seeing a tell scientists often base motives for exploration on known entities or facts which then lead them to conclude that a given location has historical or biblical significance that is worthy of serious investigation.

2. *Finding financial backing.* Expeditions cost a lot of money. Needs include travel, accommodations, equipment, salaries for both professionals and local workers, food, water and, of major consideration, fees and permits that are required by governments.

   Where does the money usually come from? Most expeditions are sponsored by foundations, educational institutions such as Harvard University, the Oriental Institute associated with the University of Chicago, Oxford and Cambridge, the British Museum, and philanthropists.

3. *Obtaining government permission to touch the site.* Permissions can be exceedingly difficult to acquire. In Israel today the approval for exploration also involves rabbinical groups opposed to disturbing any graves or often anything else.

4. *Staffing the team.* Most expeditions are headed by at least one recognized archaeologist who in turn puts together a staff of qualified individuals, often graduate students who want hands-on experience. These individuals are usually professors who either do exploration during summer months when their academic load is lighter or else they take a sabbatical from teaching to devote time to their research and work.

5. *Determining the logistics.* How can the workers be supplied and where can sufficient supplies and water be obtained? Local people have to be hired to assist with a variety of tasks—driving, cooking, procuring supplies, digging, sorting and classifying whatever is found, among other things. Finding honest laborers is not always easy. On one occasion Dr. William Albright from the American Schools of Oriental Research overheard one of the workers say that as soon as they found the gold, the workmen should cut the throats of the directors and take the loot for themselves. Perhaps fortunately for Dr. Albright and his team, no gold was discovered on that expedition.

What are archaeological expeditions likely to find?

The short answer to that question is the same kind of things that you have in your house—ordinary items that relate to your life and culture. The difference is that what was considered ordinary, say 3,000 years ago, may be considered extraordinary today.

A stroll through almost any museum reveals an abundance of things such as clothing, cooking utensils, pottery of all sizes, shapes, and descriptions (often a key to providing dates), knives, weapons, coins, human remains, statues—large and small (for example, the largest building in ancient Ephesus, adjacent to the city hall, has been identified as a house of prostitution by the artifacts thrown into a well), letters and notes (usually written on papyrus), and so forth.

What does archaeology contribute to biblical understanding?

Consider the following:

1. Archaeology has confirmed the names of literally thousands

of geographic places such as Bethlehem, Caesarea, Rome, Ephesus, Laodicea, Nineveh, Babylon, Tyre, Sidon, Dan, Beersheba, the House of Caiaphas, Corinth (including the meat market and the bema or judgment seat where Paul refuted false charges), the synagogue in Capernaum, and many other places.

2. Archaeology demonstrates that individuals such as Abraham and Sarah, Moses, David, Pilate, and great numbers of both secular kings as well as those of Israel and Judah once lived and reigned or otherwise influenced history.[6] The extensive findings at Mari, in Syria, refuted the beliefs of some scholars who taught that writing hadn't even been formulated at the time Moses wrote the Pentateuch. Thousands of tablets found here demonstrate that names such as of the patriarchs Abraham, Isaac, and Jacob, as well as many other biblical names were commonly used concurrently with the era the Bible speaks of.

3. Archaeology helps us understand events mentioned in Scripture in light of the cultures in which they took place. Remember Ephron the Hittite? Abraham needed a place to bury Sarah at her death. He was interested in buying the cave at Machpelah from his neighbor. Ephron says, "It's yours—my gift to you!" But he really didn't mean that. It was the culture, so we have learned—part of the bargaining process. Finally he says, "It's worth 400 shekels of silver," and the deal was struck. God made covenants with His people which follow the same pattern of covenants and legal documents of the times.

4. Archaeology has resulted in a vast number of manuscript discoveries (the papyri are among the finest examples of this) giving us insights to culture, the meaning of words, the vagaries of human nature and the customs of people, confirming

the data found in the Bible. For example, following the Six Days' War in October, 1967, Israeli archaeologists exploring Masada found scrolls that had been buried there for 2,000 years amidst the ruins. Says Moshe Perlman, speaking of a manuscript containing the Psalms that was found there, "The Psalms of David as recited in today's synagogues are the same as those uttered by the Zealots in their synagogues—the same Hebrew words, the same sentence structure, the same beginning and end of each chapter."

5. Findings of archaeology make biblical places and events come alive in that geography is the hook that history is hung on. The more we know of the actual environment and climate, the greater is our understanding of certain events mentioned in Scripture, such as floods, drought, earthquakes, and disasters.

6. Archaeology has shed much light on the language of Scripture. For instance, Peter told his readers to "Make your calling and election sure" (2 Peter 1:10). The word "sure," archaeologists have discovered, was used in legal documents of the Roman era. In a contract it meant the stipulations could not be changed. In a will, it meant that heirs could not alter the terms of the testament. Found in a love letter, the suitor assured his beloved that he would always love her. "Make your calling and election sure" takes on new meaning in light of this discovery about the word use of "sure."

7. Finally, archaeology provides a window to the peoples mentioned in the Bible—a very lucid and meaningful one, too, that makes them come alive even in the twenty-first century. The Bible was not written in a vacuum but in our world—a world of flesh and blood, of commerce, of intrigue, of love and death; and the more archaeologists

have unearthed, the greater is our understanding of the times in which the Word was given and the people to whom it was given. No place on earth has been better excavated than Israel, the crossroads of civilization and the birthplace of Judaism and Christianity.

The limited space does not allow an exhaustive study of important archaeological discoveries of the past century. I have, however, singled out ten representative stories that demonstrate that archaeology is a solid bridge to confidence in God's Word.

Exhibit 1: Landsat does its stuff

Satellite imagery, which was first developed with military objectives in mind, became a new tool for archaeologists who wanted to pin down the locations of long-forgotten cities—at least, forgotten to the thousands of people who thumb through the pages of their Old Testament and stumble over words like Beersheba, Zer Hammoth, Abel Beth-Maacah, Naphtali, and Tirzah. But some 4,000 years ago, these places were as meaningful to people as Manila, Frankfurt, Tokyo, or New York.

When Landsat began sending back pictures from space, scientists began seeing the faces of the earth in a new light. It was almost as if someone had switched on the light and enabled them to see ancient trade routes in the Middle East which archaeologists knew were somewhere "out there" but now precisely became "down there."

In ancient days when a city was destroyed in warfare, the survivors were usually taken away as slaves and the city was sacked and burned. Unlike the cities of World War 2, which were rebuilt, the wind and sand began to drift over these ancient cities and they were soon lost to history. Satellite imaging makes these stand out vividly and enables scientists to chart transportation routes and identify undiscovered landmarks.

Archaeologists are making some remarkable discoveries which should only enhance our trust in the historical accuracy of the Bible. You may wonder, "Like what?" For a start, the exodus of some 2.5 million slaves from Egypt to the promised land of Canaan was one of the greatest migrations ever undertaken by a nation. Can archaeologists help document this move?

According to the Bible, Moses led the group in a rather circuitous path, avoiding the immediate and direct route from the Nile River delta where they were living to Canaan. Women sometimes quip that Moses was lost for 40 years because he didn't want to stop and ask directions. Don't you believe that for a moment.

Jeffery Sheler explains,

> Recent archaeological data, scholars note, also are consistent with the Bible's explanation, in Exodus 13:17, about why Moses and the Israelites took the long way to Canaan through the desolate Sinai wilderness rather than following the shorter coastal route: Enemy military posts lay on that path. Egyptian hieroglyphics from about 1300 BC at the temple of Amun in Karnak depict a series of Egyptian installations along the coastal route. And modern excavations have uncovered a string of Egyptian citadels strikingly similar to those in the Karnak relief, stretching from the Nile delta to Gaza.[7]

Archaeologists from the Hebrew University of Jerusalem agree. The presence of the forts "is perfectly compatible with the Exodus" says Professor Trude Dothan. At the same time archaeologists don't expect to find parking meters and leftover parts from their wagons. These who came out of Egypt were slaves and traveled light. Much like the Bedouins who still trek across the Negev, their tracks being erased by the wind and sand with not much left behind.

Score one for modern technology.

Exhibit 2: Discoveries at Ein Hatzeva

An old fortress some 20 miles southwest of the Dead Sea in Israel today has been called "one of the most spectacular finds of recent decades in all Israel." Today archaeologists are unearthing the walls of a massive Iron Age fortress, built about 800 BC, which are some 300 feet on each side and had massive towers on each corner. "OK," you may be asking, "but why get worked up over a pile of very old rocks in a desert?" That is a good question. And the answer goes deeper than archaeology. It embraces the historical trustworthiness of the Bible at the same time.

Historians got excited when the old fortress was clearly identified as that which belonged to one of ancient Israel's most bitter enemies. Archaeologists got animated when they discovered an old Edomite shrine with some 67 bowls with cultic images on them. Scholars of the Bible got excited because they recalled the prophecies of both Isaiah and Obadiah—two prophets of the eighth century who predicted that Edom and its power would be absolutely smashed to pieces. I get excited when I see another instance when the spade of the archaeologist confirms the historical record, reminding us that what is found in this Book is authentic.

Among the ruins at Ein Hatzeva where the fortress and the cultic shrine are located were found seven large limestone incense altars decorated with human-like figures. The artifacts which archaeologists found had all been placed in a pit and smashed to pieces, obviously by someone who wanted to destroy them entirely. Imagine their amazement if those who stomped them so thoroughly could see them today, some 2,500 to 2,800 years later, reconstructed painstakingly by archaeologists.

Historians are surprised to find something belonging to the Edomites within territory which belonged to the kingdom of Judah, for Ein Hatzeva is located not in Edom but in Israel. Travelers to the Middle East today identify the rosy red city of Petra as the home of the ancient Edomites, but Petra in Jordan today is a long way from Ein Hatzeva, which seemingly proves that the Edomites had extended their influence and power far into territory belonging to Israel.

There are many unanswered questions, but we do know two things: First—the very presence of the Edomites was abhorrent to Judah. Edomites had—on at least three occasions—refused to let Israel pass through their territory when they came into the Promised Land. This had never been forgotten. Then, the gods of the Edomites, including their images and deities, were repulsive to Israel. The first of the Ten Commandments God had given to Moses forbade the worship of any other god, and the second restricted making any images.

How does all this relate to our lives today? The Scripture in 2 Kings 23 tells how King Josiah destroyed the idols of the Sidonians, Ammonites, and Moabites. What archaeologists have found may well be part of that massive cleansing of pagan worship. It also tells us that the prophesies about Edom were fulfilled, literally and precisely.

If what archaeologists have found gives you greater confidence as you pick up your Bible and read, then all the better. God's timetable is different from ours, yet what He says—whether it be of individuals, nations, or the world—will eventually take place. With that confidence Isaiah wrote,

> The grass withers and the flowers fall, but the word of our
> God stands forever (Isaiah 40:8).

Exhibit 3: The walls of Old Jericho

Could an earthquake have destroyed ancient Jericho at precisely the exact moment when Joshua and the warriors of ancient Israel marched around the walls seven times and then blew their trumpets? Amos Nur, a Stanford University geophysicist who has been studying the 10,000 year-long historical record of earthquakes in the Jordan Valley, thinks so. He says that Jericho "sits practically on the Jordan Fault that divides the Arabian plate from the Sinai plate."

National Geographic magazine quotes the scientist who notes that the walls of Jericho collapsed in a single direction, as they would in an earthquake, not in a variety of directions as they would if they were destroyed by an invading army.[8]

Many people presume it was Joshua's army that destroyed the walls of Jericho. But read the record: "When the trumpets sounded, the people shouted, and at the sound of the trumpet, when the people gave a loud shout, the wall collapsed; so every man charged straight in, and they took the city" (Joshua 6:20). Even a casual reading makes it clear that it was God, not the army or psychological warfare, that destroyed ancient Jericho. Could God have used an earthquake? There is nothing that would eliminate that possibility.

Actually, Amos Nur, the scientist I quoted, wasn't the first to suggest that an earthquake may have been the physical cause of the wall's collapse. Dr. John Garstang, director of the British School of Archaeology in Jerusalem, excavated Jericho between 1929 and 1936. Garstang found that the walls did actually "fall down flat" (using his terminology).[9] Garstang also noted that the walls fell outward and dragged the inner walls and houses with it, as would take place in an earthquake. Garstang contended that fire destroyed the existing grain supplies and the remains of the city, evidence that chaos resulted from this cataclysmic disturbance.

Geologists tell us that the Jordan Valley is like a giant split in a sandwich. It separates the Arabian Desert (which we know as Jordan, Iran, and Iraq today) from the gentle hills adjacent to the Mediterranean. Starting from Galilee, at an altitude of 700 feet below sea level, the Jordan River Valley drops to 1,300 feet below sea level at the Dead Sea. A giant seismic fault runs deep through that valley.

The theory that God may have used an earthquake seems to be rational, yet it doesn't, for a moment, remove God from the landscape of human history. We then are faced with a miracle of timing that defies human explanation. Even today, nobody knows when an earth-quake is going to take place. We only know when it actually happens. Apart from a supernatural revelation of God, anyone who positions himself around the walls of a city and blows his trumpet expecting an earthquake would be considered deranged and a candidate for an institution.

God normally uses the natural laws, which He puts into operation in a supernatural manner, to do His bidding. Amos Nur may well be right.

A postscript to the Jericho excavations. Subsequent to the excavations of John Garstang in the 1930s, another archaeologist, a fellow Briton by the name of Kathleen Kenyon, who was highly respected in her profession, excavated again, taking exception to Garstang's findings. Her verdict: "No, that's not how it was at all. Wrong dates." While the jury is still out, she did find something that is fascinating.

She discovered that at the time of Christ, there were at least two sections of Jericho—an old part, and a newer part where the city wall had been extended, much as we would extend the city limits today to accommodate growth. Her findings reconciled what had appeared to be a conflict in Scripture. Because walls provided protection from enemies and defined city boundaries, a second wall was erected around the perimeters of the "newer" Jericho.

The text of Matthew says that on a certain occasion Jesus was leaving Jericho when He encountered a blind man by the name of Bartimaeus, who cried out for help[10] (Matthew 9:27), and Luke says He was going into the city (Luke 18:35). Yes, it appeared to be a contradiction—that's what skeptics said for a long while. True, it's difficult to be going into a city at the same time you are departing from one. How does archaeology help us reconcile the apparent contradiction?

Kenyon's excavations have shown that as Jericho grew, an annexation prior to the time of Christ had taken place—a kind of suburban Jericho in the terminology of our day. Bartimaeus may have been blind but he wasn't dumb. He knew that sitting at the gate or passageway between these two areas would be a place of high traffic and more people would notice him. His chances of getting more alms were better. Thus, the conflict between the writers is resolved. Jesus was passing out of one part of Jericho and into the other when He encountered Bartimaeus. Score another one for archaeology.

Exhibit 4: Jezebel's makeup

An archaeological expedition digging at the site of ancient Samaria struck it rich—no, not gold! But when it became clear that the ivory palace of Ahab and Jezebel had been identified, excitement filled the camp. In the queen's chambers of the palace of the ancient monarch were the very saucers and small stone boxes which Jezebel had used in mixing her makeup. It was all there, having been preserved by the destruction of the palace. Traces of coal had been used for black; turquoise for green; ocher for red, and a small, smooth depression in the stone box was used for mixing the eye shadow.

Jezebel was one of the most powerful, ruthless, sensuous women who ever lived. Mentioned 22 times in the Bible, in both the Old and New Testaments, she became identified with the lowest dregs of womanhood.

Who was this woman? And how did she become so powerful? Born in a king's palace in Sidon across the Jordan, Jezebel knew no discipline as a child. But she did learn that her seductive ways and strong will could manipulate men. A marriage of convenience was arranged by Ethbaal, her father, and when she became the wife of Ahab, the king of Israel, little did Ahab know what he was in for!

Long before women demanded independence, Jezebel understood how to get what she wanted. Her power of persuasion involved a measure of physical beauty, manipulation and, upon occasion, raw physical power. She destroyed anyone and everyone who stood in her way. Both men and women moved quickly to get away from her wrath.

In Israel, Jezebel introduced the worship of an agricultural deity, Baal, and brought in an Asherah pole, including sexual expression as part of the worship. Eventually, human sacrifice was introduced, and archaeologists have unearthed the remains of tiny infant bones sealed in jars, hundreds of years old, a grim testimony to what took place.

There was, however, one man who withstood her fury. But even he was afraid of her. His name: Elijah. You can read about him in 1 Kings in the Old Testament. When confronted with this hideous situation, Elijah challenged Jezebel's false religious leaders and the historic battle of the true and the false took place on Mt. Carmel. But after the 450 prophets of Baal were eliminated, Jezebel vowed to Elijah, "I'm going to get you like you got my boys!"

Violence has a way of begetting violence! An eternal law of the harvest says that you reap what you sow. Eventually, all the cosmetics of the world could not erase the hard lines of sinful living, and Jezebel met her death in much the same manner as she accomplished her goals—violently and cruelly. Elijah, not given to flattery, prophesied that her end would be marked with violence. "Dogs will devour Jezebel by the wall of Jezreel" (1 Kings 21:23). When Jezebel was confronted with an invading army, according to Scripture, "she painted her eyes, arranged her hair" and went out to dialogue with the enemy. This time, though, her looks failed her, and palace attendants turned the tables on her and threw her to her death, where dogs devoured her body, exactly as Elijah had predicted.

Exhibit 5: Four coins in the Pool of Siloam

Having never studied the Bible, the skeptic considers himself to be in a better position to determine what is factual and what is mythical than the dedicated scholar who has immersed himself in the study of Scripture for a lifetime. At least that's what some college and university students are led to believe.

Take for example the belief that the Pool of Siloam you read about in John 9 didn't really exist, and that the story was more like a parable or myth than a factual encounter. Says Princeton Theological Seminary professor Dr. James Charlesworth, "Scholars have said that there wasn't a Pool of Siloam and that John was using a religious 'conceit' to illustrate a point." But then something happened.

Workers digging up a sewer line in the Old City of Jerusalem uncovered two steps—something they didn't expect to find while repairing a sewer. Work stopped. The Israel Antiquities Authority was called in, and archaeologists started excavating. They knew they were on to something big, something important. As archaeologist Eli Shukron cleared the rubble he was 100 percent certain—this had to be the Pool of Siloam where the blind man was healed by Jesus.

So how could they be so certain it was a first-century structure? The proof is almost stranger than fiction. Workers constructing the original pool had buried four coins in the plaster. All four bore images of Alexander Jannaeus, the Jewish king who ruled Jerusalem from 103 to 76 BC. Archaeologists also found another dozen coins dating from the period of the Jewish revolt against Rome from AD 66 to 70. That demonstrated for certain that the pool had been silted in or filled up by that time.

The Pool of Siloam, located near the gate of the old city where weary travelers could pause and refresh themselves, was the very pool to which the blind man was sent when Jesus healed him. Says Professor Charlesworth, "A gospel that was thought to be 'pure theology' is now shown to be grounded in history."[11] Forget about "Three Coins in a Fountain." I'll go with four coins in the Pool of Siloam—proof that was buried 2,000 years ago confirming the record of Scripture.

Exhibit 6: The old city of Dan in the north

In 1993 a group of archaeologists were working on an excavation on the gentle slopes of Mt. Hermon in the northern part of Israel. The ancient city was known as Dan in Bible days, and the city lay on the route traveled from Beersheba passing through Jerusalem, then north to Dan and on to Damascus, the ancient capital of Syria. It continued on to the old city of Haran from which Abraham journeyed.

The city of Dan was the northern outpost of Israel. Archaeologists working there discovered an old monument which may have stood in the city square. On the monument was an inscription which told about a victory Ben-Hadad, the King of Syria, had sustained against "the house of David."[12]

Interestingly enough, 1 Kings 15:20 in the Old Testament describes precisely such a battle. It reads, "Ben-Hadad agreed with King Asa and sent the commanders of his forces against the towns of Israel. He conquered Ijon, Dan, Abel Beth Macaah and all Kinnereth." For a long, long time the monument stood there. Then it was pushed aside and eventually covered by dust and debris. Dr. Avraham Biran, an archaeologist from Hebrew Union College in Jerusalem, says that this old inscription is "the first reference to David outside of the Bible." Few critics would deny that this is the David who battled Goliath and eventually succeeded Saul as King of Israel.

In the Middle East, the Bible and archaeology are intertwined in such a way that the two cannot be separated. Even scientists who harbor little sentiment for Christianity admit that they are dependent on the historical statements of the Bible. "Without the Bible," says Professor Trude Dothan of Hebrew University in Jerusalem, "we wouldn't have even known that there *were* Philistines." There is a great deal more that they would not know.

Have recent discoveries confirmed the historical accuracy of the Bible? Almost without exception. Does this mean, however, that scientists are now saying, "I guess the old Book has been right all along"? Not exactly. For those who are believers, the recent findings of archaeology only confirm their faith. For those who are unbelievers, the vast numbers of recent discoveries which affirm statement after statement are a remarkable coincidence and nothing more.

Thomas, one of the 12 who walked with Jesus, said that he would not believe that Christ had risen from the dead unless he saw firsthand and touched His nail-scarred hands. And he eventually had that opportunity as the resurrected Christ invited Thomas to "Put your finger here; see my hands. Reach out your hand and put it into my side." The conversation was ended as Jesus—perhaps seeing far beyond the encounter with a pragmatic, "gotta-see-it-to-believe-it" disciple—said, "Blessed are those who have not seen and yet have believed" (John 20:29).

Exhibit 7: The ossuary of James, Jesus' brother

It has been called the most important biblical archaeological find of the past 100 years. Others say it is the earliest archaeological evidence of Jesus Christ ever found in Jerusalem. What is it? A limestone box with a base measuring 20 inches long, 10 inches wide, and 12 inches high. Drs. Amnon Rosefeld and Shimon Ilani of the Geological Survey of Israel in Jerusalem say the little box was quarried from stone taken from Mt. Scopus during the first century. In those days it was common practice to bury a body in a niche of a burial cave, and then—say a year later—when the flesh had decayed, the bones of the deceased were placed within a box which is called an ossuary. But what makes this particular limestone box so important?

Carved on the side of the box is an inscription in Aramaic which reads, "James, son of Joseph, brother of Jesus." Now, could this be the box in which were buried the remains of Jesus' half-brother? Matthew, who was a tax-collector and whose gospel reflects a Jewish point of view, records that Jesus had at least four brothers—James, Joseph, Simon, and Judas. He also mentions "sisters" but doesn't name them (see Matthew 13:55-57).

When Jesus began His ministry, His siblings were among the skeptics. They could not explain the miracles. They were perplexed by His teaching, baffled by His insights. Some evidence suggests they even thought He was mentally deranged. But the resurrection changed all of that. Now they knew that this one who had grown up in their home was the Son of God. They believed. James became the bishop of the church in Jerusalem and played a prominent part in the life of the early church. Tradition tells us he was the first one to write a book of the New Testament—the book of James, excepting possibly a version of Matthew in Aramaic.

But is this the James the inscription speaks of? The New Testament speaks of three men by the name of James: the son of Zebedee; the son of Alphaeus; and James, the brother of Jesus. Could this be a fraud? Some Jewish scientists, not particularly sympathetic to documenting the existence of Jesus Christ, say the box is authentic and there is no evidence that the inscription has been put there in recent centuries. Others are skeptical. But why? The sad reality is the counterfeits are so convincing that it is often difficult to know the authentic from the fake.[13]

While this recent discovery is unlikely to send thousands of people to accept the Christ whose brother's bones were once placed in this box, it is one more piece of historical evidence which comes together in a massive mosaic of facts.

After I spoke recently in a church service, a man walked up and said, "I heard you preach today and liked it, but I'm not a Christian." "What keeps you from coming to Christ?" I asked him. "Well," he said, "I have a very good intellect and I'm uncertain about whether Jesus really did what the Bible says He did." Most folks who take that position hide behind an intellectual smokescreen. The life and work of no other person in all history has been as well documented as has the life of Jesus Christ.

Ultimately, the issue is not evidence but faith, as demonstrated by the man who objected to the evidence but was stopped cold in his tracks by the question, "What sort of evidence would you be willing to accept?" The final step is that of faith as you embrace the truth of what Jesus Christ did and accept the record as true and factual.

Exhibit 8: The bones of Caiaphas

A construction crew was widening a road in Jerusalem's Peace Forest, when workers stumbled across a cave which had been an ancient burial site. Within the burial cave were 12 limestone boxes and within each of those boxes were the bones of someone who had rested in peace for almost 2,000 years.

One of those boxes was carved with a rare and intricate pattern of rosettes and carried the inscription "Joseph, son of Caiaphas." It was obvious that this was a VIP, a man of great importance.

In Israel, stumbling across something like this sends shock waves through the community of archaeologists and scholars of antiquity. For almost two years, Israeli archaeologists studied the discovery, and then released their findings. Yes, they were sure. They had discovered the tomb of Caiaphas, the Jewish high priest, who condemned Jesus and sent Him to Pilate, hoping for His execution.[14]

Who was Caiaphas? Caiaphas, the high priest who ruled in Jerusalem from AD 18 to 36, was a religious leader who had become a corrupt puppet of the Roman government. Instead of honestly using his influence for good and God, he used his power and influence to amass a large family fortune. It was Caiaphas who brought the moneychangers and the sellers of animals and birds into the temple area. By doing this, Caiaphas could control the flow of money and goods through taxation, siphoning off a certain amount for personal gain.

Early in the ministry of Jesus, Caiaphas rightly assessed Jesus' growing popularity as a threat to his control. He knew that as Jesus' influence grew, his base of power was threatened, which led him to conclude that Jesus had to be silenced.

John, in his gospel, tells us that Caiaphas, as high priest, "prophesied that Jesus would die for the Jewish nation" and then set out to make his prediction come true. John adds, "So from that day on they plotted to take his life" (John 11:51-53).

Enraged by the desecration of the temple, Jesus took a whip and overturned the tables of the moneychangers and drove out those who sold doves, saying, "'My house will be called a house of prayer,' but you are making it a 'den of robbers'" (Matthew 21:13). The battle lines were drawn. It was the powerful religious establishment against one man. As Jesus, along with His disciples, prayed in the darkness of the garden of Gethsemane, the temple guard, sent by Caiaphas, took Jesus and brought Him before the religious council of the day known as the Sanhedrin.

History says that Caiaphas had more to do with the death of Jesus than any other man, including Pilate (whose existence has been verified only in recent years by an inscription found in Caesarea).

Okay, you may be thinking, *they have the bones. Now what?* Undoubtedly, another stop will be added to the itinerary of tourist buses making the rounds on Bible Land tours, while tourist guides recount the part Caiaphas played in the drama of early Christianity. But what is really significant is that one more time archaeologists have confirmed the existence of the key players in the drama of redemption.

The evidence of both history and archaeology continues to confirm the truthfulness of the gospel accounts.

Exhibit 9: "Hey, Mom, they've found Noah's Ark. I think…"

Is it conceivable that centuries after Noah and his family entered the ark, that its remains should be found in the twenty-first century? It is not only conceivable but that possibility is growing. Satellite technology as well as visual photos of Mt. Ararat reveals something at the 15,300 feet level on the northwest corner of this difficult-to-reach hunk of ice and granite. Described by researchers as "a baffling mountainside anomaly," there is something there that seems to defy identification.

For 13 years Porcher Taylor, a security analyst and senior associate at the Center for Strategic and International Studies, has been fascinated by the possibility that this just might be the remote remains of what Noah used to preserve life during the Flood. "During the what?" some people ask in amazement, as though the biblical account of the Great Flood, a deluge that lasted 40 days and nights, was only a myth.

Some describe the "anomaly" as simply being a quirk of nature, or a playful shadow, or as "a human-made structure of some sort." Taylor, though cautious as a scientist, was more optimistic. In an interview he said, "I had no preconceived notions or agendas when I began this in 1993 as to what I was looking for. I maintain that if it is the remains of something man-made and potentially nautical, then it's potentially something of biblical proportions."[15]

Why not take a team of scientists and go find out firsthand what's there? Unfortunately, that's not so easily done, for both geographic as well as political reasons. First of all, Mt. Ararat is located in Eastern Turkey on the borders of Iran, Armenia (formerly in the U.S.S.R.), and Nachivan. And none of those countries today is "user friendly." Simply put, they don't want foreigners prowling around their turf. Furthermore, their governments are not cooperative with either scientifically or religiously motivated groups. There are no airports nearby, no shuttles that will take you to the site. Nothing.

But satellite imagery defies those barriers and lets us know that something is there. Just what, though, is uncertain. A website devoted to the exploration for Noah's Ark says,

> Many people believe that Mt. Ararat is the place where Noah's Ark landed, but the Bible does not state this. It simply says that the boat landed in the Urartian mountains, of which there are hundreds, although Ararat is the highest. Since Mount Ararat is the highest location in Urartu, some people throughout history have jumped to the unproven conclusion that it was the landing place and promoted that concept as a regional tradition.[16]

To make the situation a bit more interesting, let's suppose that God in His providence should allow the fog, the politics, and the isolation to be pushed aside, and researchers, doing DNA testing, demonstrated that the baffling mountainside "anomaly" should be identified as the actual ark that Noah used, what would be the implications? After all, the actual size of whatever is there seems to approximate the size of the ark as recorded by Moses in the book of Genesis.

Should we assume that a large number of unbelievers would start believing? That didn't happen when the tremendously significant Qumran scrolls were discovered, starting in 1947 and continuing to this day.

Surprising to some is the fact that over 250 flood legends have been identified, originating all over the world. Most of these flood stories are in basic agreement with what the Torah, identified as the Old Testament, says about the event. Many, no matter what the evidence, would choose not to believe in the biblical account of the Flood for various reasons. It's not politically correct and requires a tacit, unstated acknowledgment of the possible connection between the sinfulness of humankind which resulted in God's judgment and our own personal failures that may also result in accountability before God.

Yet, should evidence be found substantiating the Flood story, some would believe. Jesus, for one, believed in the Flood, using it as evidence for the judgment of God which is not only past but future as well. Verifiable evidence isn't necessary to acknowledge the truth of Scripture. The evidence, however, only confirms the historical record, which you can read for yourself in the Bible.

Exhibit 10: The amazing light shed by the Ebla tablets

In 2250 BC, an army led by King Naram-Sin of Akkad came against an army led by a rival king whose great empire was known as Ebla, located near the modern city of Aleppo, Syria. The Royal Palace was destroyed, and the few survivors fled for their lives. Literally everything was destroyed by the conquerors—almost everything, that is. Over time the hot Syrian winds continued to blow the desert sand, and eventually Ebla disappeared—almost as though it had never existed.

Fast forward some 4,000 years—past the days of David, Solomon, and the divided kingdom, past the close of the Old Testament, even past the life, death, and resurrection of Jesus Christ, past two world wars and the rise of science and technology.

The date was 1968 and an obscure archaeologist from the University of Rome, Dr. Paolo Matthiae, was digging at a mound known as Tell Mardikh, some 30 miles from Aleppo in northern Syria. A *New York Times* reporter described the area as "a treeless desert with only a wide mound where the great city once stood," explaining, "It was destroyed and rebuilt three times before its final destruction by the Hittites around 1650 BC."[17] The tell they had been exploring was quite large—about 50 feet tall at its highest point and covered an area of about 150 acres. For four years Dr. Matthiae had been hoping to find something big.

Then he stumbled across a statue bearing the name of a king in Ebla. They now knew this was the ruins of a great Canaanite city that had flourished between the twenty-third and twenty-sixth centuries before Christ. It was only a matter of time until they found the royal library of Ebla which had not been destroyed with the rest of the palace. It was like the librarian had locked the door and walked out. Fifteen thousand clay tablets were there—not broken and smashed but in a near perfect state of preservation.

Unwittingly, Matthiae had happened upon what many archaeologists consider to be the most important find of the twentieth century, second only to discovery of the Dead Sea Scrolls in 1947. Dr. Matthiae brought in an expert on Assyriology, Dr. Giovanni Pettinato, and the two began to reconstruct the fascinating story of one of the great civilizations of all times.

Soon newspapers came alive with the story.

• The *Jerusalem Post* pictured a somber and staid archaeologist,

Dr. David Noel Freedman, holding a clay tablet. The full-page story was captioned with bold letters: THE EBLA TABLETS. The lines following the title read, "Digging into a tell in northern Syria, Italian archaeologists have come upon an archive whose contents are rocking the normally staid world of biblical and Mesopotamian scholarship. The clay tablets, written half a millennium before the Hebrew patriarch period, require a basic rethinking of biblical origins."[18]

- The *Los Angeles Times'* front-page story was captioned, "Tablets Shed New Light on the Bible." Staff reporters George Alexander and John Dart introduced the article by saying, "Beneath a dusty sun-baked mound in northern Syria, a team of Italian archaeologists has uncovered one of the most spectacular finds of all times."[19]

- Scooping both the *L.A. Times* and the *Jerusalem Post,* The *New York Times* introduced the story with the caption: "Ebla: Lost Kingdom Yields Secrets."[20]

What's the full story behind the headlines?

- Until the discovery at Ebla there had been only a few scattered references to the city with nothing of substance that revealed it was one of the great cities of the world. Gradually the tablets began to divulge their secrets.

- Ebla existed in its golden age at least 4,000 years ago—at least 500 years before the pyramids were built, more than a millennium-and-a-half before Moses wrote the Pentateuch, 2,000 years before the birth of Christ, and 1,600 years before the rise of classical Greek.

- "The language used on the tablets was a western dialect of Semitic, a language closely related to Canaanite and Hebrew," said William LaSor, professor of Old Testament studies at Fuller Theological Seminary. The tablets are windows to a world, vastly different from ours, but essentially the same where people lived, worked, married, and quarreled and fought. The tablets contain records of expense accounts, financial records of shipments, historical documents containing genealogies and exploits of kings and military personnel, some 60 different professions people were engaged in, names of plants, minerals, birds, mammals, and fish—even a list of beers, noting that one was marketed under the name "Mara Beer."

• Thousands of names of geographic locations are mentioned including many that are identical with those referred to in the Bible such as Hazor, Megiddo, Jaffa, Gaza, and Sinai. Of interest to biblical scholars is the parallel between the names of five particular cities mentioned in the Bible—Sodom, Gomorrah, Admah, Zeboim, and Bela (also known as Zoar). The list of cities in the Genesis account (written 1,000 years later) is exactly the same as those found on the Ebla tablets; however, both Sodom and Gomorrah are spoken of as being prosperous, well-established cities.[21]

• The names of individuals mentioned in the tablets parallel those whose exploits are recorded in the Bible, such as Abram, Esau, Michael, David, Ishmael, and Israel, though secular scholars are quick to distance themselves from any connection with the thought that the individuals mentioned in the Ebla tablets are the same individuals mentioned in Scripture. Nonetheless, the names appearing in the Ebla tablets prove beyond a shadow of a doubt that names such as these were common long before the individuals named in the Bible were even alive.[22]

• Ebla controlled the territory from Egypt in the south to the Persian Gulf on the southeast to the middle of modern Turkey on the north.

- Social laws very similar to those found in the book of Exodus were codified. One legal tablet contained laws with penalties for damages to be awarded if a person had been injured by a physical blow. Another specified injuries sustained by a weapon. One dealt with rape and compensation to a father if a virgin was violated against her will.

- Other tablets contained creation and flood stories that are consistent with those recorded by Moses in the book of Genesis.

How does this pre-Genesis information affirm the biblical text? The primary contribution that the Ebla tablets make is that they add a tremendous amount of light to a period of time often known as the "dark age" of Mesopotamian history and civilization establishing the fact that great civilizations existed rivaling those of much later times.

Abraham Rabinovich, writing for the *Jerusalem Post International Edition,* says, "most astonishing is that writing existed at all in this third millennium city—indeed not just writing but a highly literate society."[23] "It's like suddenly discovering an English archive showing a highly developed stage of literacy 500 years before Chaucer," says Professor Hayim Tadmor of Hebrew University and one of Israel's leading Assyriologists.[24]

For those who had denied the historicity of Old Testament individuals—including Moses, Abraham, and David—as well as those who held to the position that in Moses' day, if he even existed, writing had not developed to the point of his being able to write the Pentateuch, the Ebla tablets lit such a bright light that they will be shining for a long while.

The bottom line

Archaeology consistently authenticates biblical statements regarding individuals, geographic locations, and historical events. Professor William

F. Albright, whom I referred to in the previous chapter taught Semitic languages at Johns Hopkins University from 1929 to 1958. In an article entitled "Archaeological Discovery and the Scriptures" he summarized, "During the past century, our knowledge of the historical and literary background of the Bible has increased by a series of prodigious leaps, and it is now advancing with increasing speed."[25]

Science and technology have allowed archaeologists to better interpret the vast number of archaeological expeditions. "Phenomenal" is the word Albright used to describe the scientific contribution of disciplines such as carbon isotope dating, DNA analysis, and satellite imaging.

Gradually, expedition by expedition, we have increased our understanding of cultures, history, names, events, places, and the greater our knowledge, the stronger is the bridge of confidence that the Bible contains accurate history, that the individuals and events recorded in this text are represented exactly as they were—not fabricated composites, as some would have us believe. As Millar Burrows, a Yale University professor, puts it, "Archaeology has in many cases refuted the views of modern critics. It has shown in a number of instances that these views rest on false assumptions and unreal, artificial schemes of historical development."[26]

The case for archaeology, often intertwined with manuscript discoveries, forms a synthesis that grows only stronger as time passes.

Now, let's consider another important bridge to confidence in the Bible—that of fulfilled prophecy.

- How could archaeological evidence give you added confidence that your "calling and election" are sure?

- How do the ruins of an old fortress at Ein Hatzeva confirm the prophecies of Isaiah and Obadiah about Edom?

- The Ebla tablets prove that a highly literate society existed in approximately 2300 BC. Why is that significant?

- If you buried a time capsule in your back yard for some future generation to uncover, what would you include in your capsule, and why?

CHAPTER FIVE

✿

The Bridge of Fulfilled Prophecy

*"There is only one real inevitability:
It is necessary that the Scripture be fulfilled."* [1]

—CARL HENRY

When God decides to change the course of history, He sends a tiny baby into the world. That's the way it was when Philip II, the king of Macedonia, became the father of a little boy, born to his fourth wife. Her name didn't even rate a historical footnote, but the child she bore is included in the ranks of Genghis Khan, Napoléon, and Charlemagne. The infant was named Alexander. History calls him *Alexander the Great*. At the age of 13 he became the pupil of a slave, one whose name is almost as well known as his, Aristotle. As young Alexander grew up, Aristotle often spoke of the glories of Greece and planted the vision of taking Grecian culture to the world in the mind of his teenage prodigy.

Upon the death of his father, 20-year-old Alexander tightened his grip on power. He then set out to conquer the world. Enlisting foreign troops as well as Greeks, Alexander was formidable as he marched across central Asia Minor (now Turkey). Foe after foe fell to his assault. After he had gone east, he and his army turned and marched south into

Phoenicia, capturing Tyre after a seven-month siege. He then set his sights on pillaging Jerusalem and adding it to his roster of conquered cities. The year then was 332 BC.

Flavius Josephus, the turncoat Jew who became the interpreter of Jewish culture and history for three successive emperors, tells us that the Jewish high priest, hearing that Alexander's army was approaching the city, went to meet him dressed in a white priestly robe and bearing a scroll containing the writings of the sixth-century prophet Daniel.[2]

Showing him the passage of Scripture from Daniel 8 where the goat represented a great, powerful ruler whose ambition was to conquer the world, the high priest explained that his emergence would be sudden and decisive. With conviction he also showed him the context that explained that upon the leader's death the kingdom would be divided into four subsequent powers—exactly what happened upon Alexander's death.[3]

Alexander saw himself as the fulfillment of this prophecy and so impressed was he by this that he spared Jerusalem from destruction. It is also the nature of this very exact and precise prophecy that gives critics a difficult time. How do you explain the explicit picture of Alexander's life written at least 200 years before he ever drew a breath of Macedonian air?

What can you say about events that are predicted in vivid details— including names of individuals and world powers, spelling out the precise numbers of years or dates associated with them—even centuries before they unfold? For example, Daniel writes, "Know and understand this: From the issuing of the decree to restore and rebuild Jerusalem until the Anointed One, the ruler, comes, there will be seven 'sevens,' and sixty-two 'sevens.' It will be rebuilt with streets and a trench, but in times of trouble" (Daniel 9:25). There's no ambiguity in what he says. In a way, he was saying, "Start the clock running when the king gives the order to rebuild Jerusalem!"

When you make a prediction, you are either right or else you are wrong! And getting it entirely right is the acid test of whether or not God has spoken through a prophet. Moses said that if a man is really a prophet with insights which have come through the revelation of the Holy Spirit, there is no room for error. He's either 100 percent right, or else he is not a prophet. Thus he wrote, "If what a prophet proclaims in the name of the Lord does not take place or come true, that is a message the Lord has not spoken" (Deuteronomy 18:22), and God instructed that the person should forfeit his life. Pretty strong action. These so-called prophets could be dead wrong, literally!

No other book in the world has so many explicit and detailed prophecies as to events in the future that can be readily pronounced "fulfilled!"—verified by history—as does the Bible.

Wrote D. James Kennedy,

> In all the writings of Buddha, Confucius, and Lao-tse, you will not find a single example of predicted prophecy. In the Koran (the writings of Muhammad) there is one instance of a specific prophecy—a self-fulfilling prophecy that he, Muhammad himself, would return to Mecca. Quite different from the prophecy of Jesus who said that He would return from the grave. One is easily fulfilled, and the other is impossible to any human being.[4]

How do contemporary secular prophets differ from those of the Bible?

A Greek proverb says, "The best guesser is the best prophet!" While that may well be true of the psychics who read tea leaves or tarot cards in the mall or at the county fair, is it also true of those who back their prophecies with the words, "Thus says the word of the LORD"? If you look up the word *prophecy* in your dictionary or encyclopedia, you'll discover that it comes from two Greek words that literally mean, "to speak" or "to say beforehand." If the comments you read parallel the ones which I have noted, you'll discover such names as Elijah and Daniel are mentioned as biblical prophets, but you will also read about the Oracle at Delphi in Greece along with some of the ancient Persian prophets and astrologers who allegedly could foretell the future. The definition of biblical prophecy as being "history pre-recorded" may be simplistic, yet the framework of biblical prophecy is so precise and exact that it is not difficult to recognize the prophetic picture unfolding much as an artist creates a painting stroke by stroke.

In recent years, scores of individuals have laid claim to having prophetic genius. Michael Nostradamus is still considered to be one of the greatest of all times, yet his prophecies are cloaked in ambiguity. They are dark and foreboding—an enigma wrapped in a riddle. He was born on December 14, 1503, in southern France. His grandfather, a physician, taught the young Michael Greek, Hebrew, Latin, astronomy, and astrology. Following in his grandfather's steps, he also became a physician and had a practice in his province.

After his family died of the plague, he forsook his profession and wandered across France for six years, then married a widow and settled down. Brian Johnston, writing for *Mabuhay* magazine, says that his career in clairvoyance began when a servant pounded on his door. Going to the window of the house, Nostradamus yelled down, "You are making a great deal of noise over a lost dog. Go and look on the Orleans road. There you will find him on his leash." The servant stared at him in surprise, but went and found the dog as instructed.[5] His most notorious prophecy, however, didn't come to pass—the end of the world by the year 2000!

Another individual who gained a measure of notoriety in the twentieth century was Jeron Criswell, who was correct about 85 percent of the time. Criswell, an eccentric, flamboyant showman who wore pancake makeup in public, is best remembered for his spit-curled hair, his stentorian style of speaking, and a sequined tuxedo. Allegedly, he slept in a coffin, which later made its way into a movie. His most famous prediction was made on television in March 1963, when he predicted that President John F. Kennedy would not run for reelection in 1964 because something was going to happen to him in November 1963.[6] Kennedy, as the world well knows, was cut down by an assassin's bullet on November 22, 1963.

Other prophecies Criswell made, such as the one that Denver, Colorado, was going to be hit by an object from outer space that would turn metal into something as soft as rubber, and that the patrons of Elitch Gardens—a popular amusement park that I used to visit as a kid—would sustain massive injuries and deaths, missed entirely! He died before 1999, the year he predicted that the world would end.

Did he lay claim to any prophetic gift or insights? "No," he would have told you. He explained that he analytically looked at a situation and then drew a line from the events as he saw them to the future event. Certain individuals seem to have heightened perception—often very bright individuals with analytical minds—and they quite accurately see what is coming. Criswell seemed to fall into that category.

Vast numbers of others—psychics, frauds, and fakes—profit from playing prophet. People want to know what is out there in the future for them, whether or not "that tall, dark, handsome man I met at the theater is serious about sweeping me off my feet and including me in his life." Around New Year's Day you will find predictions of events for the forthcoming year in newspapers and periodicals, but the vast majority of them do not come to pass. A study done by *Moody Magazine,* an evangelical magazine at one time published by Moody Bible Institute, indicated that only three percent of the predictions made in newspapers and magazines at the beginning of one year actually could be said to have been accurate.

The question, though, that confronts us is this: Where do prophets get their information? Are they just good guessers? Do they have "connections" normal people do not have? Or, rather, are they playing mind games with people who are frightened and desperately wanting to know what the future holds? Even more important is the question: "How do secular and biblical prophecies differ?" In confronting those issues, please observe five ways in which biblical prophecy and non-biblical or extra-biblical prophecies differ:

1. Biblical prophecies differ from secular ones in their source of revelation

The Bible declares very plainly that biblical prophecies came through common, ordinary men by means of the Spirit of God. Here's the statement confirming that: 2 Peter 1:21 says, "Prophecy never had its origin in the will of man, but men spoke from God as they were carried along by the Holy Spirit."

Take a sheet of paper and make three columns or headings representing the sources of prophecy. On the left side I would write Satan. On the opposite side write God, and in the middle write human intellect or heightened intuition.[7] Under these three you can list all the prophets who have ever lived.

Can Satan reveal certain things which are to happen in the future? Yes, to a certain extent. Think of the possibilities. If you knew the future, you would know where to invest money, how much to bet on the game, or whether or not you should marry that stunning girl. But the thought comes with a very dark side. In the New Testament Paul encountered a slave girl who could predict the future, the result of being controlled by a demonic spirit,[8] which thereby brought financial gain to her master. As he was on his way to a prayer meeting in Philippi, Paul being grieved with what he saw, turned and commanded the evil spirit to leave her. It did! And when the spirit departed, her ability to foretell the future was gone, incurring the wrath of her owner, who managed to have Paul and Silas unlawfully thrown into prison. (See Acts 16:16-19.)

You will never have to convince Bud and Shirley James that Satan has limited powers to foretell the future. When the couple went to a party and things began to drag, someone got out an Ouija board. A friend who was a Christian asked, "Will I have a baby?" The woman already had several children, and she and her husband didn't plan for any more. However, the person operating the Ouija board replied, "Yes—twins!" Everybody had a good laugh! But six months later, nobody was laughing. The same woman gave birth to twins, who were still-born. What no one knew, including the woman herself, was that she was pregnant at the time they played with the Ouija board.

Séances, Ouija boards, tea leaf reading, and astrological fortunes have been consulted for centuries. The Bible has a lot to say about the unseen world, or the spirit world. Men such as Professor Kurt Koch, Dr. Merrill F. Unger, and Mark Bubeck, who have made a study of demonic power, warn Christians against playing games with the supernatural or satiating their curiosity.

The book of Revelation says, "The devil has gone down to you! He is filled with fury, because he knows that his time is short!" (Revelation 12:12). His knowledge of the future, however, agree most theologians, is extremely limited.

But what of those in the middle column, whose ability comes neither from Satan or God? Consider those individuals who have a heightened sense of perception thus enabling them to foresee events that have a very high degree of probability of being fulfilled. Just as some have better physical skills than do others, some people have a superior intellect, a brain that works like a computer, allowing them to see in shadow form what others completely miss. Jeron Criswell, the person I've already described, seems to be such a one.

The column of prophets under the heading "God" was clearly identified in the New Testament church. Over 150 times the New Testament alone speaks of prophets—many of whom actively exercised the gift of prophecy in relationship to the church and the world in which they lived.

One whose name was Agabus "stood up and through the Spirit predicted that a severe famine would spread over the entire Roman world," says Luke, quickly adding the seal of authenticity as he pinned down the historical period, saying, "this happened during the reign of Claudius" (Acts 11:28).

In the church at Antioch there were prophets and teachers, and Luke mentions five by name—Barnabas, Simeon, Lucius, Manaen, and Saul. Women had prophetic ability as well as men. The evangelist Philip had four unmarried daughters, says Luke, all of whom had the ability to prophesy.

Paul, writing to the Corinthians, mentions prophecy as one of the spiritual gifts bestowed on believers, one to be sought because "everyone who prophesies speaks to men for their strengthening, encouragement and comfort" (1 Corinthians 14:3). Though that gift is not widely seen today in churches, in the absence of any New Testament statement restricting it to a first-century phenomenon, we can assume that it is still a gift given to believers today. God, through His Holy Spirit, does on occasion use prophecy to give individuals or groups direction or a glimpse of the future which is vivid in scope and particulars, something that can only be described as supernatural.

※

When I was speaking in a Russian church in Woodburn, Oregon, several years ago, the pastor, Alex Shevchuk, said, "After the service tonight we will invite several people to our home for fellowship. Ask Brother Joseph to tell you his story."

Brother Joseph, a bearded, somewhat frail man then well into his 80s, was revered in the church as a man of God, one who had seen affliction as well as the hand of God directing his life. From notes that I made immediately after our conversation, I'm reconstructing the story as he related it.

Living in Eastern Russia in the early 1930s was difficult. The economy was in shambles, and the iron grip of communism grew tighter and tighter, making life especially difficult for those who were Christians. Joseph, the son of a mill owner, was part of a Christian family and regularly attended the "house of prayer," as churches are called in Russia even today.

As things grew darker and more difficult, God seemed to speak through several of the brothers. The Holy Spirit said, "Great trouble is coming!" But the question was, "What should we do? How should we cope with the threat?" Then a prophecy was given with clear instructions that deliverance was to come by leaving almost everything behind and striking out through the Gobi desert to China. Clear instructions were given that people should assemble on a certain date at the hour of midnight and bring with them only what they could carry or push in a handcart. Those like Joseph's parents who had recently moved into a new house were uncertain—walk away from everything because someone said, "God said *that*"?

Joseph, with his parents' blessing, chose to depart. On the day he was set to leave, a terrible storm hit their village with thunder and lightning, thus driving the soldiers who would have detained them into the barracks. A group of 43 people met together and quietly filed through deserted village streets and out into the darkness. Their escape was undetected until they were too far gone to be pursued.

The little group made their way into the desert, but their problems were not over. The heat became intense and the water supply quickly was depleted. Children were crying and the adults were plodding on, wondering what to do.

Finally the group stopped, came together, and fervently began to pray. Then one of the group said, "The Spirit of God is telling me to go forward so many steps, turn left, and dig in the sand." With anxious hearts some of the men paced the distance and knelt down, scooping the hot sand with their hands. After a few inches of sand had been removed, tufts of green vegetation were found, and in moments the hole that they had dug filled with water! Not once but seven times this procedure was followed, and every time, said Joseph, there was sufficient water to alleviate their thirst.

Then it was my turn to ask questions that came not because of an ingrained skepticism but as one who wants to know how you test the prophecy to determine whether God has, indeed, spoken. I asked the obvious, "How did you know this was the Spirit of God that was speaking and leading you?" quickly followed by the question, "Did some disbelieve that this really was God?"

In response to the first question, he doubled his gnarled right fist and, placing it over his heart, said, "It was something you felt right here." *And did everyone believe that God was speaking?* "No!" *And what happened to them?* "Those who remained behind had things stolen from them, and most of those who stayed in the village were killed or imprisoned by the communists, who closed the church."

From China the group eventually went to Argentina and from there to the United States, where they presently live.

Did dark days come to Russia as prophesied? History's bloody answer is that Joseph Stalin, having come to power in 1928, found his country in a state of disarray by the 1930s. Food shortages were widespread. Purges, including the persecution of the church, were being carried out with relentless and ruthless brutality. You decide whether or not the prophecy given in a Russian village church was accurate.

2. Biblical prophecies differ from secular ones in their scope and detail

The prophecies of Scripture, unlike secular ones which are often couched in broad, sweeping strokes, are precise and detailed. For example, Cyrus, the king of Persia, is mentioned by name years before he became a ruler (Isaiah 44:28). Jeremiah prophesied that the children of Israel would be in captivity in Babylon for 70 years, and history verifies that to the year. How could anything be more precise than what Jeremiah wrote, "This whole country will become a desolate wasteland,

and these nations will serve the king of Babylon seventy years" (Jeremiah 25:11)? Names, dates, places, events—all of these make the likelihood of the prediction "just happening" preposterous.

The destruction of Tyre was predicted long before its actual demise. Ezekiel was a civil servant in Babylon, having been taken there from his native Jerusalem during the assault by Nebuchadnezzar in 586 BC. In the text that we know as Ezekiel 26, this young man is God's spokesman. In nine different passages he uses the phrase, "Thus says the LORD"—directly acknowledging God as the source of his authority.

He prophesies the fall of Tyre to Nebuchadnezzar's army the following year—an event which took place. Then he describes the siege of Tyre so graphically that it almost seems he could see Alexander the Great's siege that took place some 250 year later. He explicitly tells the manner in which the invaders would tear down the ruins and throw them into the sea.

Says Ezekiel,

- "They will destroy the walls of Tyre and pull down her towers; I will scrape away her rubble and make her a bare rock. Out in the sea she will become a place to spread fishnets" (26:4).

- "They will plunder your wealth and loot your merchandise; they will break down your walls and demolish your fine houses and throw your stones, timber, and rubble into the sea" (26:12).

- "I will make you a bare rock, and you will become a place to spread fishnets. You will never be rebuilt, for I the LORD have spoken, declares the Sovereign LORD" (26:14).

Historian Phillip Meyers says, "Alexander the Great reduced Tyre to ruins in 332 BC. Tyre recovered in a measure from this blow, but never regained the place she had previously held in the world. The larger part of the site of the once great city is now as bare as the top of a rock—a place where the fishermen that still frequent the spot spread their nets to dry."[9]

It is little wonder that without reasonable grounds for their position, critics have tried to deny that prophecies such as this could have been written prior to the actual event. To admit their legitimacy would be to certify the very nature of prophecy—the supernatural prediction of events, names, and the movement of nations long before these became realities.

3. Biblical prophecies differ from secular ones in significance

A reading of the prophecies of secular prophets reveals that most of them deal with trivia, yet the prophecies of the Bible deal with the sweep of nations, the events of the end time, and the coming of Jesus Christ. William F. Albright said, "Fulfillment of prophecies was only one important element in the validation of a 'true' prophet. More important still was the moral and religious content of a prophet's message."[10]

Let's consider one of many major prophecies in Scripture—the fulfillment of which has been a matter of interest to the entire world—the establishment of the modern state of Israel.

The development of modern Israel—the most significant fulfilled prophecy of the twentieth century. It was September, 1967—barely 90 days from the Six Days' War—when I visited Israel for the first time. Taking a small tape recorder, I interviewed as many people as I could, asking a basic question: "How do you account for the remarkable victory that Israel won?" Taxi drivers, tourist guides, government workers, soldiers in uniform, and people on the street all were quick to relate how the odds were stacked against them. Fifty million Arabs were intent on driving some two millions Jews into the Mediterranean. But there was singular and unanimous agreement. "God gave us the victory," they said. Forget about military hardware, superior equipment, better strategy, or bravado.

Hardened soldiers told me their parents had been victims of the Holocaust and that they had not wept openly from the day their parents were taken from them until the day they stood at the Western Wall of the temple; but as they stood on the perimeter of what had once been the foundation of the temple something inexplicable happened, something deep inside broke up in a flood of tears and emotions.

What is the fascination with this piece of stone wall about 150 feet long and 90 feet high—the remnant of the foundation of the first-century temple—overlooking the Kidron Valley? Here stood the temple originally built by Solomon, destroyed by the Babylonians, rebuilt following the captivity under Zerubbabel, then enlarged and refurbished by Herod the Great about 20 BC. On this spot the Holy of Holies and the Ark of the Covenant stood. It was sacred ground, the meeting place of God and man.

You might also wonder, "What's so special about Israel?" It's not a large country—just a narrow piece of land sandwiched between the Mediterranean Sea and the Arabian Desert. Yet, the establishment of the modern state of Israel and how it came about when never before in all history have a people so scattered across the surface of the earth come back to their roots, constitutes one of the most astonishing and remarkable prophecies of Scripture, one fulfilled in the past century.

To understand why the re-establishment of Israel is significant, you need to know something of the historical developments. Following the destruction of Jerusalem in AD 70 when the temple was demolished, the Jewish people were spread across the face of the earth—some going into Egypt, some to Europe, some to Asia; and wherever they went they took the Torah, or Old Testament Scriptures, and for centuries observed the Passover with the words, "Next year in Jerusalem!" That hope never died.

Meanwhile Jerusalem was overthrown some 43 times by various and assorted armies including waves of Crusaders in the Middle Ages intent on driving infidels from the holy places.

In 1897, however, an unlikely candidate for God to use significantly, Theodor Herzl, an atheist, convened the first Jewish Congress in Basel, Switzerland. From all over the world prominent Jews came to talk about how wonderful it would be to have a homeland for the Jewish people.

Victor Hugo once said, "Nothing in all the world is as powerful as an idea whose time has come," and his words described the quickening impulse in the hearts of Jews to immigrate to this tiny territory between Lebanon and Syria on the north and Egypt on the west. Then a trickle of immigrants returned to the land their ancestors had once fled, buying what Arab locals consider to be worthless pieces of property—often swampy land infested with mosquitoes and malaria—for inflated prices. Those who sold land to the immigrant Jews later sat in coffeehouses laughing at the ridiculous prices they had been paid for the desolate land. Their smiles, however, soon faded as they watched the Jews, undaunted, drain the swamps, plant trees, dig out rocks, and plow the ground—often physically pulling the plow behind them. Frequently fighting disease and sickness, the immigrant Jews gradually gained a toehold on this land that was once taken by Joshua.

At the same time a lad by the name of Arthur James Balfour was growing up in Britain. He attended the local Anglican church, where an evangelical rector told his parishioners that the Bible says eventually the Jews will return to their promised land. That thought was planted in Balfour's mind, and he never forgot it.

Then World War 1 broke out taking the lives of 13 million people, and in the aftermath of this conflict, anti-Semitism reared its ugly head as failed politicians blamed the Jews—especially the bankers and industrialists—for the post-war economic failure. As the war was winding down, General Allenby, leading the British troops, routed the

Turks from Jerusalem and rode into the city on a white horse. He saw himself as a liberator.

In the mandate bringing resolution to the war, Lord Balfour, now the British Prime Minister, undoubtedly recalling that his Anglican pastor talked of the return of the Jews, persuaded the British crown that it was in the interest of Her Majesty's government to establish a homeland for the Jewish people. Thus Lord Balfour was responsible for the adoption of a position paper, known as a *white paper*. It carried no legal clout but was an expression of the goodwill of the British government. It read that it was "pleasing to Her Majesty's government to allow the Jewish people to have a homeland." That was 1917. And the creation of the paper known as the Balfour Declaration became a significant and meaningful step towards the creation of the modern state of Israel.

The aftermath of the war created almost unbearably harsh conditions in Germany. The economy was in shambles, and reparations caused unrest among the people. Adolf Hitler, then a student in Vienna, so goes a story disputed by some and embraced by many, was walking down the street one day, when a Jewish rabbi, wearing the traditional black garb, side curls dangling over a book he was reading, didn't see the young student and bumped into him. Losing his balance, Adolf fell into a mud puddle. Rising to his feet, Hitler shook his fist at the rabbi, cursing him and vowing that some day he would kill every Jew in Europe.

Exactly how the bitter cauldron of anti-Semitism was born in the heart of this young man may never be fully known, but his legacy of hatred—a demonic kind that knows no logic or sense—resulted in embroiling the whole world in a devastating conflict.

Some six million Jews died in the concentration camps of Europe, for Hitler was intent on wiping out a race—genocide—who had been made the scapegoats of Germany's failed economy.

Today reminders, memorials to those who died, are found in such places as Auschwitz and nearby Birkenau, Dachau, and Mauthausen. Yet until you see a map showing the vast network of concentration camps numbering in the hundreds, you have no idea of the horrible extent of the sites—many of which were death camps.

Following the end of World War 2, Zionists were offered land for the establishment of a Jewish homeland in Argentina and elsewhere. But other locations were not the same! The hearts of Jews all over the world, both religious and secular, were drawn to the place where Abraham offered his son on Mt. Moriah, and the city of David, where the great temple built by Solomon had stood. This was their land, so they reasoned, and they wanted it back.

Meanwhile, Eliezer Ben-Yehuda, a Lithuanian Jew, moved to Jerusalem. Upon arriving in the Holy Land, he determined to speak nothing but Hebrew—the same Hebrew spoken by Isaiah and the prophets. Yiddish—a mishmash of Hebrew, German, and Balto-Slavic spoken by most Jews in Eastern Europe, he declared, was not the language of the Book. "When his first son, Ben-Zion Ben-Yehuda (or, as he is more commonly known, Itamar Ben-Avi), was born in 1882, Ben-Yehuda made his wife, Deborah, promise to raise the boy as the first all-Hebrew speaking child in modern history," writes Jack Fellman.[11] He single-handedly waged a battle to give biblical Hebrew a rebirth—the first time in the history of the world that a language fell into disuse and was resurrected.

When there were no Hebrew words to describe such things as "plastic" or other items with no adequate equivalent, Ben-Yehuda coined them. They became standard usage for modern Hebrew. And he succeeded, with Hebrew eventually becoming the official language of Israel. Should Elijah or Daniel be resurrected and walk down Dizengoff Street in Tel Aviv on a Saturday night, following the end of Sabbath, he could read the menu at a local restaurant and eat his meal while he read the weekend edition of the *Jerusalem Post*—in the same language spoken centuries before.

Finally the tide of public opinion turned, and at 4:00 PM on May 14, 1948, just before the Sabbath began, that lion of a statesman, David Ben-Gurion, walked to the podium in the Museum of Art on Rothschild Boulevard in Tel Aviv and, with a voice that was steady and firm but fueled by intense emotion, read a Declaration of Independence, announcing the establishment of a Jewish nation to be known as the State of Israel. Inside that room were 200 people who saw history made. They applauded, then wept, then spontaneously broke into singing "Hatikvah" ("hope"), which was to become the national anthem. Outside a vast crowd of people had massed. Soldiers on the roof, Sten machine guns ready, scanned the crowd for terrorists. Even as Ben-Gurion spoke, gunfire erupted outside, and the War of Liberation was on. The coalition of Arab states was intent on finishing the task Hitler had attempted—the complete destruction of the descendants of Abraham.

How does the modern state of Israel relate to fulfilled prophecy? Some seven centuries before Christ, Isaiah recorded an amazing prophecy, and one powerful phrase of the prophecy certifies this indescribable tug in the hearts of Jews all over the world to come back to this desolate, arid country. Isaiah said, "In that day the Lord will reach out his hand *a second time* to reclaim the remnant that is left of his people from Assyria, from Lower Egypt, from Upper Egypt, from Cush, from Elam, from Babylonia, from Hamath and from the islands of the sea" (Isaiah 11:11).

Let's go back and take a closer look at how this prophecy was fulfilled. In 603 BC Nebuchadnezzar, king of Babylon, laid siege to Jerusalem and eventually destroyed the city (586 BC), taking the finest of the youth back to Babylon. The prophet Jeremiah, who had predicted the destruction of the city, gave specifics when he said they would be in captivity for 70 years. He wrote,

> "This whole country will become a desolate wasteland, and
> these nations will serve the king of Babylon seventy years.
> But when the seventy years are fulfilled, I will punish the
> king of Babylon and his nation, the land of the Babylo-
> nians, for their guilt," declares the LORD, "and will make
> it desolate forever" (Jeremiah 25:11-12).

The day eventually came when the great Tigris River flowing through the city of Babylon was diverted, and while the king partied, the armies of the Medes and Persians crept under the city walls through the dry bed of the Tigris, overthrew the garrison and took the city. Wanting to placate some of the subjects, Cyrus, the new king, issued a decree allowing the Jews to return—70 years after the captivity.

When they returned to their homeland under Ezra and Nehemiah, that was Isaiah's *first* return. There was no second recorded in history until the twentieth century, when a gradual exodus resulted in plane after plane of exiles from all over the world coming back to till the land once trod by the patriarchs.

∞

In my library is a nondescript little book of 74 pages that my father-in-law, Guy P. Duffield, had acquired secondhand, and I eventually inherited from him. The price on the inside cover tells me it sold for 60 cents when it was written in 1941. Its intrinsic value is limited; however, I smile every time I take down the book and browse through it. Why? Because 1941 is the year remembered by us who are Americans for the Japanese attack on Pearl Harbor on December 7. The next day, December 8, the U.S. Congress declared war on Japan. A mere three days later Germany declared war on the U.S., which meant the U.S. became involved in Europe. Well prior to those fateful days, though, Dr. Harry Rimmer, a Presbyterian pastor, archaeologist, scientist, and staunch defender of the faith, wrote this book I now own, entitled *Palestine: The Coming Storm Center*.

Rimmer believed that coming events cast their shadow before them, and based upon Ezekiel 37–39 and other Old Testament prophecies, he saw Israel as a nation that would be rebirthed with great travail. The premise of his book is that Palestine was about to become embroiled in major conflict involving much of the world and that the conflict would culminate in the establishment of the modern state of Israel.

What makes Rimmer's book a source of mirth, though, are the notations written in the margins of the pages by a skeptic who disbelieved what Rimmer had written. Comments include the following: "Who says? Silly reasoning. Dogmatic. Monstrous reasoning," and so forth.

Rimmer concludes his book saying,

> So the storm which Ezekiel foretold is even now gathering, and no man can say when it will break! The only certainty is that it will come, and it may be very soon. But this will not be the last world attempt to blot out the Jew.
>
> As the dark clouds of the final storm gather before our very eyes, may God grant that we shall not be taken unaware by the swift flight of events. When the hearts of natural men are literally fainting with the fear of what the future may unfold, we can lift up our heads, knowing that Jesus is coming again, and our redemption is nearly complete.
>
> Even so, Lord Jesus, come quickly![12]

When the skeptic penned words in the margins reflecting his incredulity, he was blind to the dark, ominous clouds that were settling over Europe at that very time which would bring the cauldron of hatred against the Jews to a boiling point resulting in the horrors of the Nazi Holocaust, which would turn the tide of public opinion in favor of a homeland for the Jewish people.

4. Biblical and secular prophecies differ in satisfaction

Most of the prophecies of Scripture are not terribly pleasing. Many biblical prophecies cut to the bone and outline dark, difficult days ahead. "You will surely die and not live!" or "You will be overthrown by Babylon. Your children will go into captivity, and you will be slain by the sword" is typical of many prophecies found in the Old Testament. So dark and gloomy were the prophetic statements made by Jeremiah that the term "a jeremiad" came to represent anything gloomy and dark.

5. Biblical and secular prophecies differ in their accuracy

A traveler who was growing weary of rainy weather asked an old-timer, "Is it ever going to stop raining?" With a dry sense of humor, the old-timer replied, "Always has!" Right! But if he had said, "Yes, by three this afternoon, the sun will be shining and we'll have sunshine for the next week," you would be impressed, correct? If, however, he was accurate 100 percent of the time, you would have to say, "This guy is phenomenal. He knows more than the weather bureau!" Under the Mosaic law a false prophet paid for his charade with his life—something that would make any false prophet think twice before he proclaimed, "This is what the LORD says..." (see Deuteronomy 18:22).

P.T. Barnum, the man whose name became synonymous with the traveling circus, used to say that people like to be fooled. But God didn't want Israel to be taken in by fraud or sleight of hand. In Deuteronomy Moses laid down tough caveats. He said that even if a prophet was able to do apparent miracles or wonders, that prophet was still not to be received as being from God unless what he prophesied came to pass.[13] God's standard for His people was that a prophet be 100 percent accurate, neither 70 percent or even 85 percent, but 100 percent. Nothing was to be added to His message or taken from it.

God considers prophecy to be important

The Spirit of God would not have impressed upon individuals the importance of lifting their voices in prophetic utterance had prophecy not mattered to God. J. Barton Payne, who spent a lifetime studying prophecy, says that 27 percent (8,352 of 31,124 verses) of the Bible is prophetic, and because most of those prophecies have been fulfilled and can be historically verified, this produces a solid bridge to confidence that what the Bible says cannot be treated lightly. This means that when the Scriptures were originally given to humankind, about one-fourth of what was written was prophetic—yet to be fulfilled!

What are the chances of the prophecies of Scripture "just happening"?

To what degree is chance involved when it comes to the laws of probability? If you answer, "Not much!" you are right, because the laws of probability are carefully defined and mathematically calculated. There is no real element of likelihood or chance whatsoever. For example, take a coin and toss it in the air. If the coin is perfectly balanced, it has a one in two chance of coming up heads, right? Now, what chance is there in it coming up heads twice in a row? The odds are two in four. Again, what chance is there of the coin coming up heads three times in a row? If you answer, "One chance in eight," you are right, and I suspect you have given this matter some thought on previous occasions.

Now with this in mind, consider another question: Have you ever applied the laws of chance or probability to the remarkable prophecies which were made prior to the coming of Jesus Christ to earth? Dr. Charles Ryrie says, "Someone has calculated that actually there are more than 300 prophecies concerning various aspects of the first coming of Christ." Another scholar says that there are 332 prophecies relating to Jesus Christ, 61 of which are major prophecies.

To help you grasp the immense improbability of these being fulfilled by chance, let me give you something to think about. Let's begin by pondering the possibility of just eight of those being fulfilled. One college math class that investigated this likelihood concluded that it would be 1 possibility in 10 to the seventh power. The chance of 48 of those being fulfilled is 1 in 10 to the fifteenth power.[14]

Another mind-boggling illustration puts it in a different perspective. If you had a ball of electrons the size of our universe (which is six billion light years in diameter), and you could make these balls at the rate of 500 per minute for six billion years (the estimated time of the existence of our universe), and you could do this 100 billion times over, and one of those balls was marked with a black "X" and you could locate it, you would have the chance factor of one person fulfilling even 48 of these prophecies. Frankly, that is more than I can really grasp.

Here's another way to grasp this: Let us suppose that the state of Texas was covered with silver dollar coins to a thickness of 12 inches, and one of those coins was marked with a red "X." The probability of diving into that pile at random and coming up with the coin marked with the red X would be the same as even eight of those prophecies being fulfilled.

When Jesus was here on Earth, He had a keen sense of understanding that He was fulfilling the prophecies of old. Repeatedly He would say, "This was done that it might be fulfilled which was spoken by the prophet saying…" and Jesus would document the quote. The average person has little understanding of the complexity of prophecies and their importance when it comes to documenting what Jesus did. But Jesus stressed their importance. Immediately before the crucifixion Jesus said, "I am telling you before it comes happens, so that when it does happen you will believe that I am He" (John 13:19).

There were three prophecies, at least, over which Jesus Christ had absolutely no control this side of heaven.

- the place where He was born
- the time of His birth, and
- the manner in which He was born

The chance of these three being fulfilled, if it were as simple as tossing a coin in the air, would be 1 in 8, but the chances of these three prophecies being fulfilled in the detailed manner predicted goes far beyond chance. Simply put, in the natural it could never have just happened.

The place of Jesus' birth in the village of Bethlehem

At least 500 years before Jesus was born, Micah predicted the village where His birth would take place. He wrote, "You, Bethlehem Ephrathah, though you are small among the clans of Judah, out of you will come for me one who will be ruler over Israel, whose origins are from of old, from ancient times" (Micah 5:2). Being born in Bethlehem to a descendant of David (whose home was in this same Judean village of Bethlehem) fulfilled the prophecy made centuries before.

The timing of Jesus' birth

The events leading to the birth of Jesus were much like the components of a fine Swiss watch consisting of a variety of cogs, springs, and gears working with synchronicity so that the hands of the watch are trustworthy. Some of those events surrounding His birth were relatively minor, some were major, but timing was everything. Thus, Paul, looking back over the series of occurrences which had to come together, wrote, "When the fullness of time had come, God sent forth His Son, born of woman, born under the law" (Galatians 4:4 NKJV).

The scenario had begun many years before the birth of the infant Jesus, when Julius Caesar was assassinated in 44 BC and his grand-nephew Augustus became Caesar. Considered weak by most Roman senators, Augustus teamed up with Marcus Aurelius and purged the Senate, ensuring he had a powerful grip on his future.

Augustus was no different from politicians today. He wanted to leave behind a legacy in marble and stone, and to get the money for his beautification program, he did what politicians still do—tax the people! Luke tells us,

> In those days Caesar Augustus issued a decree that a census should be taken of the entire Roman world. (This was the first census that took place while Quirinius was governor of Syria.) And everyone went to his own town to register. So Joseph also went up from the town of Nazareth in Galilee to Judea, to Bethlehem the town of David, because he belonged to the house and line of David (Luke 2:1-4).

Once the decree was given, a messenger—probably a centurion—made his way from Rome to the harbor at Puteoli. From there he boarded a ship, taking the order across the Mediterranean—a journey of six to eight weeks depending on the vagaries of winds and currents. Had the decree not been given ordering men to register in their ancestral homes (Bethlehem, for Joseph, because he was a descendant of David), a poor carpenter would never have undertaken a journey of this distance with a wife well more than eight months pregnant.

Furthermore, Daniel some six centuries before Christ was born, prophesied an elaborate timetable (Daniel 9:24-27) that seems to pinpoint the exact time sequence leading to His birth—something so phenomenal that only God could have known this.

In order for the details of Jesus' birth to fulfill the prophecies made centuries before, the timing had to be precise. The pace that the ship was borne on the waves, the speed at which the order was posted in Palestine, and even the pace of the journey that brought Mary and Joseph to Bethlehem—all of this, of course, had to synchronize with the timing of Mary's pregnancy for prophecy to come to pass.

Had any of these events leading to the birth of Christ taken only a few days longer—say, for instance, had the winds which bore the ship blown a bit more sharply—Jesus would have been born in Nazareth, where Joseph lived, rather than in Bethlehem. You begin to see immediately that the chance of just three of these prophecies happening is remarkable.

The manner of Jesus' birth

"The Lord himself will give you a sign: The virgin will be with child and will give birth to a son, and will call him Immanuel," wrote Isaiah the prophet (Isaiah 7:14). "Does it really matter whether or not Jesus was born of the virgin?" asks J. Edward Barrett in an article carried by *Bible Review* magazine. Barrett doesn't think so. He contends that the language of Matthew and Luke is poetic, "not to be taken literally," and that their primary intention is to "highlight the role of God."[15]

The final paragraph of his article says, "Surely it is possible to believe in the virgin birth of Jesus, and not be a disciple. Muslims do just that. But surely it is also possible to be a disciple who takes the virgin birth seriously, but not literally."

I disagree, along with Augustine, the reformers, and millions of believers down through the centuries. If Jesus Christ was not born of a virgin, Christians of all faiths have been misled for 2,000 years, and obviously Matthew and Luke were deceived as well. Neither Matthew nor Luke were writing poetical couplets but literally telling what transpired—an event celebrated by all Christendom every December 25.

Luke happened to be a doctor, a Syrian physician, who had been at the side of scores of women who brought infants into the world. I acknowledge that a doctor can be a poet, but when Dr. Luke wrote to Theophilus and described the birth of Jesus, he was just plain factual, as factual as he would have been in filling out a birth certificate. He says plainly that the angel appeared to Mary, who was a virgin, and when the angel told her that she would bear a son, she objected, asking quite directly, "How will this be...since I am a virgin?"(Luke 1:34).

Matthew was a tax-collector-turned-disciple of Jesus Christ, who wasn't accustomed to poetic license when he filled in the great tax ledger he kept for the provincial government. In the book which bears his name, Matthew makes careful note of details, something I would expect a tax collector to do, as he accurately traces the lineage of Joseph back to Abraham, the father of the Jewish race. He records father and son relationships until he gets to Jesus' father and then he switches genders: "Jacob was the father of Joseph the husband of Mary, by whom Jesus was born, who is called the Messiah" (Matthew 1:16 NASB).

Interestingly, Matthew doesn't say Jesus was born of Joseph, the pattern he followed with all the previous generations. He used a feminine gender in the Greek text, and says, "Of Mary was born Christ," leaving Joseph's DNA entirely out of the picture as to being the actual father of Jesus.

Even critics have to admit that Matthew and Luke believed Jesus was born of a virgin. The early Church Fathers were convinced that the event of Jesus' birth in Bethlehem was the intersection of man and God in a unique being who was both fully man and fully God. They debated it, sought to understand it, but never denied it. It was part of the very fabric of Christianity, which was recognized not only by the Church but also by Muslims.

Does it really matter today whether or not Jesus was born of a virgin? If fulfilled prophecy is important, the reality of the virgin birth is an issue of primary concern. If Christianity matters, the virgin birth of Christ matters greatly. Great men have died as martyrs, but our redemption could take place only in the death of a sinless man whose lineage was not tainted with human failure and sin.

When God detailed the circumstances relating to the coming of His Son, He was making the odds so great that it was absolutely impossible for them to have "just happened." Knowing this strengthens the bridge to your confidence in what the Word says.

The bottom line

The prophecies of the Bible clearly foretelling events, naming individuals, and even predicting dates are accurately verified by history and thereby attest to the supernatural character of this book.

Numerous books fill library shelves on the subject of this chapter, good ones, too, written in far more detail than I can go into with the space allotted to the topic.

Suffice it to say that you have been confronted with the reality that one of two things is true: either the prophecies of the Bible have been fraudulently created, written after the fact, fabricating history so that it appears to have been written before the event, or God through His Holy Spirit revealed things to men that are impossible to predict apart from supernatural knowledge.

The evidence points to the latter premise and it provides a bridge of confidence allowing you to assess the unique character of the Word in a broken world that so badly needs guidance and direction.

- How do you explain the explicit picture of the life of Alexander the Great written in the book of Daniel at least 200 years before his first breath of Macedonian air?

- Contrast the prophecies of Buddha, Confucius, or Muhammad with the prophecies give in the Bible about Jesus.

- If you had friends playing with Ouija boards or consulting palm readers or astrologists, what would you tell them?

- What is the significance of the rebirth of the modern state of Israel?

- Why is the manner and timing of Jesus' birth of any importance?

CHAPTER SIX

The Bridge to a Truce with Science

"Looking at the doctrine of Darwinism which undergirded my atheism for so many years, it didn't take me long to conclude that it was simply too far-fetched to be credible." [1]

—LEE STROBEL

When Moses wrote the first sentence in the book of Genesis, he began by penning, *"Bereshit bara Elohim ath hashamayan wath harets."* Our English Bibles say simply, "In the beginning God created the heavens and the earth." In writing those words, Moses broke with accepted Hebrew grammar in how he recorded the first phrase, "in the beginning." Proper grammar is to link the phrase to something, like "in the beginning of (whatever)" but Moses knew there was no antecedent or precedent to attach that phrase to so literally he says, "In beginning, God!" That's it! He assumes God's existence. There is no footnote striving to establish proofs of His existence. He's there. He has always been there and always will be, contended Moses.

Blaise Pascal, the French scientist and theologian, put it,

> "Either God exists, or he does not." But which side shall we take? Reason cannot decide for us one way or the other; we are separated by an infinite gulf…Let us weigh the gain and

the loss in betting that God exists…If you win, you win
everything; if you lose, you lose nothing. Do not hesitate
then, to gamble on His existence.

"I take exception to what you have written about creation and God,"
commented an acquaintance. Somewhat taken aback, I said, "Really?
What in particular bothers you?" "Well," he began, "from what you
have written, I conclude that you believe God is the author of creation."

Those words surprised me—not because they came from a Ph.D.,
a tenured biology professor at the University of Southern California—
but because the statement came from a man who is actively involved
in his church, which holds to reformed theology, the kind that was
first articulated by Martin Luther and John Calvin. I suspect that this
man had bought into the belief that the Bible's validity has pretty well
been dissolved in a vat of nitric acid.

"Yes," I confessed, "I do believe that creation is the direct act of
God because that's what the Bible says, and it is far more rational and
plausible to me than to accept evolution." The problem today is that
science has become almost exclusively naturalistic, which leaves little,
if any, possibility for God's existence. Many people think that if you
believe in God, you cannot be scientific; and if you believe in science,
there is no room for faith in anything other than the evolutionary,
naturalistic approach to creation and to life.

This dichotomy is sad, not only because it is unscientific, but
because it results in an either/or situation which discredits valid research
conducted by first-rate scientists. It also results in capable, intelligent
individuals turning their backs on careers in science because they hold
their faith to be dearer than a career in science.

In his book *The Game of Science,* Richard Dickerson, whose spe-
cialty is chemical evolution, says, "Science, fundamentally, is a game.
It is a game with one overriding and defining rule…Let us see how
far and to what extent we can explain the behavior of the physical

and material universe in terms of purely physical and material causes, without invoking the supernatural."[2]

Has science become unscientific in its bias against religion? That was the contention of Dr. Henry Morris, a hydrologist and a specialist in his field, who for many years served at the Virginia Polytechnic Institute. Morris agreed with Dickerson that science plays games, and he charged that science plays at least three games with the truth; all of which violate the scientific method. The first game of science, believed Morris, is a search to explain the physical and material universe in purely physical causes. This, of course, is based upon the premise that there is no God who could have had anything to do with creation. It is the attitude, "Don't confuse me with the facts; my mind is already made up."

Morris recalls a conversation he once had with a biology professor in charge of doctoral candidates. When Morris asked the professor whether or not someone could get a Ph.D. in his department who believed that God created the universe, the professor answered, "No!" Morris added, "No matter how outstanding his grades or his dissertation or even his knowledge of evolution might be, if he did not believe in evolution, he could not get the degree. That's the rule of the game."[3]

The premise of science's second game, according to Morris, is that the end justifies the means. In other words, it's okay to bend the facts if it helps to substantiate what a scientist wants to prove. (Did you say, "Science does this? It sounds more like the pitch of a used-car salesman.") In his book *The Inferiority Complex,* Harvard University Professor Richard Lewontin says, "Scientists, like others, sometimes tell deliberate lies, because they believe that small lies can serve big truths." It's like saying, "No evidence for creation as an act of God will be allowed because everybody knows that God did not create the world."[4]

The objective of the third game which science plays, said Morris, is to insist that all true scientists are evolutionists; therefore, to believe that God created the world automatically discredits your research and work as a scientist.

That's like saying that cottage cheese makes you fat since fat people eat cottage cheese. Isn't that a bit absurd? Could it be that to admit that there is a God and that He had something to do with the creation of humankind as well as our universe brings a measure of personal, moral accountability into existence which scientists want to avoid?

Have you ever wondered why some scientists are so opposed to recognizing a Creator God as the force of creation—the One who formulated the laws of cause and effect which resulted in our beautiful planet? The very fact that some are so violently opposed to recognizing His existence is a powerful proof of His reality, so claimed G.K. Chesterton, the British author and writer.

Chesterton wrote, "I was a pagan at the age of twelve and a complete agnostic by the age of sixteen." He abandoned whatever faith he grew up with, and then as an adult began to ask why some people were so opposed to Christianity. He began asking himself, "What is it about the God of Christianity which they so want to deny?"

In his own words:

> As I read and reread all the non-Christian or anti-Christian accounts of the faith…a slow and awful impression grew upon my mind—the impression that Christianity must be an extraordinary thing. It was attacked on all sides and for all contradictory reasons…And it did for one wild moment cross my mind that perhaps those might not be the very best judges of the relationship of religion to happiness who, by their own account, had neither one nor the other.

Seemingly, the deeper the probe of science, the closer we come to the reality of the God who spoke the Word and brought our world into being. The Cosmic Background Explorer (COBE) satellite, which was put into orbit as part of the U.S. space program, confirms that immediately following what scientists refer to as the big bang there were ripples of matter that seemed to form in patterns. But what was observed was not a chaotic explosion such as follows when you put a firecracker under a tin can or in an ant hill, but a systematic pattern that reflects design.

But the question immediately follows, "If there is design, then who is the designer?" A newspaper editorial asks, "Does this new discovery prove God exists?" Says the editorial: "The proofs are not theological but philosophical. Though religion acts as a guide, the proofs must stand the test of strict rationality." But the editor who wrote the column admitted that design raises a question that Thomas Aquinas posed: "If there is design, does not this bear witness to the fact there had to be a designer?" And, reasoned Aquinas, neither can there be design in creation apart from a designer who is God, the Creator.

Aquinas drew from Aristotle, the Jewish Rabbi Maimonides, and Arab philosophers in putting together his five proofs for the existence of God, one of which is that design proves a designer. Aquinas, who lived seven centuries before modern science came into its own, argued that something cannot be created from nothing, and when you acknowledge that creation followed a pattern of development, you have recognized the power of a creator. That creator, believed Aquinas, was the God of the Bible who described the creative process in the book of Genesis.

Moses not only began with the premise that there is God but that this one was the Creator of what we live on and what we see. It is the argument posed by the story of one who is walking a trail in the mountains who crosses a stream and encounters three large rocks stacked one upon another. All three are approximately the same size and of the same composition. *So what does it mean? Who put them there? Is this a trail marker made by someone in the long distant past? Is it a warning that the traveler should not proceed further?*

It is obvious, however, that these three rocks did not happen to align themselves by chance. Someone was responsible for their being placed where they were, and all the earthquakes the Ring of Fire can produce would not so position them this way.

The gifted intellectual Samuel Johnson spent nine years of his life producing his *Dictionary of the English Language*. One of his biographers described him as "a genius—a man with a computer-like memory and a mind that could assemble, analyze, organize and present ideas so uniquely that the greatest people of his day clamored to sit and listen to him."

Do you think that anyone could ever be convinced that the dictionary which bears Johnson's name was the result of an explosion in a London print shop when someone forgot to turn off the gas lamp? No, of course not!

Here's one last absurdity to ponder. The Eiffel Tower in Paris rises some 984 feet into the air. When it was built for the exposition of 1889, it was considered to be one of the greatest engineering feats of all times. It contains some 7,000 tons of iron and steel, and for many years was the highest structure in the world.

You could never convince Alexandre Gustave Eiffel that it just happened to exist. Why? Because the idea for the magnificent tower first existed in his mind. Eventually, he developed his idea on paper. Then the idea evolved into blueprints, which eventually became a reality.

A tourist who visits Stonehenge in the English county of Wiltshire in Britain cannot be convinced that someone at some far distant time in the prehistoric past did not have something to do with the placement of those stones. A dictionary does not come into existence without a lexicographer having spent years in compiling it. A building does not appear apart from an architect's concept. Behind each is an intelligence, a designer, a plan which eventually became a concrete reality.

Evidence for creation lies all around us—the complexity of the human body including our emotional make-up, the fine tuning or preciseness of the solar system, the laws of thermodynamics, the ongoing exploration of the solar system as well as the laws of chemistry which allow two atoms of hydrogen and one of oxygen, both combustible, to combine and form a molecule of water which extinguishes fire.

The response of Darwinian atheism

How do you discount the argument that design demands a designer? A group of scientists and philosophers argues that everything can be explained by natural causes—including the concept of God. Leading the group who charge that a belief in the supernatural and anything going beyond nature is passé, is the Oxford professor Richard Dawkins, author of the book *The God Delusion*. In his book Dawkins attacks belief in a creator, contending that anyone who believes in the miraculous has lost any scientific credibility.

In a debate with Francis Collins, the genome pioneer who headed a multinational team of 2,400 scientists that mapped the 3 billion biochemical letters of our genetic blueprint, Dawkins attempted to explain how he thought Darwinism could have produced a seemingly "designed" product:

> For centuries the most powerful argument for God's existence from the physical world was the so-called argument from design: Living things are so beautiful and elegant and so apparently purposeful, they could only have been made by an intelligent designer. But Darwin provided a simpler explanation. His way is a gradual incremental improvement starting from very simple beginnings and working up step by tiny incremental step to more complexity, more elegance, more adaptive perfection. Each step is not too improbable to countenance, but when you add them up cumulatively over millions of years, you get these monsters of improbability, like the human brain and the rain forest. It should

warn us against ever assuming that because something is complicated, God must have designed it.[5]

Collins rebutted the logic of his opponent saying, "I actually find the argument of the existence of a God who did the planning more compelling...less a stretching of the imagination."[6]

On the personal side of the argument I would be more inclined to look seriously at Dawkins's premise if I saw some positive movement in our world towards longevity, towards growing stronger as the years progress, and toward seeing my receding hairline reverse itself. The trend of both history and science is that left to its own, things move towards decay and disintegration, not towards complexity.

Embracing the implications that Darwin's theory leads to requires a far greater leap of faith than to accept the verdict of a shepherd boy named David who on the hills of Bethlehem wrote, "The heavens declare the glory of God; the skies proclaim the work of his hands" (Psalm 19:1).

Physicist Charles H. Townes, who won the 1964 Nobel Prize for his work on lasers, explains that a person must have faith whether he or she believes in creation as an act of God or as a random act of chance. In *Think* magazine, then published by IBM, he says,

> Faith is essential to science too, although we do not generally recognize the basic need and nature of faith in science. Faith is necessary for the scientist even to get started, and deep faith necessary for him to carry out his tougher tasks. Why? Because he must have confidence that there is order in the universe and that the human mind—in fact, his own mind—has a good chance of understanding this order.[7]

Whether an individual is a theist (one who believes in God) or an atheist (one who disbelieves God's existence), faith is a prerequisite for any worldview. President Dwight Eisenhower used to say that an atheist is a person who goes to a Notre Dame–Southern Methodist

University football game and doesn't care who wins. Why go to the game in the first place? The reality is that at the same time secularists accuse theists of blind faith in a Creator, they appropriate faith in a somewhat indefinable, unguided process called evolution.

Says Alister McGrath, Professor of Historical Theology at Oxford University: "The truth is that claims of atheism simply cannot be proved. How do we know that there is no God? The simple fact of the matter is that atheism is a faith, which draws conclusions that go beyond the available evidence."[8]

It would take much more faith, however, to believe that three stones stacked on a trail just happened apart from the explanation of human hands placing them one on top of the other, or that Johnson's dictionary resulted from an explosion, or that Eiffel's tower evolved from a building project gone out of control, than to believe that our universe—far greater than anything man has ever thought up or created—just happened!

This line of logic has also produced convulsions in the world of science in the past few decades even without invoking the mention of the word "God." The movement is known as Intelligent Design and what follows is the background of its development.

The argument from a mousetrap

"If it could be demonstrated that any complex organ existed, which could not possibly have been formed by numerous, successive, slight modifications, my theory would absolutely break down," so wrote Charles Darwin in *Origin of Species*.[9] If Darwin were alive today, it is well possible that Darwin would rethink his premise of natural selection.

What's happened? A simple mousetrap—yes, the kind that I have in my garage to control the vermin which slip under the door intent on making their home there—was part of the logic that eventually caused an unassuming looking microbiologist named Michael Behe to rethink the logical steps or building blocks of life. And what does a mousetrap have to do with the building blocks of DNA and life? Simply put, a mousetrap consists of five parts that must each function independently and be in place for the simple apparatus to work. Likewise, theorized Behe, for life to be sustained certain systems had to function and operate all at the same time. Behe was not out on an anti-evolution, pro-creation crusade at all. He is a simple man who has been likened to an accountant who finally held Darwin accountable and discovered he had come up short. Behe calls it "irreducible complexity."

After pointing out the fact that a mousetrap consists of five simple but necessary parts, he says, "You need all the parts to catch a mouse. You can't catch a few mice with a platform, then add the spring and catch a few more, and then add the hammer and improve its function. All the parts must be there to have any function at all. The mousetrap is irreducibly complex." And as a microbiologist who takes apart the building blocks of DNA, he is convinced that certain systems had to be working and in place for life to have been sustained.

In his ground-breaking book *Darwin's Black Box,* which is now in its ninth printing, he says,

> To Darwin, the cell was a "black box"—its inner workings were utterly mysterious to him. Now the black box has been opened up and we know how it works. Applying Darwin's test to the ultra-complex world of molecular machinery and cellular systems that have been discovered over the past 40 years, we can say that Darwin's theory has "absolutely broken down."

Behe further says, "The question for evolution is not whether you can take a mousetrap and use its parts for something else; it's whether you can start with something else and make it into a mousetrap."[10]

And, of course, the entire scientific community readily recognizes the truth of what Behe is saying, right? Well, not exactly. Some Darwinists have praised the author for his insightful analysis—not quite sure what to say or to make of it but recognizing that the molecular biologist's findings cannot simply be dismissed. Others overtly denounce him as being unscientific.

❧

Jim Holt, writing a 1999 *Wall Street Journal* article entitled, "Science Resurrects God," says, "If the scientific findings of the nineteenth century eroded belief in God, those of the twentieth century have had just the opposite evidential force, although few intellectuals outside science have come to terms with this."

Far more than the opponents of Intelligent Design will admit, however, scientists are now rethinking the accepted dogma of science that you can't be a real scientist and not believe in natural evolution. That mentality is well represented by a cartoon that appeared in a newspaper showing a boy sitting on a stool in a classroom, a dunce cap on his head, obviously being punished for something. He explains, "I defined evolution as 'unintelligent design'!"

The argument for design was impressive enough to cause at least one legendary atheist to do an about-face, abandoning his commitment to atheism and accepting the existence of God. Antony Flew, the British philosopher and creationism antagonist, has discarded what he argued for during his 50-year professional career. No, Flew hasn't joined the ranks of the creationists just yet. He says he can now best be described as a deist—a person who believes there is a God but is not sure how involved He is in people's lives today. But he leaves the door open. He's on a journey, and he's come a long way from where he started. Now in his mid-80s, perhaps he's "cramming for his finals."[11]

On May 11, 2006, Flew received the Phillip E. Johnson Award for Liberty and Truth from Biola University, an evangelical institution in La Mirada, California. In accepting the award he said that he simply "had to go where the evidence leads." He also said that "in light of...the criticism I've received for changing my position, I appreciate receiving the award."[12]

Michael Behe, who dislikes being labeled a creationist, believes that God—not chance—was the Intelligent Designer. And he stresses that "science itself may not have the ability to ferret out the identity of the designer any more than astronomers can determine from their measurements the one who caused the expanding universe to spring into being out of nothing." Behe believes that neither science nor religion should usurp the other. Nor does he see them as being in conflict with each other.

Some, such as Louis Pasteur, have completely compartmentalized science and religion, seeing no interaction between the two. Others, however, do recognize the interaction. Charles H. Townes, the Nobel Prize-winning physicist previously quoted, has written,

> Some accept both religion and science as dealing with quite different matters by different methods, and thus separate them so widely in their thinking that no direct confrontation is possible. Some repair rather completely to the camp of science or of religion and regard the other as ultimately of little importance, if not downright harmful. To me science and religion are both universal, and basically very similar.[13]

Francis Collins, whom I have previously identified, agrees with that premise. In an interview with John Horgan, Collins said, "The God of the Bible is also the God of the genome. He can be worshiped in the cathedral or in the laboratory."[14]

Resolving the conflict between the Bible and science

Yale psychologist Paul Bloom says, "Religion and science will always clash." He has a lot of history on his side, but the issue is this: Can the tension between science and religion be resolved? If so, how is resolution possible? That was the issue that confronted a former British chaplain who did a doctorate at Oxford following World War 2. In his lifetime J. Edwin Orr received 11 graduate degrees, including degrees from the University of South Africa, Semaphore University in India, and two doctorates from the University of California in Los Angeles (UCLA).

Orr held to the premise that there is one God—not two, a God of the Bible and a god of science—and that this sovereign God has revealed His words in Scripture and His works in science. He rejected the premise that science and faith occupy two separate, airtight boxes with no interactions between them.

Orr reasoned that God's word has been recorded in the Bible in passages (texts). But going beyond the statement recorded in Scripture is what men say the Bible says, which is an interpretation of the text. Orr wouldn't argue for the validity of interpretations of Scripture (for example, the duration of creation) but rather the textual statement that "In the beginning God created the heavens and the earth."

On the other side of the paradigm, Orr contends that God's awesome works are the subject of science—what nature reveals—the "what happened" of our world, and when something can clearly be demonstrated and proved, it ceases to be theory and must be recognized as a scientific fact. But the extension of the fact into the realm of possibility or probability is a scientific theory.

"The sky is blue because that's the way God made it," says the Christian. "The sky is blue because of wavelength dependence of Rayleigh scattering," says the scientist on the other side of the issue. So, are these two statements in conflict and, therefore, contradictory? Not really. The first statement describes the color observed by the naked eye. But the other statement describes *why* the sky is blue. Both are correct. The Bible deals with the *what;* science deals with the *how.*

The logic of Orr's paradigm can be visualized as follows:

ONE GOD

Who has revealed His

WORD   WORKS

in the   in

BIBLE   SCIENCE

TEXTS ⟵ ⟶ FACTS

INTERPRET   THEORIES

What people *say* the Bible says (which is often pushed beyond the actual statement of the biblical text) and what it *really* says often contradicts each other. Likewise the same conflict is present when theories are presumed to be factual. Any premise that can be logically verified under the same set of circumstances anywhere ceases to be a theory and can legitimately be recognized as factual. But when theories are considered as factual (that is, "Doesn't everyone believe that evolution is factual?") and those theories contradict the actual statements of Scripture there is unresolved tension.

What's the solution? Orr believed the conflict is resolved by ensuring that the theories of science are cross-checked with the factual statements of biblical text, and the interpretations of Scripture are cross-checked with demonstrable facts of science.

Creation—the act of God, or random chance?

When Astronaut Jim Irwin stood on the moon 229,000 miles from planet Earth and held his arm out straight with his thumb raised, he said that the blue planet, as Earth has been called, was approximately the size of his thumbnail. On several occasions Jim Irwin was my guest on a television series I produced, and never have I seen a more gracious, accommodating individual who patiently answered the most elementary questions about his journey into space and took the time to be photographed with everyone who asked.

On one occasion we were casually chatting before the cameras rolled, and Jim told me of one of the most challenging moments in his space career. It happened after the lunar module had taken him to the moon. As he reentered the spacecraft that was to take him back to Earth, he saw shards of glass floating in the air. Glancing at the instrument panel of the spacecraft, he saw that the protective glass on one of the instruments had shattered. For a moment his heart sank because he knew that their lives were dependent upon the functioning of that particular instrument. The glass could be sucked into a space vacuum built for that kind of use, but if the instrument behind the shattered glass malfunctioned, they were in big trouble that would make it impossible to return to Earth. But when the power was turned on, to his great relief and delight, the instrument functioned properly.

Getting to the moon and getting home again was dependent upon many different systems working perfectly in harmony with precise navigation. When the spacecraft had blasted into orbit, someone commented, "Wasn't that blast-off a great entry into space?" "Yes," acknowledged the wife of one of the astronauts, who added, "But I'm more interested in re-entry!"

Planet Earth rotates on its axis at a speed of 1,000 miles per hour, orbiting the sun at the speed of 19 miles per second or about 66,000 miles every hour. It makes this journey of 595 million miles every year; every 365 days, 6 hours, 9.54 seconds, to be precise.[15]

The issue of re-entry is compounded by the fact the moon is not stationary. As Earth's only natural satellite, it rotates around the Earth every 29.5 days. So two moving objects have to be synchronized for astronauts to return safely from the moon.

One scientist likened getting a spacecraft back from the moon to shooting an apple off the head of a person standing in the open door of a freight train traveling at the speed of 100 miles per hour from a distance of 100 yards—an analogy that is a huge oversimplification of the problem! Getting back to Earth in one piece requires tremendous mathematical precision, especially, if you remember, that there were no onboard personal computers when the space program was inaugurated.

When the *Apollo 8* capsule was heading back to Earth, Mission Control at NASA asked, "Who is driving up there?" (meaning, "Who is piloting the spacecraft?"). Colonel Bill Anders replied, "Sir Isaac Newton." What he meant was that they were simply demonstrating the precise laws concerning gravity that Newton had defined some 300 years before. Newton, the great mathematical genius, was also a student of Scripture as well as physics and astronomy. He spent years striving to synthesize science, prophecy, and history. On one occasion he was accused of having removed God from the universe only to replace Him with his *Principia,* one of the most exhaustive and comprehensive books on calculus and astronomy ever written. Newton was horrified at the very suggestion. In his book he had written, "This most beautiful system could only proceed from the dominion of an intelligent and powerful being."

Who is responsible for the calculated order of the solar system and our universe? Who determines that the laws of gravity should be so precise, so accurate that there should be order in the universe allowing "one small step for a man, one giant leap for mankind"? Who put into effect the laws of physics that allowed *Apollo 11* astronauts Neil Armstrong and Michael Collins to reach the moon 229,000 miles from earth and take the first steps on earth's only satellite on July 20, 1969—and then come back home?

The case for a Creator

Lee Strobel was a Yale Law School grad, the award-winning legal editor of the *Chicago Tribune,* and an investigative reporter who went digging to find motives others overlook. He was also an inveterate skeptic. In high school his belief in God's existence had been dissolved by what he then thought was the airtight logic of Darwin's evolutionary hypothesis. In his thinking, four things in particular seemed to destroy belief in what Moses wrote, "In the beginning God created..."

1. A 1953 experiment conducted by Stanley Miller in a University of Chicago laboratory whereby amino acids were produced by sending an electrical current through a chemical soup (evolution contends that all life evolved from a kind of primordial substance like a gooey soup).[16]

2. Darwin's "Tree of Life"—starting with the ape who transmigrates into someone you might recognize on the street today—bearded and slump-shouldered, arms dangling at his sides as if he had just walked out of the cave onto your street—homeless and forlorn.

3. Sketches of embryos drawn by German biologist Ernst Haeckel demonstrating that all forms of life are related to the one original cell.

4. The missing link—a half-bird, half-reptile known as the *archaeopteryx,* allegedly having been discovered in Germany shortly after the publication of *The Origin of Species.*[17]

Then, quite unexpectedly, something happened that upset the status quo: Strobel's wife, Leslie, became a Christian. Lee was afraid that from this point on that she would wear black, drink vinegar, and stop smiling and enjoying life with him. But Lee saw something in her that he had not seen before—a change within making her a kinder, more compassionate, and loving person.

Intrigued by what he saw, he decided to investigate the claims of Jesus Christ much as he would a serious crime to determine whether or not He was a fraud or was who He claimed to be. That quest ultimately resulted in his conversion, which he tells about in his award-winning book *The Case for Christ.*

In a subsequent book entitled *The Case for a Creator,* Strobel directs his investigative genius towards separating the actual findings of science from the dogma that has become accepted in research and education—that you can't believe that God created the world and be a first-rate scientist.

The 400-plus pages analyze and respond to the premise of Darwinism and make the case for a Creator in logical, step-by-step fashion, as he devotes the entire book to what I have only a few paragraphs to deal with.

The Genesis account of creation states that God created the heavens and the earth, and the Hebrew word *bara,* translated *to create,* is used at three critical junctures in the text—the creation of matter, the creation of lower forms of life, and the creation of human life. (Genesis 1:1, 1:21, and 1:27, respectively). The word generally means to create from no previous existing materials, and it is here that the biblical account and Darwinian evolution stand in sharp opposition to each other.[18]

Moses' contention that God was the cause of creation has the finality of a stake driven into the ground without reference to how long it took,[19] the manner in which He did it, or the full extent of what happened.

The dropout minister who walked away from Moses

In 1827, Charles Darwin, the man who has been vilified by the Christian world as the father of evolution, entered Christ's College in Cambridge University to prepare for Christian ministry. Darwin was a young man without purpose, frustrating his father who thought he was wasting his life in trivial pursuits that he was convinced would deter his son from a pastoral ministry. In 1831 Darwin finagled an invitation to join the H.M.S. *Beagle* headed out from Plymouth to the South Seas. The ship sailed with a crew of 73 under clear skies and a good wind.

For the next four years, nine months, and five days, Darwin explored, collected fossils he knew practically nothing about, and gained a rich hands-on appreciation of creation. At the same time the philosophies of Benedict Spinoza, David Hume, and natural science slowly changed Darwin. Biographies cannot pinpoint any specific event or encounter that pushed Darwin the direction he eventually went. It seems that whatever faith in God he had was more institutional than warm and personal.

Finally Darwin settled down and married. In spite of a generous endowment from his father, he became agoraphobic, beset with physical afflictions, and intrigued with the possibilities of transitions from lower forms of life to higher ones. He abandoned theism and embraced naturalism.

In 1842 Darwin wrote a 35-page treatise of his ideas on mutation but hesitated to publish them, not wanting to be labeled an atheist or scorned by the church. "He continued to struggle with his health, which was becoming much worse with new symptoms showing up. He was experiencing bouts of depression, dizziness, twitching spells, and seeing spots before his eyes. He feared he was going to die soon."[20]

He didn't die, but his four-year-old daughter did. Rick Cornish explains, "The final impetus for his unbelief may have been the death of his daughter Anne in 1851. Darwin was deeply grieved and angered. By the time Anne died, his views on evolution had solidified."[21]

Darwin or the evolutionary hypothesis he espoused never explained the cause of the orderly process that decreed electrical current through a primordial substance should result in the creation of life. But from that time on there seemed to be no turning back for him.

Darwin's assumptions led to the full-fledged evolutionary hypothesis that has become widely accepted today. There are, however, still no clear answers to questions such as, "Who established the principle that condensation and cooling should result in mass? And how were the building blocks of simple life produced by passing an electrical current through amino acids?"—something that Stanley Miller attempted to demonstrate in 1953. Still unanswered is the simple logic that if all life today is related through descent from some primitive form of original life, why is continuity in the fossil record lacking?

Darwin's Achilles' heel. Darwin himself asked the question, "Why, if species have descended from other species by fine gradations, do we not everywhere see innumerable transitional forms?"[22] The lack of fossil evidence was what he considered to be "the most obvious and gravest objection...against my theory."[23]

Darwin died on April 19, 1882, clinging to the anticipation that eventually the fossil record would support his premise. Since then vast numbers of books have been written by scientists purporting that the fossil record is falling into place—or explaining why it isn't, while, in fact, there is yet no conclusive evidence that shows the existence of fossil transitions from lower to higher forms of life.

Walter Brown, in his book *In the Beginning: Compelling Evidence for Creation and the Flood,* summarizes:

> If evolution happened, the fossil record should show continuous and gradual changes from the bottom to the top layers. Actually, many gaps or discontinuities appear throughout the fossil record. The fossil record has been studied so thoroughly it is safe to conclude these gaps are real; they will never be filled.[24]

So certain have been scientists (paleontologists in particular) that the missing link would be found, there has been an ongoing chorus of voices saying, "This is it! We've found it!" only to discover that the newly discovered "missing link" wasn't quite what it was supposed to have been, and the great discovery turned out to be a fraud, hoax, or a premature diagnosis driven by the desire to come up with something conclusive. Such was the demise of the Piltdown Man, discovered in 1912 at Piltdown, England. No fewer than 500 doctoral candidates made this skull the subject of their dissertations, only to learn in 1953 that they (as well as the scientific community at large) had been the victims of a colossal fraud perpetrated by a Hastings dentist who pieced together the find as a practical joke from a hodgepodge of bones not even from the same animal.[25]

"So God created man..." wrote Moses. George Gallup, the man who gained fame as a poll-taker, has said, "I could prove God statistically. Take the human body alone. The chance that all the functions of the individual would just happen is a statistical monstrosity."

The intricacies of your body

- Let us start with your *brain*—the control center of your body. It weighs about three pounds (two percent of the weight of your body) and consists of 100 billion neurons in two major hemispheres connected by a broad, thick band of fibers—a kind of interface known as the corpus callosum. Ten thousand thoughts (so estimates one scientist) pass in and out of your mind every day. Your brain has storage vaults that contain bits of information recorded years before. Yet as an average person you use less than 10 percent of your brain. No computer has ever been invented that comes even close to rivaling the powers of the brain. (After all, who invented computers?) In spite of the marriage of science and technology in the past centuries, the human brain has been called the last frontier of science, and only in the 1990s have scientists begun to unravel its marvels and its interaction with the rest of our bodies.

- Then, there is that organ in your body about the size of a man's fist called the *heart*. It is a muscle that contracts and forces blood through over 60,000 miles of veins, arteries and capillaries, pulsating 100,000 times every day. It pumps about 75 gallons of blood every hour or 1,800 gallons every day. Simple math shows that working 24/7 it pumps 12,600 gallons a week or 50,000 gallons every month.[26]

- No camera ever invented comes even close to the intricacies of the human *eye,* with an iris that automatically adjusts to different lighting and has a lubrication system that allows dust or grime to be whisked away with a blink of the eye. Your eyes are also protected by eyelashes—some 200 hairs per eye that last from three to five months before you grow a new set of them.

- Bose speakers are considered to be some of the world's finest (at least among the world's higher-priced ones), yet no laboratory in the world can produce the stereo system you were born with, one that detects sound waves at a frequency of about 16 to 20,000 cycles per second. Your *ears* are hardwired to your brain, which gives you a special reference to what you hear because sound arrives in one ear a hundredth of a second before it reaches the other ear.

- No air-conditioning system has ever been designed as efficient as the one that keeps the *body's thermostat* at a steady 98.6 degrees when it's working right and sends chills or fever when the system is threatened by disease.

- Your *nervous system* links all the systems of your body, advising the brain of what is happening, monitoring feelings, sensations, pain, and pleasure. Each of the 100 billion neurons in your nervous system is comprised of three parts: Dendrites receive information from another cell and transmit the message to the cell body. The cell body stores the information for retrieval. The axon conducts messages away from the cell body.[27] Nerves in different parts of your body—say the tongue, for example—are specialized to perform certain tasks.

- Your *skeletal system* forms a framework that anatomically

adapts to your movement whether you are a graceful bal-
lerina on a stage or a pole-vaulter arching your body over
the high bar. No bridge ever built surpasses the symmetry
of the arch in your foot.

• Dr. Paul Brand, the renowned missionary surgeon famous
for his research and reconstructive inventiveness helping
lepers become functional, used to say that the *hand* is the
epitome of God's creative genius—unduplicated by science.
Rotate your hand, flexing your fingers, and compare what
you see with the mechanical hands attached to a robot.

Your DNA and the image of the Father

On the last day of February in the year 1953, biochemist James
Watson announced to the patrons of the Eagle pub in Cambridge,
"We have discovered the secret of life." Watson knew he had discovered something very, very important. He had teamed up with fellow
scientist Francis Crick, and eventually the two of them issued a paper
entitled, "Molecular Structure of Nucleic Acids: A structure of deoxy-
ribose nucleic acid." "If life ever had a secret," says Brian Hayes, "the
double helix of DNA was surely it."

It took no more than ten minutes to read that 900-word paper
which appeared in the April 25, 1953, edition of *Nature*, a British scientific journal. But their research opened the door to some tremendous
possibilities that have not only convicted killers but have resulted in
remarkable medical breakthroughs for genetic defects.

"The six-feet of DNA coiled inside every one of our body's 100 trillion cells contains a four-letter chemical alphabet that spells out precise
assembly instructions for all the proteins from which our bodies are
made," explains Lee Strobel.[28]

At conception more than 500 million sperm compete with
each other to fertilize an ovum. At the moment of fertilization 23

chromosomes come from the father and an equal number from the mother. A fertilized ovum contains 46 chromosomes, and attached to every chromosome are genes, which determine the color of hair, eyes, bone structure, and a complex genetic code, which has been passed down on either side of the family for untold generations.

At birth there are more than 100 trillion cells and all of them carry the genetic record in them. When a current of electricity is passed through a DNA segment, enzymes serve as markers that define sequences. This allows the segments to be mapped, noting specific genes. No wonder they call it the fingerprint of life.

In more recent days, scientists have demonstrated that you leave DNA evidence on almost everything you touch—coffee mugs, car keys, your desk, your automobile—just about anything. Even a one-second handshake leaves DNA evidence behind. That evidence proves who you are and where you were or were not. In other cases, it proves what you did or did not do and who your forebears were or were not.

DNA evidence brought the American president Bill Clinton to his knees, painfully forcing him to admit that he had been intimate with an intern not much older than his own daughter. It also proved beyond reasonable doubt that some two hundred years earlier the American president Thomas Jefferson took Sally Hemings, a slave, for his mistress and fathered one—or perhaps all—of her children.

In recent days DNA has forced individuals to admit what God already knew, as the unassailable truth finally came to light. The Bible tells us clearly that eventually we shall give an account of what we have done, whether it is good or evil. Paul wrote, "Each of us will give an account of himself to God" (Romans 14:12). God hardly needs the DNA evidence to support His charges. He is fair and just. But He knows. Hebrews 4:13 says, "Nothing in all creation is hidden from God's sight. Everything is uncovered and laid bare before the eyes of him to whom we must give account."

The complexity of DNA offers a compelling argument that this kind of programmed information demands an intelligent source. Dr. Paul Brand says,

> DNA is estimated to contain instructions that, if written out, would fill a thousand six-hundred-page books…The DNA is so narrow and compacted that all the genes in all my body's cells would fit into an ice cube; yet if the DNA were unwound and joined together end to end, the strand could stretch from the earth to the sun and back more than four hundred times.[29]

This, believes Brand, constitutes evidence that we were made in God's image, by His design, and according to His plan and specifications. As for scientists Watson and Crick, they didn't set out to discover DNA. They stumbled across it. But what they discovered demonstrates how awesomely we are made.

The work of the Designer was described by the psalmist who said, "Thank you for making me so wonderfully complex! Your workmanship is marvelous—how well I know it" (Psalm 139:14 NLT). And surely the greater the complexity, the more remarkable is the intelligence of the designer. As the concluding book in the Bible says, "You created all things, and by your will they were created and have their being" (Revelation 4:11).

The physical is merely one aspect of life. What about the way that your mind works? Scientists have spent years in the field of behavioral psychology, yet these same men cannot understand their own wives! What about your emotions such as love, hate, and fear—complex emotions? Samuel Alibrando asks, "From an impersonal rock to single-celled organisms to fish to who knows what, where and why did a craving for attention and affection get put in the evolutionary DNA strands?"[30] When you stop and think about the complexities of the body and mind, and their interaction, the questions arise: "What is life? What makes us truly human—more than a composite of elements?"

Of all the 6.5 billion people on planet Earth, no one is exactly like you. No one else sees through your eyes or feels what you feel.

Suppose for a moment that we contend humankind was created by chance. Then we are confronted with unanswered questions such as: "Why death? What is beyond the grave, if anything? What is the purpose of life itself? Who is to say what is moral or immoral, and by what standards do we determine what is right or wrong in an existential search for meaning?" But if God created man, as the Bible simply states, there is an answer to the question, "Where did I come from, why am I here, and what is beyond the grave?"

"In the image of God, he created him; male and female he created them"[31]

But what does it mean when the text says that humankind is created in the image of God (Genesis 1:27)? Does that include the baby you brought into the world, as well as your gray-haired, feeble grandfather who talks about "going home and being with the Lord"?

The image of God—what does that mean? As author Philip Yancey suggests, "The word *image* is familiar to us today, but the meaning of the word has leaked away so now it connotes virtually the opposite of its former meaning of 'likeness.'" In advertising, *image* refers to the projected, often contrived picture or representation of something—what a marketing firm wants you to perceive a product as being. The image and the reality often are quite diverse. "Image is everything," was the punch line of an ad for Minolta cameras depicting tennis star Andre Agassi making a terrific shot.

Frankly, "image" is the popular definition that has been pinned on God. The popular notion or image of God is far less than what He really is. But the point is that you were made in God's image, in His likeness, touched by the finger of the Almighty. This dramatically distinguishes you from the "smartest animal" that walks the planet.

Dr. Paul Brand, along with coauthor Philip Yancey, argue that not only is the physical body an amazing creation that could never have happened by chance, but that the spirit of man is what really testifies loudly to the contention that we are created in the image of God. In his book *In His Image*, Dr. Brand wrote,

> Increasingly I have come to realize that the physical shell I devote so much energy to is not the whole person. My patients are not mere collections of tendons, muscles, hair follicles, nerve cells, and skin cells. Each of them, regardless of deformed appearance and physical damage, contains an immortal spirit and is a vessel of the image of God.[32]

In every war, and every crisis, including the heroic response of police, firemen, and rescue workers following the 9/11 World Trade Center disaster, there are individuals who demonstrate they were created in the image of God by their actions. The chaplain who goes back into a building to pray with someone crushed under the wreckage, the passerby who stops at an accident and crawls into a burning vehicle to pull someone to safety, or the observer who plunges into a raging river to rescue a child being swept away with the current—they are the heroes of an often selfish, "me-first" world. Created "in the image of God" explains human kindness in ways that are not reflected by lower forms of life nor explained by science.

The following news note was three inches high, one column wide on the twelfth page of a newspaper following the terrible tragedy that resulted in the death of five young girls in an Amish school in central Pennsylvania. The story of the disaster brought on by a deranged gunman intent on molesting the girls was titled, "Amish Victim Tried to Protect Younger Girls." It read in its entirety:

> In a cold drizzle, the Amish drove in horse and buggy to a cemetery in Georgetown to bury the fifth girl shot to death by an intruder as details emerged of heroism inside the school.

> Two of the survivors told their parents that 13-year-old Marian Fisher, one of the slain girls, asked to be shot first, apparently hoping the younger girls would be let go, according to Leroy Zook, whose daughter was the teacher who ran from the school to call police.[33]

The willingness of that teenage girl to sacrifice herself in the hopes of saving the lives of others mirrors the love of the Creator for His creation. That is what Jesus was talking of when He said, "Greater love has no one than this, that he lay down his life for his friends" (John 15:13).

❧

In the year 1908 Sir Ernest Shackleton took a group of adventurers and headed for the South Pole. On this expedition he got closer to the Pole than any other person had ever been—within 97 miles, but then realized their food supply would not allow them to reach their goal and also return. In those days there were no planes to drop supplies, no helicopters, no satellite phones, no McDonald's or KFCs. They had no choice but to do a 180-degree turn and head back.

Before they reached help, however, their food was exhausted. The time came when Shackleton had to call the men together and inform them of the gravity of the situation. There was one hardtack—a kind of biscuit often used by explorers—for each member of the expedition and that was it! Nothing more until they could return—when and if only God knew at that point.

Telling of the situation in his diary, Shackleton said that some of the men boiled water, made tea, and then slowly and pensively ate the biscuit. Others, though, waited, wanting to save this last morsel of food for a future, more desperate time. Finally the fire was built up and the men slowly settled into their sleeping bags, furs piled over them, and restlessly dropped off to sleep.

As he was about to fall asleep, Shackleton noticed one of the men sit up in his sleeping bag and quickly scan the others to ensure that no one was watching. Quietly he began to reach for the small food bag tucked under the sleeping bag of the man next to him. Shackleton's heart sank within him. This was one of his most trusted men; he never thought the man was capable of taking food from his friend. But then he realized that in times of desperation sometimes our instincts switch into basic-survival mode.

Yet nothing prepared him for what he saw. He watched out of the corner of his eye as the man took the food sack of his neighbor, opened it, and then *placed his own biscuit in the other man's bag.*

In a world which threatens to reduce your uniqueness and individuality to a digital imprint or the black strip of information on the reverse side of a credit card, it is time to acknowledge you are a unique individual created in the image of God—fully human and with a soul that will live forever.

Walk through a museum and view the magnificent paintings of the masters and see the image of God reflected in their works. How else to explain what came from the brushes of Rembrandt, Michelangelo, or van Gogh? Read some of the great literature that fills the shelves—the classics. Read a sonnet from Shakespeare, a poem from Longfellow.

Listen to the music of George Frederick Handel, a symphony from Beethoven, or a stanza written by a slave-trader-turned-minister that we call "Amazing Grace," and you will see these expressions of beauty mirror the image of the Almighty. At the same time, remember that what makes your response to music, the delicate fragrance of a rose, the love of another person, the beauty of our world, and the pathos of someone who suffers argues compellingly that you were created in the image of God—a composite of body, soul, and spirit.

While you may not be the "spittin' image" of your Father, you will see within your life the reflection of the image of God, the Father. That's what sets you apart from the rest of God's created beings—that demonstrates you are a living soul and spirit, not an animal. It is the spiritual nature of humankind that separates him from all other mammals and defies simple explanations that humans are the result of natural selection—mere chance that evolved from lower forms of life.

What about statements the Bible makes of a scientific nature?

While the Bible is not a book on science but rather a book on life and living, what biblical writers penned centuries ago is in harmony with what we now consider to be scientific. At the time, what they wrote must have seemed strange to those who heard or read their comments. Their statements were often in sharp contrast to the scientific thought of the writer's day.

Consider the following:

1. Who told Moses God did it?

Take, for example, what Moses said about creation. The New Testament quotes Stephen, saying that Moses was schooled in the wisdom of the Egyptians (Acts 7:22). From secular history we know that the Egyptians of the twelfth to fourteenth century BC, the era in which Moses lived, believed that the earth was hatched from an egg. If you question that fertility model, check out the number of eggs on ancient sarcophagi and tombs in Egypt. Moses, though, didn't advance the egg theory. He said, "In the beginning, God created the heavens and the earth."

2. "The world is round"—really?

"Come on, now," you may say, "Doesn't everyone believe today that the world is round?" Surprisingly, no. The oldest continuous society in the world, having begun in 1547 is—*are you ready for this?*—The Flat Earth Society. Their website says they are "deprogramming the masses...dedicated to the Flat Earth principles which define our organization." A 1980 *Science Digest* magazine quoted the president of the society, Charles K. Johnson, as saying, "The facts are simple. The earth is flat!"[34]

The person who now serves as spokesman for this group lives in the shadow of Rockwell International, where the Space Shuttle was built, and a short distance across the rolling hills of Southern California from Edwards Air Force Base, where numerous Space Shuttles have landed. "The Space Shuttle is a joke—and a very ludicrous joke," he says. No, he's not kidding. He believes it. The twelve astronauts who have walked on the moon, however, would grimace and give you a "he-can't-be-serious" look at such nonsensical ignorance.

Seven centuries before Christ, the prophet Isaiah wrote these words: "He [God] sits enthroned above the circle of the earth, and its people are like grasshoppers." (Isaiah 40:22). Isaiah lived during a period when the Persian astronomers were convinced that the Earth was flat. But not Isaiah. In a written statement, Columbus said he got the idea of a round Earth from reading Isaiah's writings.[35]

"But," you say, "doesn't the Bible talk about the 'four corners' of the Earth?" Yes, twice the book of Revelation uses that term denoting the broad expanse of the world's population—a figure of speech familiar to the readers, and that's the "flat-out truth."

3. How many stars are out there?

One of the interesting facts about the statements of a scientific nature which the writers of Scripture made about our world is that what the authors wrote was usually in sharp contrast to the philosophic or scientific ideas of their day. Nowhere is this more apparent than when Jeremiah recorded the statement found in the book that bears his name: "I will make the descendants of David my servant and the Levites who minister before me as countless as the stars of the sky and as measureless as the sand on the seashore" (Jeremiah 33:22).

That statement—that the stars cannot be numbered—was contrary to the wisdom of the ancient astronomers, but ultimately science demonstrated how right Jeremiah really was. As late as 150 BC (even several hundred years after Jeremiah) the Greek astronomer Hipparchus said there were 1,026 stars in the universe. A hundred-and-fifty years later, Ptolemy, a scientist who was alive at the time of Christ, said, "No! Hold it. There are not 1,026 stars…but 1,056 stars."

That wisdom held sway until the year 1610, when Galileo pointed his first primitive telescope at the starry host of heaven and said, "Wait! There are more stars than we had any idea!" Then came the 200-inch Mt. Palomar telescope, at that time the largest in the world, followed by NASA's Hubble Space Telescope, the renowned orbiting telescope, the discoveries of which changed everything, and astronomers concluded that nobody really knows how many stars there are, but they estimate that there are more than 200 billion billion stars out there.

Got any idea how many 200 billion billion are? To help you grasp this, try this picture. There are over 6 billion people in the world. If every person in the world started counting stars and counted 50 billion stars, no two stars would have been counted twice.

That's not the end, either. In a "try to top this one," Australian astronomers more recently panned strips of the starry sky in both the Canary Islands and in New South Wales (Australia). The team, working from the very powerful Anglo-Australian observatory in Australia, decided that there are about 10 times as many stars in the sky as grains of sand on all the deserts and beaches of the world. That figure, so they estimate is 70,000 million million million, or 70 sextillion! Dr. Simon Driver, who reported the findings to the General Assembly of the International Astronomical Union in Sydney, said there were likely many million more stars in the universe but the figure of 70 sextillion was the number visible by modern telescopes.[36] Actually the number of stars may be infinite. Who knows?

Who told Jeremiah that the stars were without number? Obviously, he didn't learn that from the scientific thought of his day. Nor did he learn that from the ancient astrologers. Jeremiah's insights could have come only from God. The Spirit of God gave witness to Jeremiah, who wrote truths and facts far beyond his times.

The Bible, surprisingly enough to some, mentions stars more than thirty times. It refers to some stars by precisely the same names as they are known today. Psalm 147:4 says that God counts the stars and calls them all by name.

One of the earliest dramas chronicled in Scripture is recorded in the Old Testament book of Job. This ancient writing says God made the Bear, Orion and the Pleiades, and the constellations of the southern Zodiac, using the same names which astronomers use today (see Job 38:31). Psalm 33:6 says candidly, "By the word of the LORD were the heavens made." The next time you look towards heaven on a dark night and marvel at the starry hosts, start counting and remember the words of Jeremiah. He well made a point that science has verified.

4. Are they still laughing at what Peter wrote?

For centuries people read the following and couldn't comprehend what Peter was trying to say: "The day of the Lord will come as a thief in the night, in which the heavens will pass away with a great noise, and the elements will melt with fervent heat; both the earth and the works that are in it will be burned up" (2 Peter 3:10 NKJV).

Obviously, Peter was speaking of Christ's Second Coming—an event that would be accompanied by cataclysmic disturbances in the atmosphere. He says the elements (*stochia,* meaning the materials comprising the planet) will melt with fervent heat. For centuries this seemed to be completely irrelevant to anything educated men and women had learned and more like science fiction than biblical prophecy.

In 1867 the French scientist Pierre Vichelieu wrote in his diary, "The day will come when man will not only toy with the atom but will split an atom, and the energy of the sun itself shall be harnessed.

When that day comes, God with his long beard will come down to earth and say, 'Gentlemen, it is time to close up shop.'"

Less than a century later it happened! On a cold wintry day in December, 1942, utilizing a squash court beneath the football field, a nuclear chain reaction was achieved as Enrico Fermi and his colleagues at the University of Chicago unleashed the power of nuclear fission. What took place that day enabled scientists to produce "Little Boy," the code name for the Bomb that fell from a B-29 bomber, the *Enola Gay,* over the city of Hiroshima on August 6, 1945.

The bomb exploded in a yellow ball of fire that morphed into a mushroom-shaped cloud that rose to an altitude of 9,000 feet. Within minutes 80,000 people had died and a final toll of those killed or injured was twice that many. Yet, all of the firepower of World War 2, including the A-bombs dropped on Hiroshima and Nagasaki, equaled only 3 megatons of nuclear power. Three hundred megatons of nuclear power would destroy every major city in the world and create a colossal holocaust in the genre of the one that Peter described. But today only God knows how many megatons of destructive nuclear power are presently available and could be unleashed in our world as the planet's "nuclear club" grows.

After the war a news reporter standing at Hiroshima began his broadcast with these words, "I am standing at the spot where the end of the world began." In his famous position speech at Fulton, Missouri, Winston Churchill, who had led Britain through the war, said, "The Dark Ages may return on the gleaming wings of science—beware, I say, time may be short." With that horrible specter forever etched on the consciousness of the world, nobody laughs at what Peter wrote. Suddenly those words have become a grave possibility.

5. What did Moses know that Sir William Harvey proved?

Moses contended that the life of all flesh is in the blood (Leviticus 17:14). No one with medical knowledge, not even Hippocrates, the

Greek father of medicine, would have agreed with Moses. It actually took science 3,000 years to catch up with that one. In 1628 Sir William Harvey discovered the principle of circulation. His contemporaries scoffed at him then, but he eventually proved his findings.

How did Moses know that the life of all flesh is in the blood if it was not that God revealed something to him which was eventually borne out by science? As the adopted son of an Egyptian princess, Moses' mind-set and education should have reflected that of his Egyptian tutors, but it didn't. Moses' Egyptian contemporaries bathed in blood, thinking it would restore their vitality. Both cultured Romans and their pagan enemies thought that drinking blood—something forbidden in the Bible—would give them the physical strength of their enemies.

Remember seeing pictures of the old-fashioned barber pole outside barbershops? That barber pole originally meant that more than haircuts were given there. It was a sign indicating that "bloodletting" was done on the premises—a practice that was believed to release the "bad blood," allowing healing to take place. History tells us that more than a few renowned individuals might have lived longer, including George Washington, had they not been victims of the well-meaning but ignorant practice of "bloodletting." For centuries humankind knew that blood was significant but never understood what Moses wrote—that it is the source of life itself.

6. Does color or ethnicity matter?

Two of the commodities in the world that control our lives are oil and blood. The price of a barrel of oil fluctuates—depending on market supply and demand; whereas if blood were sold by the barrel it would cost about $20,000 for the same volume. (Here's a trivia: If all the blood that is donated annually in the world was collected—about 16 million gallons—it would fill 32 Olympic-sized swimming pools.)

When someone in an oil refinery makes a mistake and fuel is corrupted, cars may sputter and choke but nobody dies; however, if a mistake is made in a laboratory, the contamination may result in the large-scale loss of lives. For centuries racial prejudice tainted our understanding of the nature of blood. Different nationalities were thought to have different kinds of blood and because of attitudes of racial superiority, blood was neither universally donated nor received. Even in World War 2 separate blood stocks were maintained from white and black donors for fear of offending people.

It was actually in 1900 that a Viennese doctor demonstrated conclusively that there are four major universal blood types which have nothing to do with racial heritage. Your color does not matter to God and never has! Addressing the philosophers and intellectuals of Athens, Paul declared, "He has made from one blood every nation of men to dwell on all the face of the earth, and has determined their preappointed times and the boundaries of their dwellings" (Acts 17:26 NKJV). Over 400 times the Bible speaks of blood, elucidating its significance and underlining its importance to life and wholeness.

Is there resolution to the tension between science and religion?

In the twentieth century science and technology have united to change the world and the way we think, shrinking our boundaries and limitations. It has produced what Canadian philosopher and media theorist Marshall McLuhan described as a "Global Village." The scientific-technological breakthrough of the past century unleashed the frightening power of the atom—like a genie uncorked from a bottle, never to be recaptured, threatening to incinerate the planet.

In the laboratory miracle medicines and drugs were birthed that transformed the way we live and the way we view life itself, bringing into focus a vast plethora of moral and ethical issues—how life is conceived, whether or not it should be sustained, but far more cogent, what life means, and what lies beyond our last breath here. Transportation, communication, education, and spatial boundaries have all been transformed. Changes in the past century have quantitatively been greater than in the previous 19 centuries combined.

The great questions confronting us today involve our origin, purpose, and destiny, and it is the issue of purpose that will be the driving philosophical and religious issue of the twenty-first century. Nigel Brush, in his book *The Limitations of Scientific Truth,* so aptly summarizes the impotence of science to speak to these pressing questions:

> Only two answers have come to dominate the modern world. One is that humans were purposefully created by God in the past, are meant to serve Him in the present, and have the opportunity to dwell with Him forever in the future. The alternate answer states that random processes created humans, that we have no particular purpose in the present, and that we will cease to exist when we die.[38]

Surveys state that at least 80 percent of the population believes that humankind had a Creator and that design and purpose are evident in our world leaving a scant 20 percent holding to the position that human existence and life on the planet is the result of random selection and change. Those who deny that humankind was created in the image of God struggle with the very concept of purpose—either in their personal lives or in history. The resolution of tension between science and religion involves both theology and philosophy.

The bottom line

Large numbers of qualified scientists in literally every field of science believe our world reflects creative design and that it did not "just happen." Some are quiet believers; others are outspoken in their faith, yet they are theistic. Many of them not only believe in God but acknowledge He sent His Son to bring redemption and healing to humankind.

While an entire book could be dedicated to this premise (some authors have done just that), the testimony of the German-born father of the U.S. Space program, Dr. Wernher von Braun, is exemplary and representative of those who are out of step with "political correctness," yet still adhere to a belief in God.

The historical library of NASA contains a copy of a letter written by von Braun dated January 3, 1972 in response to the inquiry of a Canadian woman asking if he believed in God. He replied,

> In my education, as I became exposed to the law and order of the universe, I was literally humbled by its unerring perfection. I became convinced that there must be Divine Intent behind it all. It is one thing to accept natural order as a way of life, but as I asked the question, "Why?" then God entered in all his glory. My experience with science led me to God.[39]

While it is unlikely that we will ever see a truce declared between science and religion, many individuals are quietly finding middle ground and declaring a private peace. Such is Robert Jastrow, a renowned astronomer and physicist. Founding director of NASA's Goddard Institute for Space Studies, he is the director of the Mount Wilson Institute and Hale Solar Laboratory. He is also the author of *Red Giants and White Dwarfs* (1967) and *God and the Astronomers* (second edition, 2000).

In an article written for the *New York Times* magazine, Jastrow concludes with this:

> For the scientist who has lived by his faith in the power of reason, the story ends like a bad dream. He has scaled the mountains of ignorance; he is about to conquer the highest peak; as he pulls himself over the final rock, he is greeted by a band of theologians who have been sitting there for centuries.[40]

I, for one, believe he is right.

Think It Over, Talk It Over

- How did a simple mousetrap cause microbiologist Michael Behe to rethink evolution?

- Russian astronauts said they saw no sign of God when they went into space. American astronaut Jim Irwin, however, described the moon as a holy place where he sensed the presence of God. Why do you think he said that?

- Since an alphabet or code is not a random assemblage of symbols, how does the DNA code imply the existence of God?

- While the Bible is not a scientific book, all of its writings penned centuries ago are in harmony with what is now considered scientific. Describe one of these confirmations.

CHAPTER SEVEN

The Living Book That Changes Lives

"When you read God's Word, you must constantly be saying to yourself, 'It is talking to me, and about me.'" [1]

—SOREN KIERKEGAARD

It all began with a coded radio message wafted across the South China Sea that read, "Expecting so many people that we have arranged 21 teacups and cooked 18 bowls of rice." The cryptic message was to alert Christians in China to stand by for a delivery. The 21 teacups meant 2100 hours or 9 PM. The 18 bowls of rice meant the delivery would be on the eighteenth of November. The year was 1981, and this was no ordinary shipment.

The cargo to be delivered was one million Chinese Bibles weighing some 232 tons—a delivery that was extremely dangerous and fraught with logistical problems. In 1981 you couldn't just drop off a million Bibles at your local post office and tell them to "send 'em to China!"

Project Pearl, as the operation was known, was engineered by a hero of mine—Doug Sutphen, a man who knew no limits in believing that God can do what no one else can do. Some 15 years before, after I became the pastor of a Southern California church, I learned that there was a need in the Philippines for someone to serve with the Far East

Broadcasting Company's print division. Two of our members, Doug Sutphen and his wife, had quickly volunteered even if they lacked financial support. Getting to know Doug, I learned that the greater the challenge, the more fervently he prayed for the impossible.

When Doug learned that Mao's *Little Red Book* containing quotes by Chairman Mao Zedong was widely read in China, he said, "Hey, let's print New Testaments with red covers on them, just like the Little Red Book." Some 25,000 copies of these were printed in the Philippines and taken to China, where they were joyfully received by Christians eager to have pages of Scripture in their hands.

Then one day the idea was conceived: *Why not do it big time? Get a barge and take a million Bibles to China!* Doug then teamed up with Brother Andrew, a Dutchman known for his daredevil exploits in smuggling Bibles into Communist countries who describes himself as "the son of a blacksmith employed by a Jewish Carpenter." Several abortive attempts were made to launch Project Pearl. The sailing date was on, then off. Finally it was a go—21 teacups and 18 bowls of rice meant "Get to the beach; we intend to deliver." The tugboat named *Michael* played hide and seek with Chinese patrol boats as the crew lay in the cabin praying for God to blind the eyes of the authorities. Snaking their way between Chinese vessels, they gradually made progress. At last three smaller rubber boats ferried the bundles of Bibles close to the shore. Wrapped in bubble paper, the Bibles floated the rest of the way to shore on the tide.

Some of the Bibles got wet and were eventually dried out. They were known as "Wet Bibles." When authorities intercepted other packages, they threw them into a latrine, and, yes, you guessed it, they were eventually retrieved by the believers, washed and sprayed with Chinese perfume, later to become known as "Perfume Bibles."

The operation was a smashing success and a tremendous embarrassment to Chinese authorities—a situation which contributed to the establishment in China of the Amity Foundation, which has now printed and distributed 39 million copies of the Bible and counting.

Today Bibles can be purchased in China at most registered churches.[2] Malcolm Muggeridge put it so well, saying, "The truth is that the light which shines in this incredible Book simply cannot be put out."

When Doug Sutphen engineered Project Pearl, putting a Bible into the outstretched hands of a Chinese Christian was tantamount to giving him a block of gold the same size. Isaiah was right when he wrote, "The grass withers and the flowers fall, but the word of our God stands forever" (Isaiah 40:8).

Brother Andrew, the founder of Open Doors, reflected on this heroic undertaking of Project Pearl:

> [It] was the biggest action any mission had ever undertaken in the history of missions. For us it was also a big thing in that it was a miracle. The vision was born inside China. We never do things at our own initiative. We always work with the churches. We go there, we say, "What is your need? What can we do for you?" And then they always say first, "Prayer." Secondly they say, "Give us Bibles." So they devised the plan. They actually told us how to execute it—and we have taken in tens of thousands of Bibles in backbreaking expeditions.
>
> But this one million—that was a very, very big project and we have, unfortunately, never done it anymore. And later I heard from Chinese pastors and I said, "Well, was that bad for you? Some of you have been arrested. You had trouble afterwards." They said, "Well, the only thing that we marveled at is that you didn't do it again, because we were waiting for you for another million Bibles."[3]

What difference does it make?

The question that must be addressed is simply, "Why? Why risk imprisonment or even death to take a Bible to people? What difference does it make?" The answer is straightforward: In a despondent world, this book brings hope. In a world of darkness, it gives light. In a world of hatred, it shows the way of love as does no other book in the world.

Having talked with dozens of men and women over the past 40 years who were imprisoned for their faith in various countries, I can tell you that repeatedly in different locations and situations, I have heard the words, "Without a Bible, I don't think that I could have made it!"

In his book about the struggles of Chinese Christians under the persecution of communism after the Bamboo Curtain came down in the 1950s, Carl Lawrence says that when Christians had memorized Scripture or had access to a Bible, they endured, whereas, those who had neither often succumbed to their doubts. He tells of a conversation with an old man who had felt the iron fist of deprivation and persecution. He told Carl, "We as pastors who refused to recant our belief in Jesus were held in solitary confinement, with total silence, unable to speak or sing aloud. Later I found out that those who did not know Scripture or sing hymns, either recanted and denounced Christ or committed suicide. I know of no exceptions. It was the Word of God that kept us from doing any of the three."[4]

I was sitting in a teahouse in China with a godly pastor in his 70s when two workmen passed by carrying a large stone suspended on a heavy chain attached to a pole which bit deep into their shoulders. Their muscles were taut. Jugular veins bulged and beads of perspiration covered their faces. Pointing to the two men who carried the piece of rock weighing perhaps 300 pounds, the pastor said, "I used to have to do that as a forced laborer!"

Gradually, his story began to unfold. When Joseph (not his real name) was a young man, the senior pastor of the church he attended was executed by Communist forces who radically took over the government in 1949. Not liking what happened, he brashly spoke out against the persecution. Within days he was arrested. The people's court who tried him forced him to sit on a high stool in public view, with a dunce cap on his head and a sign on his chest which read, "I am a tool of the Running Dog Imperialists," referring to the Americans.

Following that humiliation, he was sentenced to 20 long years of forced labor in northern China, throwing railroad ties off a train and carrying heavy stones to build dikes and dams; the bitter cold winters and harsh conditions gradually wore down those who were prisoners. "I smuggled a little Bible into the camp when I was taken there," he explained, adding, "Without that Bible I don't think I could have survived."

Eventually Pastor Joseph was released from prison, and several years later, quite unexpectedly, on a Saturday night he received a phone call. It was a government official who said, "Tomorrow we are opening a church and since you are a religious man, you will be the pastor. There is only one condition: you must use only the Bible, nothing but the Bible." And now, years later, this brother who survived the times of testing nourished by a book called the Holy Bible, continues to faithfully proclaim the Good News of that book in a bad-news world.

In this chapter you will meet other individuals whose lives have been transformed by the Bible, the book described by the writer of Hebrews as being "living and active" (Hebrews 4:12).

Exhibit 1: Gaylord Kambarami and the man who smoked Matthew, Mark, and Luke

Few people ever struck a stranger deal than did Gaylord Kambarami, the General Secretary of the Bible Society, who tried to sell a New Testament to a man in Zimbabwe. As Gaylord talked with the man, he could see he was interested. The stranger, however, was not interested in the content of the New Testament but was eyeing the size of the pages and the texture of the paper. It was just the right size to use to roll his cigarettes. In fact, he told Gaylord that he wouldn't buy it, but if he gave it to him, he would take it and use the pages for cigarette paper.

"I understand that," Gaylord replied. "I will make a deal with you. I will give you this book if you promise to read every page before you smoke it." Pleased with himself that he indeed had the better end of the bargain, the man agreed to do so. Gaylord gave him the New Testament and the man walked away.

Years passed. Then one day Gaylord was attending a convention in Zimbabwe, when the speaker on the platform recognized him in the audience. Pointing to him excitedly, he said, "This man doesn't remember me, but I remember him." He explained, "About 15 years ago he tried to sell me a New Testament. When I refused to buy it he gave it to me, even though I told him I would use the pages to roll cigarettes." He continued this strange testimony saying, "I smoked Matthew. I smoked Mark. Then I smoked Luke. But when I got to John 3, verse 16, I couldn't smoke any more. My life was changed from that moment!"

Now the former smoker is a full-time church evangelist devoting his life to showing others the way of salvation he found in this little book which had just the right size pages to roll cigarettes.

Strange isn't it, how God honors the power of His Word to impact the lives of people! Paul Finkenbinder, known as Hermano Pablo in Latin America, tells the story of a man in El Salvador who discovered that the pages of a Bible were just the right size to wrap little purchases of produce at the market which he operated. He would rip a page or two from the book and wrap beans or rice for his customers. And when they got home and unwrapped their purchases, the villagers began reading the stories contained on this strange paper. Some of the people were keenly interested in what was happening. The stories were continued on the page of the next customer, so they began to compare pages, and through this strange method of evangelism people were converted and a church was born.

Exhibit 2: Professor William Ramsey

Countless individuals have embarked on a "search and destroy mission" only to experience a life-changing encounter with this living book. Some have been intellectuals, some ordinary individuals, some historians and through a diversity of different paths, they ended up acknowledging that the Bible is no ordinary book.

Sir William M. Ramsey was born in Glasgow, Scotland in 1851, the youngest son of a family of lawyers. His ability as a linguist helped him win a scholarship to Oxford, where he graduated with honors. Then in 1880 he won a three-year grant for travel and research in Greece. Ramsey thought of himself as a kind of "archaeological detective," and an innate skepticism prodded him to sift truth from fable. In his day he was considered to be the world's most eminent authority on the geography and history of ancient Asia Minor, eventually being knighted by Queen Victoria—a unique and distinct recognition. Incidentally, he was also a thorough, outgoing skeptic and a Bible critic.

Ramsey, according to friends, got tired of hearing the Bible quoted as authoritative and decided that he would take a sabbatical and visit Turkey and Greece for the purpose of gaining the knowledge to demonstrate how the book was full of errors. How better to approach this than to take the book of Acts, thought Ramsey, and prove it was filled with historical inaccuracies? Of the book of Acts, he wrote that it is "a highly imaginative and carefully colored account of primitive Christianity."[5]

After years of research and study, however, Ramsey's writings on the book of Acts amazingly became the definitive sourcebook on this portion of Scripture. Gradually he became convinced of the historical accuracy of the Bible, even in the most insignificant details. As one biographer records it, "The absolute historical accuracy...captured first his brain and then his heart."[6] To the great surprise of many of his friends, Ramsey acknowledged that in the process of discovery, he became a believer, a Christian, and accepted the Bible as the Word of God without reservation.

Exhibit 3: General Lew Wallace—the man who wrote the story of my favorite movie

The 1959 movie *Ben Hur*, starring Charlton Heston, was one of the first Hollywood-produced movies I ever saw. The chariot race in that movie is one of Hollywood's finest hours, as Judah Ben Hur battles the cynical Messala, his one-time friend who has become his archrival and enemy.

But what makes the movie meaningful for me is the story behind the story. The film was based on a novel by General Lew Wallace, a man who served as a general in the American Civil War and later became governor of the state of Kansas. A friend of Wallace's, Robert Ingersoll, who was an outspoken agnostic, challenged Wallace to write a book debunking the myth of Jesus as recorded in the Bible and picture Him as Ingersoll believed He was—an ordinary man no different from any of us.

Wallace took the challenge, but he was quickly confronted with the fact that he knew practically nothing about Jesus Christ, so he decided to research the subject before he started writing. And where do you find biographies of Jesus' life but in the New Testament? The more he studied, the more Wallace became convinced that Jesus was the person He claimed to be, and thus he wrote the book *Ben Hur—A Tale of the Christ*—a story that represents the testimony of his own changed life as a result of his study of the Bible.

Exhibit 4: Viggo Olsen—the agnostic doctor who knew he could debunk the Book

His biodata reads like a "who's who" in medicine which includes details about his professional honors, international recognition and credit for establishing a hospital in southern Bangladesh, where modern medical care was previously unknown. Recognizing him for his work with the people of Bangladesh, an ambassador declared him to be "a true friend of Bangladesh" and honored him with visa # 001 "in recognition of [his] service to our country."

The remarkable story of what Dr. Viggo Olsen accomplished is written in the award-winning book *Daktar/Diplomat in Bangladesh* and in *Daktar II*. Should you have had the opportunity of meeting Dr. Olsen, as I once did, you would never think that this rather quiet, self-effacing gentleman with graying hair and expressive eyes once set out to discredit Scripture, to prove that it is not only unscientific but irrational and full of errors—historically, scientifically, and logically.

Dr. Olsen tells the story of his encounter with the truth in an autobiographical book entitled *The Agnostic Who Cared to Search*. It wasn't that Olsen cunningly set himself against generations of believers. He simply could not believe that educated men and women living in an era of enlightenment and scientific advancement could believe some of the preposterous-sounding things recorded in the Bible.

Olsen's challenge to the credibility of the Bible was the result of the irritation caused by his wife's parents. They were committed Christians who shared their faith by letters, pamphlets, and newspaper clippings with pointed comments from a Christian perspective—most of which were immediately trashed. But it was when Viggo and Joan visited her parents' home that the encounters grew more heated, more intense, and more challenging.

After a debate over Christianity that lasted until 2 AM, Viggo and his wife agreed to look at the business of God and faith, and make a reasoned decision as to why they were rejecting the whole thing as an outmoded and leftover practice from a bygone era.

Says Olsen, "We would prove the Bible is not the Word of God, that Christianity is *not* the true religion of God, and that Christ was but a man, *not* the Son of God."[7]

Their starting point was to survey all of the arguments against God he had heard and believed during his years of study—God is invisible, all roads lead to God (if there is one), and the touchstone issue of suffering, thereby proving God's disinterest and weakness in what happens to humankind.

Part of the agreement they made with Joan's parents was that during this "search and destroy mission" they would attend church—something which, at times, made them very uncomfortable.

In his study Olsen stumbled across a book by Dr. Henry Morris (mentioned in the previous chapter), a top-notch scientist with ample credentials, and read other publications written by scientists who believed in God and the record of Scripture. Slowly the Olsens' airtight logic began to develop some hairline-thin cracks. Gradually the balance tilted as it made more sense to accept the historical record and to believe than to disbelieve.

Then unexpectedly Olsen's world took a hit! His wife gave birth prematurely to an infant baby boy—the "spitting image" of his father—who lived for only 40 hours, then died. Seeing others die is one thing; seeing your first-born son die is entirely another matter.

Something struck Olsen with awe. He loved this tiny baby—his own flesh and blood, and then he began thinking of the Father who also gave His Son, who died outside the walls of Jerusalem. By this time, Olsen had accepted the historical record that—yes, Jesus did live and die and that God does love us and wants to communicate that love to us through His Son.

"If I could love an infant son who looked like me," he wrote, "how much the Father must have loved His Son so much like Him. My very human love focused on a tiny son I didn't even know; God's love—infinite, divine—enfolded a Son whom He had known for eternity."[8]

When tragedy strikes, you either turn to the Lord or turn against Him, and Viggo and Joan Olsen took refuge in Him who not only loves us but comforts us in our times of sorrow.

The Olsens never turned back, and the agnostic who dared to search redirected his life and energies into making a significant difference in our world.

Exhibit 5: C.S. Lewis—the apostle to the agnostics

He is known simply as C.S. Lewis. When he died on November 22, 1963, most newspapers never mentioned that fact. Some papers carried a brief news note on an inside page, stating that the Cambridge Professor of Medieval Literature had died of heart and kidney failure. On page one of newspapers, on the day Lewis died, was the vivid picture of an American president, John F. Kennedy, who had been cut down by an assassin's bullets. No wonder Lewis's passing drew only scant mention.

His full name was Clive Staples Lewis, which may account for his using only the initials "C.S.," or simply "Jack," to his personal friends. Lewis was a brilliant man, and a keen thinker. He wrote on a vast number of themes including English literature, theology, and children's stories such as The Chronicles of Narnia, filled with mythical beings and fairy tale characters.

The cover of a *Time* magazine featured Lewis dubbing him "Apostle to the Agnostics." Some refer to Lewis as an apologist, or one who defends Christianity, yet Lewis never really intended to defend anything. His book *Mere Christianity,* which came from a series of radio lectures broadcast during World War 2, was the tool that brought Chuck Colson, known as "Richard Nixon's hatchet man," to an understanding of who Jesus Christ is. Since the conversion of Colson, he has spoken to the hearts of millions of people. His logical, intuitive mind simply concluded that it is more rational to accept the gospel and its implications than to disbelieve it.

As a youth, Lewis was a believer. Then, partly because of his struggle with his sexuality, he abandoned his faith and claimed to be an atheist. Eventually, however, the gospel again became meaningful to him, and he fully embraced Christianity, this time with commitment.

Lewis never based his salvation on feelings or emotional experiences. To the contrary, he later wrote that before he was converted there were times when Christianity seemed very logical, and after his conversion there were times when atheism also seemed logical. He believed that you have to tell your emotions where to get off; otherwise, you dither back and forth, uncertain of who you are or what you believe.

His personal life was complex and his path to faith was marked by intense struggles and personal conflicts. He never learned to drive a car and he was a failure when it came to practical things like fixing something around the house. Though book royalties eventually amounted to large sums, he generously gave most of it away and never could handle money well. But he was a master at handling words. When it came to making complex things simple, he was good—very, very good.

Lewis met Joy Gresham, an American writer who admired him. He eventually married her and became a father to her two children. When they were first getting acquainted, Lewis was attracted to Joy but didn't really love her. Forced, however, with either the choice of marrying her or losing her because the British government was going to deport her, he married her. He eventually fell deeply in love with Joy, and she became an indispensable part of his life.

When she died of cancer, Lewis was shattered. He felt as though God let him down. "I turn to God now that I really need Him," said Lewis, "and what do I find? A door slammed in my face, the sound of bolting and double-bolting, and after that…silence."[9]

Yet Lewis held on to his faith, not based on his feelings of pain and loss. If there is one very powerful thing about which the life of C.S. Lewis speaks to my heart, it is that faith must never be based on our emotions but on the truth of the gospel, which rises above sensations or feelings. It was the Bible that became his bridge from skepticism and doubt to faith and commitment.

Exhibit 6: Barry Taylor—the rock musician who opted for the Rock

Barry Taylor, a one-time rock musician turned pastor, was part of the anti-war, drop-out-and-do-your-own-thing rebellion of the late

1960s and early 1970s. Then one of his best friends became a Christian—"a Jesus freak," as Barry called him. He describes what happened in a conversation with author Philip Yancey:

> I thought he was crazy, so I started searching the Bible in order to find arguments to refute him. For the life of me, I could not figure out why God was concerned with the bent wing of a dove, or why he would give an order to kill, say, 40,000 Amalekites. And who were the Amalekites anyway? Fortunately I kept reading, plowing through all the hard books. When I got to the New Testament, I couldn't find a way around Jesus. So I became a Jesus freak too![10]

When Taylor encountered the real thing, he found reality in a superficial world, and the rebel stacked arms and surrendered to the Prince of Peace. He has continued to use his music to touch the lives of people around the world. A website describes him as "an award winning multimedia musician who specializes in sound design, electronic music composition and acoustic drumming."

Exhibit 7: Genya Gvozdenko—the schoolteacher who had to know the truth for himself

You have never heard of the little village of Chuguyevka in the Russian Far East some 350 kilometers from Vladivostok, right? I'm not surprised. How I found myself in this remote village where strangers must register with the police and having a refrigerator is the exception rather than the rule, is part of the remarkable story behind the conversion of Genya Gvozdenko. A man who, having grown up under Communism and never held a Bible in his hands, was eventually changed by the power of the Book.

Genya, along with his wife, Lyena, and children, was living in the distant Russian province of Primorye, where he taught school and spent his spare time working in his garden. Then one day shortly after perestroika began to change the face of Communism, Genya went to market and noticed someone with a display of Bibles laid out on a rickety table. Although he had heard about the Bible, in all his life he had never seen one. Curious, he picked up one and looked through it. He knew that under Communism it had been impossible to buy a Bible even if you had money for one—which this poor schoolteacher did not have.

Seeing that he was interested in the Book, the missionary who displayed the Bibles agreed to let the schoolteacher take one home if he returned it the next day. Genya showed the book to his wife, then sat down and started reading. He read all night, and by the time daylight had pierced the eastern sky, the light of God's love had penetrated his heart. He decided then that he wanted to know more about God.

Returning the next day, Genya asked the missionary where he could learn more about this Book and the God who says He loves us. The missionary told him about a fledgling new Christian school in Donetsk, Ukraine. Now, if you should draw a straight line between Chuguyevka and Donetsk, you would note that it stretches across 11 time zones and thousands of miles across the vast expanse of the former Soviet Union. Making the decision to go to the Christian school, Genya quit his job, sold his cow, and bought train tickets for the long journey, which took eight days and nights.

Finally arriving in Donetsk, the family made their way to the school, which had not received their application and so did not expect the schoolteacher and his family. But they could hardly send them back, so they accepted Genya as a student. That's where I met the Gvozdenkos and was impressed by their sincerity and commitment to the cause of Jesus Christ. Now having completed his training, Genya and his family have returned to the remote area in the Far East and have planted an evangelical church.

Is theirs an easy task? No way. I've been there and know what they are up against. First, there is the physical difficulty. Would you care to raise five children in a log house consisting of three rooms? Thirty meters from the house is a pipe coming out of the ground, a faucet attached, with cold water—when the pipe is not frozen. A broken mirror is attached to the wall of the cooking house, which also serves as a bathhouse, and behind this is a little shack with no modern plumbing. In the winter temperatures dip below minus 50 degrees centigrade, and the snow can be a meter deep.

Are Genya and Lyena discouraged? Not for a moment. They are positive and upbeat, pleased that they have planted a church where needs are so great. The two-edged sword of God's Word still cuts through the gloom of our old world, bringing hope and life.

Exhibit 8: E.V. Rieu—the honest agnostic who found the truth

It has been said that there are several kinds of agnostics—ordinary agnostics (those who look for truth like a thief looks for a policeman), ornery agnostics (those who hide behind the truth), and honest agnostics—the kind who will accept the truth once they are confronted with it.

Such was the classical scholar E.V. Rieu, best noted as the translator of Homer for the Penguin Classics series. A lifelong agnostic, Rieu was asked by the Penguin editor to undertake a fresh translation of the Gospels. At the time his son, who was a lay reader in the Church of England, quipped, "It will be interesting to see what father makes of the four Gospels. It will be even more interesting to see what the four Gospels make of father."

And what happened? Rieu explained, "I approached them in the same spirit as I would have approached them had they been presented to me as recently discovered Greek manuscripts...That is the spirit in which I undertook my task, to find out new things." Within a year he embraced the faith he had scorned for his adult life, was thoroughly converted, and joined the Church of England.

In a radio interview with J.B. Phillips, he was asked, "Did you not get the feeling that the whole material was extraordinarily alive?" Rieu agreed, saying, "I got the deepest feeling. My work changed me. I came to the conclusion that these words bear the seal of the Son of Man and God. And they're the Magna Charta of the human spirit."[11]

Exhibit 9: Alexander Solzhenitsyn and what he learned from Alyosha the Baptist

It was the power of the Word in the life of a fellow prisoner called Alyosha the Baptist that spoke to the heart of the Russian dissident Alexander Solzhenitsyn when he was in the Siberian Gulag. In *One Day in the Life of Ivan Denisovich,* Solzhenitsyn tells how a man in the bunk over his remained cheerful, brotherly, and distinctly different from the rest of the prisoners amidst filth, squalor, half-rotten food, and bitter cold.

Solzhenitsyn observed that when this man lay down on his bunk in the evening, he would pull from his pocket little scraps of paper on which something was scribbled and meditate on them. And what were they? A letter from his wife? Thoughts about how to escape? No, words from the Bible—from the Gospels. The man who slept in the bunk above him had been transformed from a broken, bitter, and angry human into a "brotherly, loving, fellow human," and he was impressed.[12] Solzhenitsyn never forgot what he saw in this man. Upon his release he later thanked God—not that he was again free—but that he had been sent to that particular prison camp.

Exhibit 10: Glen Chambers—the man who never lived to see the fruit of his death

When he was a young man Glen Chambers felt God was speaking to his heart about serving Him as a missionary, and eventually Glen combined a love for adventure with his desire to serve the Lord. Finally he was ready to go. His support was raised (yes, most missionaries do raise support, for without it they can't serve), he had had enough shots to immunize him from just about everything, and his bags were packed, hopefully with enough to last him for several years. Farewells had been said and the tears had been wiped away. At last he was off, headed for Ecuador where he was going to serve with the pioneer Christian missionary radio station HCJB, situated in the heart of the beautiful Andes in Quito, Ecuador.

What went wrong will never fully be known. But we do know that the commercial plane he was in crashed, and there were no survivors. Strangely enough just before he left Miami, Glen scribbled a note to his mother on a travel poster which had the word "Why?" in large letters, and that was the burning question on her heart following the death of her son. "Why, God?" her heart cried out. "How could this happen when You called him, and he never had a chance to proclaim Your Word to the people he wanted to serve?"

Fast forward several years. A stranger knocks on the door of the home where Glen's mother lives and introduces herself as a missionary serving in Colombia. She tells a story that is stranger than fiction.

Going into a remote village in Colombia to give the Gospel to unreached people, to the missionary's great amazement she discovers that there are already believers in the village and that they meet together for worship. "Who was the one who came and gave you the gospel?" she inquires.

One of the men answers, "You are the first person ever to come to this area." Then he explains that several years prior to this, he was out hunting in the jungle one day and he found "this little case," which he showed to the missionary. "It was badly burned," he said, "but in it was a book called the Bible. We have read it and believe in Christ. That is how we got the message."

The missionary looked at the slightly charred Spanish Bible. Opening the cover of the Bible, she read a dedication addressed to Glen Chambers—the man who never was privileged to preach to the Indians of either Colombia or Ecuador. When she returned to the U.S. she made it a point to share the story firsthand with Glen's mother and to continue to tell the story you have just read.

Long ago God gave a promise to His people, one we can only understand in retrospect. He said,

> As the rain and the snow come down from heaven, and do not return to it without watering the earth and making it bud and flourish, so that it yields seed for the sower and bread for the eater, so is my word that goes out from my mouth: It will not return to me empty, but will accomplish what I desire and achieve the purpose for which I sent it (Isaiah 55:10-11).

The story of Glen's Bible is one of thousands where someone inadvertently finds a Bible, and reading that Book changes his life. In other situations it was only a few verses written on scraps of paper that resulted in a changed life. That power of the Word to bring hope in a hopeless situation in a truth-is-stranger-than-fiction scenario is told in this final story.

Exhibit 11: Hien Pham—the man who found comfort in a Vietnamese prison

In his autobiographical book *Walking from East to West* Ravi Zacharias tells a story so remarkable that I have saved it for last.

In 1971, Ruth Jeffrey, a descendant of Jonathan Goforth, the renowned Presbyterian missionary to China, insisted that a young evangelist by the name of Ravi Zacharias consider going to Vietnam, then being torn by warfare. When a check arrived in the mail for the precise amount Zacharias needed along with a note, "May God bless you!" the stunned young man could not say no to the invitation.

Arriving in Vietnam, Zacharias fought both fear and homesickness. Soon invitations to speak started coming from rather remote corners of the country and 17-year-old Hien Pham was designated as both his driver and interpreter. Riding on the back of Hien's motorbike, Ravi and his young friend began going from village to village. As the two evangelized, a bond of love and friendship developed between them.

After several months Zacharias returned to the United States and because of the devastation of the war, completely lost touch with the young man who had ministered alongside him.

Skip ahead about thirty years. Now Zacharias has gray in his hair and a worldwide ministry as a kind of apologist-successor to the Cambridge professor C.S. Lewis. He was in Vancouver for a lecture when the phone rang. "Brother Ravi," said the caller, and immediately Ravi recognized the voice he had not heard for years.

After Vietnam fell, Hien was arrested by the Vietcong on trumped up charges that he had worked with the CIA, imprisoned, and repeatedly brainwashed by his captors. His Bible was taken from him, and hour after hour, day after day, he was bombarded with the message, "You have been deluded; there is no God and you have been a victim of American imperialism."

Finally Hien broke. "Maybe they are right. Maybe there is no such thing as God," he thought, and that's when he made the decision to walk away from it all. "I'm through with God," he said, adding, "When I wake up in the morning, no more God, no more prayer."

The next morning Hien was sent by the commanding officer to clean latrines—one of the most despicable, humiliating, shameful and degrading tasks anyone could perform. The filth was excoriating as flies swarmed freely and the smell was overpowering. Hien's last task was to empty the trashcan full of paper soiled by human excretion. As he was about to empty the can, one piece of paper got his attention—it contained English words, something he had not seen for a long while.

Hien gingerly picked up the paper, washed off the filth and hid it. That night when others had fallen asleep, he dug it from his pocket. In the upper right-hand corner, he saw the words "Romans 8." It was from the Bible. His eyes fell on familiar words such as, "We know that in all things God works for the good of those who love him, who have been called according to his purpose." As he read on, shocked by the discovery, his eyes misted, then filled with tears.

The next morning, to the amazement of the commanding officer, he asked to clean the latrines again! Permission granted. The officer in charge must have thought he was crazy. Nobody ever volunteered for this task. "You are going to clean them every day until I tell you to stop," he said.

In coming days, Hien added to his collection—page by page, torn from the Book and used for toilet paper—and faithfully Hien would clean the pages as best he could and study them at night when it was safe. Says Ravi, telling of the incident, "He ended up collecting numerous passages from the book of Romans, as well as from other books of the Bible."[13] In a series of events that can only be described as a miracle, following the end of the fighting Hien escaped Vietnam and eventually made his way to the United States. Only God could have so ordered the timing of the circumstances I have just related.

The bottom line

The impact of the Bible in changing the lives of people for the better is unrivaled. Have you ever heard anyone say, "When I began reading books on science and technology, my heart was strangely drawn towards God"? Or, "When I began studying philosophy and history, I was converted and gave my life for Christian service"?

When a newspaper asked people, "What is the most impressive book you have ever read?" the Bible was mentioned more than any other book. One person responded, "My life and my seven-year-old son's life were forever changed when someone gave me a Bible in a translation I could understand." Another gave this testimony,

> The Bible remained on my bookshelf gathering dust while
> I had feelings of guilt for not reading it. I'm still not sure
> why I picked it up one day and began seriously reading it.

> I remember thinking that if Christians were right about Jesus, I had better know what God was saying to me...My intent was to read it for intellectual purposes, but something happened that day and to my surprise I began to understand the words with my heart and spirit. That was the beginning of a very different life for me.[14]

If you have never made a serious study of this Book that tells you how to connect with God, you'd better get started. It can make the difference between spiritual survival and failure when the winds of adversity blow and the dark winter of trouble begins to engulf you. The writer of Hebrews describes the Word as "an anchor for the soul, firm and secure" (Hebrews 6:19).

Accepting what the Bible says isn't a matter of trying to convince yourself to believe something that isn't true. It is acknowledging the historical record of what God tells us about life, about His love and His concern for us. Not knowing this is an ignorance you can ill afford.

There is great comfort in knowing that the promises of God's Word have your name attached to them, so when you face the inevitable troubles and difficulties of living in a broken world, you know God is not indifferent to your needs but will see you through. This assurance is found only in the Bible. A stanza from "No Other Plea," a nineteenth-century hymn with words by Lidie H. Edmunds, puts it so well:

> My heart is leaning on the Word, the written Word of God,
> Salvation by my Savior's name, salvation through His blood.
> I need no other argument, I need no other plea;
> It is enough that Jesus died, and that He died for me.

- Why do you think some people risk imprisonment or even death to take a Bible into restricted countries? What difference will it make?

- E.V. Rieu described the Bible as "the Magna Charta of the human spirit." What do you think he meant by that phrase?

- Describe someone you know who has undergone a significant transformation in their understanding about God.

- How has Jesus changed *your* life?

Chapter Eight

The Implications of Uncertainty

*"The deathless book has survived three great dangers:
the neglect of its friends; the false systems built upon it;
the warfare of those who hated it."*[1]

—Isaac Taylor

In 1911 thieves broke into the world's most prestigious art gallery, the Louvre, in Paris, and took the most famous painting in the history of art, Leonardo da Vinci's *Mona Lisa.* It can never be said that the thieves did not have good taste. During the two-year period when the haunting image of the woman with the semi-smile was missing, more people came to the gallery to stare at the empty spot on the wall than had gone to look at the masterpiece in the previous twelve years. Think about it! People were going to see *what wasn't there!*

No wonder that Muscovites, having been denied the privilege (a right, as we would consider it) of being able to purchase a Bible for 73 years under Communism, lined up outside Moscow bookshops—100,000 of them, so said the press—the first day a collection of Bible stories was made available. A newspaper editorialized, "It is only natural such people should seize a permitted opportunity to study the strange book which has affected the lives of so many other people for thousands of years."[2]

Have you ever pondered how much we take for granted? When we are blessed with health, we never stop to think about our circulatory system working, our legs and arms moving, or our eyes focusing properly; but then let illness strike and suddenly we understand how much we have taken for granted and how much we desire to regain what has been lost.

It is only when there is a blank spot on the wall of our lives that we begin to realize the value of what is missing—something that is precious and meaningful that we took for granted. The empty place speaks loudly and clearly.

For many—perhaps you as well—that blank spot on the wall of your life has resulted in uncertainty, a lack of definition as to who you are, where you are going, and what your life is all about. C.S. Lewis once used the analogy of a ship that was on the ocean and he said that three questions have to be faced: First, how do you keep the ship from sinking? Then, how do you keep it from running into other ships? But more important, why is it out there at all?

The answer to what your life is about will never be found through the study of science or philosophy, but it will be found in this Book that is a reliable bridge across the dark chasm of uncertainty that obscures the future.

Consider your options

By now you have walked with me across a number of bridges. This evidence is what has led me to have confidence that the Bible is what it claims to be: the Word of God. The Bible's uniqueness, the manuscript evidence, fulfilled prophecy, the findings of archaeology and science, and the lives of people who have been changed by this book—all point to its writing being more than human endeavor could have accomplished, and therefore, of supreme importance. Reading the book causes you to conclude, "Yes, God said that!"

Some truths are so profound and meaningful that it becomes

intensely painful to confront them. Furthermore, embracing them at times requires changes in our lifestyles that we don't want to make, so we tend to look the other way or give feeble intellectual assent to truth apart from a commitment to its direction.

On one occasion Peter came to Jesus and asked, "Lord, to whom shall we go? You have the words of eternal life" (John 6:68). That yearning or passion to know God and commune with Him often lies dormant in our hearts and lives. Yes, we believe, at least theoretically, that the Bible is God's Word and confirm that belief by adding new editions and translations to our overburdened shelves. But, and here is where the whole equation turns the corner, we often feel that our duties are complete by acknowledging those beliefs and making token commitments to them.

When people, however, choose to ignore what a map or compass says, preferring to rely on their feelings—such as, "What I want to do seems okay to me,"—they may well be in for a rough ride. The Bible is not only cross-cultural in the sense that it embraces all humankind, but is also cross-cultural in that it provides a clear understanding of right and wrong, often rejecting practices that are socially acceptable today. It postulates moral absolutes that are as unchanging as the North Star, the same regardless of the weather or the vagaries of human opinion. It tells you who God is, who you are, and how you can get through life without falling on your face.

Just a minute, you may be thinking. *Does it really matter that much what my views are of this Book?* If the Bible is true, it matters tremendously. You then have four options:

Option 1: You can ignore this Book and what it says

I often think of the instruction manual for a small single-engine aircraft that says something like this: If you are flying at night and you lose power, try to restart the engine. If that fails, when you reach an altitude of 200 meters, turn on your landing lights. *If you don't like what you see, then turn them off again.*

The sad fact is that a lot of people have turned off their landing lights when it comes to very important things. Some do it in a high school or college classroom. Some do it simply because they don't like what the Bible says—too confining, too limiting, too—well, puritanical. They like what they are doing and don't want to change, so they just "turn off the lights."

Actually, that is what vast numbers of people do, many of whom even go to church every Sunday, have a half-dozen or more Bibles in their homes, put *ixthus* (fish) symbols on the bumpers of their cars, and support humanitarian causes. That's about as far as their faith really takes them.

At times the neglect of the personal encouragement and direction that the Bible gives is nothing less than tragic. Consider the following: Dick Johnson was serving as a police chaplain for the Urbandale–Des Moines Police Force, when he received an urgent summons to report to a home where there had been a disturbance. Dick is often called upon to provide counseling, help, encouragement, and support when it is needed. For one couple, however, his help was too little and too late. A husband had become jealous over the attention that his wife had been giving to a mutual friend. Pointing a gun at the head of his wife, asleep on the sofa, he pulled the trigger, then took his own life as well—a double murder-suicide.

As Dick came into the living room, the scene of the crime, he noticed that a Bible was lying two feet from the head of the woman who had become the victim. He picked it up. It was a confirmation Bible that had been presented to the husband when he had finished his religious instruction and had become a church member.

"The answer to their problems," said Dick, "was there, only 24 inches away. In that Book was the solution to their conflict and all of their anger and frustrations. The answer was so close physically, yet ignored."

Option 2: You can trivialize this Book

You can reduce it to the level of good literature and nothing more. Many people, having never read or studied the Bible, mock or scorn the Book as a collection of myths and fables, making light of anyone who takes the Bible seriously. Thousands of young adults, having grown up in a Christian home, having gone to Sunday school as youngsters, hit college campuses and suddenly find that anyone who actually believes the Bible is considered an "intellectual throw-back," a kind of weird non-conformist, who has no real academic future.

Howard Stern is a talk show host whose trademark is insulting vulgarity and profanity. Stern, so I have read, refused to let his three daughters listen to his daily radio talk show or watch his TV program as they were growing up. He doesn't seem to mind, however, that other people's kids watch him or listen to his filth—just not his own kids.

When Stern appeared on *The Tonight Show* hosted by Jay Leno, he held up a Gideon Bible and then said, "The Gideon Company is now putting *my* book in the place of Bibles in hotels." In the event that you are not familiar with the work of Gideons International, they are a group of businessmen who for more than a century have placed Bibles in hotels around the world. Though their work is somewhat of a thankless task, Gideons can tell you of literally thousands of lives that have been changed because someone picked up a Bible in a hotel room, read it, and found the answer to their searching, lonely heart.

Annoyed by Stern's comments, Jay Leno, who isn't exactly the prototype of a Sunday-school teacher himself, rebutted the comments, saying, "Howard, something horrible is going to happen to you...This Book [meaning the Bible] will strike you down as you go down the road. It will go through the windshield and pierce your heart." He continued, "I am sounding like an evangelist now, but I predict that's what will happen suddenly, all that is in this Book is making perfect sense to me."

Touché! Surprised by what Leno said? Why make light of this

book? Why not pick on Karl Marx and what he wrote, or something
that came from the pen of Plato? Or take a shot at Brown's *The Da
Vinci Code?* The Bible is often made the brunt of jokes because it
condemns the very lifestyles that many embrace today. For centuries
individuals have attacked this Book, predicting its demise; yet like the
old blacksmith who wears out his hammer while the anvil remains,
these individuals pass from the scene and yet this grand old Book of
all books remains.

Option 3: You can flat-out deny the truth of this Book

You then are faced with the task of explaining how the Bible has
been the inspiration for the world's greatest literature, art, and music
down through the centuries. You are forced to offer psychological
explanations for the life-changing conversion experiences of people
who say, "Reading that book changed my life!" You can interpret
and explain the influence of the Bible however you wish, yet the fact
remains that denying something doesn't change the consequences of
truth, no matter how you choose to ignore or deny it.

I once had an unexpected encounter with this issue as I sat down
in a restaurant across the aisle from two men who were engaged in
a rather heated discussion. Attempting to mind my own business, I
began reading the menu, but it was impossible for me not to overhear
their conversation. It went something like this: "You call yourself a
Christian? Why do you believe in Jesus Christ?"

The friend having lunch with the interrogator hadn't expected the
inquisition. He hesitated, then responded, "I believe that He died for
me and that His death took away my sin."

"How do you know that Christ ever lived anyway?"

"Because the Bible says so." And that settled the issue—right?
Not exactly.

Then, the antagonist launched a rather loud and caustic oration,
stating that the Bible was a collection of myths and fables that came

out of the superstitious Middle Ages, and if God existed at all we could not know Him. Then he said, "Besides this, all religious faith is based on 'what men think'—not facts."

At this point the conversation was a great deal more interesting than the list of soups and sandwiches on the menu in front of me so I spoke up. "Please excuse me for interrupting your conversation, but I couldn't help overhearing, and what you have said is of interest to me. Would you mind if I asked a question?" Both said, "Certainly not."

Then, turning to the fellow who was quite certain that his friend had been deceived by Christianity, I asked, "Suppose that your friend, who is a Christian, is entirely wrong. Suppose that there really was no such person called Jesus Christ and that the Bible is a fraud—not God's revelation to humankind at all. Let's suppose that life ends when you die—that's it, and there is no heaven or hell and no life hereafter. Now suppose this is true, what has this fellow lost?"

He answered, "I suppose that he has not lost anything, because he believed in something that did not exist."

Then I said, "On the other hand, suppose he is right, suppose that there is a God, a heaven and a hell, and that He sent His Son to pay the price of our sin and give us eternal life, what have you lost?"

He sat in stunned silence for a moment and then blurted out, "Well, that is not the question, but I...I never thought of it like that."

Option 4: You can embrace this Book and what it teaches

The implications of the contents of the Bible are tremendous, touching every part of my life including my business, my marriage, my money, my ethics, my work, my morality, my sex life, my views of men and women, how I treat the elderly, what I think about abortion and stem-cell research and on and on.

The greater your knowledge of this Book, the greater will be your respect for it, and when you come to understand that it is a Book given by God, you gradually begin to recognize that God gave us His direction for our benefit, not to make us miserable, but to show us how to live.

The inertia separating the widely-held beliefs of people today and the counsel of the Bible can be overcome by persuasion that is stronger than our indifference and our neglect. Ben Jonson, the seventeenth-century poet, once said that the prospect of being hanged "wonderfully concentrates the mind," and so does a challenge to your security or future.

For Viggo Olsen (see the previous chapter) it was the death of a child. For some it is a divorce and the loneliness that follows. The somber words of a doctor, "I am sorry to tell you that you have an inoperable cancer," suddenly makes a person search for something to dispel fears and provide security. For others it is simply the quiet persuasion of the Holy Spirit speaking to your heart saying, "This is the way, walk in it!"

Steps to embracing the truth of Scripture

If you are now convinced about what the Bible truly is, then what? What are the steps you can do to fully embrace the truth of Scripture?

Step 1: Make a commitment of faith

Act upon the evidence that I have discussed in the various chapters of this book. The subtitle of this book, *Bridging the Distance Between Your Heart and God's Word,* means you have to cross that chasm of doubt that keeps you from embracing the truth of Scripture. Crossing this bridge may mean you take one step at a time, perhaps even a few inches at a time. The Archbishop of Canterbury once said that "the longest journey in the life of one's belief is from the head to the heart."[3] With your intellect you acknowledge truth but with your heart you appropriate that truth.

When social critic Malcolm Muggeridge gave the Blaise Pascal Lectures at the University of Waterloo, eventually printed in a little book called *The End of Christendom,* he was asked, "At what point in your life did you believe in Christ Jesus?" He responded, "It's a question I often get asked, but I can't answer it. For me there has never been a moment when I would say at that point I believed. It's been much more like the journey of Bunyan's Pilgrim." [4]

That commitment came as Muggeridge hit the bumps of life. In his youth Muggeridge had a tongue that was as sharp as a sword, and he never spared anyone of position or influence when it came to using it. He referred to Britain's monarchy as "a royal soap opera." He wrote of the American president Dwight D. Eisenhower as "a meandering, old President." When he edited *Punch* magazine, he wrote a lot of things that caused a wisp of smoke to rise as people read them.

A variety of experiences slowly caused his doubt and skepticism to erode, such as the time he was serving with British intelligence in Mozambique during World War 2. Depressed, he decided to terminate his life by drowning. He started swimming but saw a great light which caused him to turn back towards the shore. Later in life he admitted that he had moments of doubt when he secretly read the Bible. He said that he actually read it at all stages of his life—in Egypt, India, the USSR, and, of course, at home in his native Britain. In the Gospels he "discovered a new world" which was vastly different from twentieth-century life.

In his *Confessions,* which he wrote at the age of 84, he admitted that the most marked-up passages of his Bible concerned the Passion, and bear "stains that might be from tears." On November 27, 1982, Muggeridge was received into the Roman Catholic Church, but this does not really date his time of conversion. It was his way of making a statement condemning the carnality and depravity of life today, and a reaffirmation of his commitment to life, including his opposition to abortion.

For others, however, the commitment of faith that the Bible is trustworthy comes as a conversion-like encounter with the truth, driving a stake in the ground settling the truth of what this Book is about. Visit Forest Home Christian Conference Center in the mountains of Southern California, and there on a tree near one of the paths, you will find a brass plaque where a young man the world has come to know as Billy Graham wrestled with the issue of whether or not the Bible could be trusted. He crossed the line and said, in effect, "From now on I take this Book by faith."

Billy's crisis had been precipitated by the challenge of a friend, an intellectual, who chided him saying, "Billy, you're 50 years out of date. People no longer accept the Bible as being inspired the way you do. Your faith is too simple. Your language is out of date." Chuck Templeton, the man who challenged Billy, eventually left ministry, divorcing his wife, and opted for a career in television. Billy, though, knew he had to decide. He describes crossing the Continental Divide of doubt, saying,

> Dropping to my knees there in the woods, I opened the Bible at random on a tree stump in front of me. I could not read it in the shadowy moonlight, so I had no idea what text lay before me.
>
> The exact wording of my prayer is beyond recall, but it must have echoed my thoughts: "O God! There are many things in this book I do not understand. There are many problems with it for which I have no solution…" At last the Holy Spirit freed me to say it. "Father I am going to accept this as Thy Word—by *faith! I'm going to allow faith to go beyond my intellectual questions and doubts, and I will believe this to be Your inspired Word.*"
>
> When I got up from my knees at Forest Home that August night, my eyes stung with tears. I sensed the presence and power of God as I had not sensed it in months. Not all my questions were answered, but a major bridge

had been crossed. In my heart and mind, I knew a spiritual battle in my soul had been fought and won.[5]

That commitment allowed Billy Graham to authoritatively use a phrase that has become almost synonymous with his ministry: "The Bible says..."

❧

Charles Farrah grew up in a Christian home, but when he began working on his Ph.D. at the University of Edinburgh, little by little his belief system was undermined by men he held in high esteem. The battle for his faith came to a crisis as he walked the streets of that beautiful city at two o'clock in the morning one cold night, struggling with the issue, "Is there a God who is personal and caring? Is the Bible really true? Or should I abandon the whole thing?"

In telling of his battle with doubt Farrah said that the Scriptures he had memorized as a child kept rolling over and over in his mind and he could not shake them. Finally, returning to his little apartment, he got down on his knees and settled the issue once and for all, committing himself to the truth of the Word of God.

Crossing the bridge to confidence in what the Bible says requires a commitment—not a blind faith but one based on evidence that dispels uncertainty and hesitancy. Apart from it your faith will surely falter. W.H. Murray,[6] one of the team members of the 1951 Scottish Himalayan Expedition, in an often quoted statement about the importance of commitment, wrote,

> Until one is committed, there is hesitancy, the chance to draw back, always ineffectiveness. Concerning all acts of initiative (and creation), there is one elementary truth, the ignorance of which kills countless ideas and splendid plans: that the moment one definitely commits oneself, then

Providence moves too. All sorts of things occur to help one that never would have otherwise occurred. A whole stream of events issues from the decision, raising in one's favor all manner of unforeseen incidents and meetings and material assistance, which no man could have dreamt would have come his way.[7]

It was commitment that Joshua had in mind when he challenged his hearers,

If serving the Lord seems undesirable to you, then choose for yourselves this day whom you will serve, whether the gods your forefathers served beyond the River, or the gods of the Amorites, in whose land you are living. But as for me and my household, we will serve the LORD (Joshua 24:15).

Step 2: Live up to the knowledge that you have

Quite often what we do not understand doesn't bother us nearly as much as what we do understand. Frankly, that's what growing in the grace and knowledge of the Lord Jesus Christ (2 Peter 3:18) is about. You may not understand everything. Nobody does. But when the Holy Spirit gives you enlightenment as to what He wants you to do, you need the courage to say, "Yes, Lord, yes, I will."

Bob Vernon spent 38 years in the Los Angeles Police Department, finishing his illustrious career as Assistant Chief of Police. He rose through the ranks from a rookie street cop to second in command of a highly important police force. During a stint as an undercover agent for the department, he was working the streets when he sat down on a curb next to a bearded, somewhat disheveled young man with long dirty hair, then known as a hippie. The conversation went like this:

Vernon asked the hippie, "Hey, where are you from?" And the young man told him. With his interest piqued, Vernon inquired, "What do they sell pot for back there?" The hippie replied, "I don't use that stuff anymore," and then went on to tell the story of his conversion. Then Vernon, explaining that he, too, was a Christian, reached out and shook hands with the young man.

"What do you know? A *Christian* cop!" exclaimed the young man.

The conversation then turned to what he was going to do in Southern California, and Vernon, wanting to lend a hand, volunteered to help him find employment.

"Work!" he exclaimed, "That's not for me!"

Vernon then reached for a well-worn New Testament he carried in his pocket and turned to Paul's second letter to the Thessalonians where it says, "If a man will not work, he shall not eat."

"That's in the Bible?" the young man asked with incredulity.

Vernon then showed him the text, and with surrender he said, "Well if that's in the Bible, it's for me!" And Vernon helped him connect with employment.

That attitude quickly closes the gap between the lives we live and the counsel of God's Word.

Step 3: Strive to know the truth that will set you free

That's what Jesus told the disciples (recorded in John 8:32). But the truth is divisive, and the only way you can be sure that your persuasions are right is when you have confidence that the Bible is trustworthy. The harsh reality is that today we are in a cultural and spiritual war that will repeatedly put you, if you are a believer, at odds with our society and force you to swim upstream.

Large numbers of individuals today are reinterpreting what faith is about, suggesting that we have moved into a new era characterized by an "openness of God" with new interpretations of old truths.

Let's back up for a few minutes. Two terms that are almost

synonymous and quite often used interchangeably describe religious, sociological, and cultural changes that are vitally affecting our lives today—postmodern and post-Christian. Both, accusing Protestants and Roman Catholics of being sons of Aristotle who follow an intellectual tradition marked by rigidity and adherence to religious authority, reject historical Christianity as being unworkable and out of touch with life today. The terms are somewhat elusive when it comes to accurate definitions; however, both describe a society or person whose foundational philosophy originated with Christianity but has gone far beyond the "confines of Christianity and the Bible" in an attempt to encompass a wider worldview, one that seeks an "authentic Christianity" through feeling and experience. "Post-Christian" says *Wikipedia,* an online encyclopedia, "is a term used to describe a person, religious movement or society that is no longer rooted in the language and assumptions of Christianity."[8]

Having rejected the caricature of cultural Christianity, some of those who are part of the quest for authentic Christian beliefs in a world they would describe as post-Christian are sincere in their searching for an authentic relationship with God. However, relationships (usually with other individuals in small groups), subjective personal experiences, and opinions based on conjecture and feelings often transcend the authority of "thus saith the Lord"—an expression found over 400 times in Scripture as a final appeal to what God has revealed.

The path to the post-Christian world began with the Enlightenment, that intellectual movement of the seventeenth and eighteenth centuries that ultimately resulted in an industrial revolution in the Western world. The offspring of science and technology then formed a powerful catalyst that shifted the focus in both religion and education from the mysterious to the concrete, from the unknown to the known, and from God to man. Gradually we ceased to bow in reverence before a Creator and began to worship the human spirit and intellect.

One of the ground-breaking pioneers in this social and religious transition undermining biblical authority was a German-born professor who taught at the University of Basel. His name was Friedrich Nietzsche, the father of the "God is dead" movement that created a lot of noise in the 1960s. He was not actually suggesting that God suffered a stroke and died, or that he had dealt Him a death blow; but that he no longer saw a need for a belief in God and visualized a world in which men lived as though there were no God—no ultimate accountability and no absolutes that serve as moral anchors for a drifting society. Of course, God didn't die. Following Nietzsche's exodus from the scene, babies continued to be christened, churches kept their doors open (though fewer people went through them), and life went on.

On one occasion I was in the village where Nietzsche grew up and walked through beautiful forests and by lakes that mirrored the sky and clouds. I marveled at the wildflowers growing in the meadows, treading some of the same paths that he had once hiked. As I reflected upon the beauty that surrounded the village, I pondered the sad and tragic fate of a man who denied the existence of a Creator and His revelation to humankind. And how did Nietzsche's belief system work for him? Having rejected God and traditional values, his mind snapped. For the last 11 years of his life, he was insane, drawing his last breath in a mental institution. Nietzsche, admiring only one person in history—Pilate who asked the question "What is truth?"—unwittingly laid the foundation for twentieth-century existentialism and a post-Christian world.

In the novel *The Brothers Karamazov* by Russian novelist Fyodor Dostoevsky, a contemporary of Nietzsche's, there is a line: "If there is no God, then anything is permissible." The "God is dead" mind-set of Nietzsche laid the groundwork for two oppressive world powers—Hitler's Third Reich and the USSR.

Charles Darwin, Nietzsche's contemporary and fellow runaway from God, wrote, "A man who has no assured and ever-present belief in the existence of a personal God or of a future existence with retribution or reward, can have for his rule of life, as far as I can see, only to follow those impulses which are strongest or which seem to him the best ones."[9] This philosophy prompted Adolf Hitler without conscience to send 14 million people (6 million Jews and 8 million Gentiles—priests, pastors, politicians, and those who opposed him) to their deaths in the concentration camps of occupied Europe.

A onetime seminary student, who as a lad won the village prize for Scripture memorization, also bought into Nietzsche's philosophy and led a society where for practical purposes God's existence was denied. His name? Iosif Vissarionovich Dzhugashvili. History identifies him as Josepf Stalin—the butcher responsible for the deaths of 15 million people. Svetlana Stalin, the dictator's daughter, defected to the West and declared, "I could not live without God," and neither could the millions of repressed citizens who survived 73 years of communism.

The impact of what I have just described on the twentieth century has resulted in a rather universal philosophical transition to a world where the line between biblical authority and expedience is blurred, a world that interprets truth in a subjective framework. In a postmodern or post-Christian world decisions are often based on expedience or relativism—not upon absolutes clearly defined as being right or wrong, moral or immoral, more upon what we think the Bible should say or what we think it must mean (as opposed to what it says and actually means). The post-Christian mindset strives to find meaning to life through ritual, community, literature, music, art, and nature. It is an endless search for meaning without God.

In his book *A New Kind of Christian* Brian McLaren describes the emergence of postmodernity as a "spiritual resurgence" which is "unconventional and irreverent at times" based far more on sensitivity to your feelings than *sola Scriptura* (Scripture alone).

In the final chapter of his book McLaren contends that the Bible should be read "as a pre-modern text, emerging from a people who believed that truth is best embodied in story and art and human flesh rather than abstraction or outline or moralism."[10] In other words, he is saying that the Bible has limited relevance when it comes to defining what life is about today.

Jude, the half-brother of Jesus, would not easily be convinced of that premise, having exhorted believers of his day to "contend for the faith that was once for all entrusted to the saints" (Jude 1:3). Neither would those who spearheaded the Reformation at great personal cost, such as John Calvin and Martin Luther, be easily convinced either! Sensing the direction the church is headed today Malcolm Muggeridge predicted the end of Christendom—but not the end of Christ. He recognized that the institution is in trouble—but not the Incarnate Word.

At the same time society will tell you in no uncertain terms that you are narrow and intolerant because you do not embrace the "I'm OK; you're OK; anything you want to do is OK, too" philosophy that has swept aside biblical values, replacing them with a lifestyle that the Romans would have enjoyed but the apostle Paul would have condemned. So you don't want your child subjected to social reeducation in school and taught by a teacher who tells your son that homosexuality is an alternative lifestyle? That makes you stand apart from the crowd and often a target of derisive criticism. The farther society moves from the biblical norm, the more His people will be strangers and pilgrims. The darker the world becomes, the more obvious will be those who stand in contrast to it.

C.S. Lewis contended that you need to know what a straight line is before you know what a crooked one is, and, like it or not, the truth of this Book is the straight line that says, "Do this!" and "Don't do that!" It has the same ring of authority that a guide who knows the jungle has when he speaks to a lost traveler, telling him how to come out safely on the other side. The negatives of this Book are not to inhibit you or keep you from finding happiness but to guide you through the hazards of life.

But once you close the door on post-Christianity or lifestyles that, of necessity, reject the position that the Bible is true, and you have embraced what it says, you draw a line in the sand and take a rather narrow path—one trod by countless of pilgrims and sojourners who like Moses of old "chose to be mistreated along with the people of God rather than to enjoy the pleasures of sin for a short time" (Hebrews 11:25).

When Alexander Solzhenitsyn was in prison for the first time he said he was forced to accept the reality that there is both good and evil in our world. Here's how he described it: "It was there [in prison] that I realized that the line between good and evil passes not between countries, not between political parties, not between classes, but down, straight down each separate individual human heart."[11]

In the midst of sin and depravity—including our own failures—there is the marvelous grace of God that brings forgiveness and allows us to separate ourselves as pilgrims and sojourners from a world that is hostile to truth.

Long ago Jesus said that a commitment to truth and uprightness would result in schism. He told the disciples,

> Do not suppose that I have come to bring peace to the earth. I did not come to bring peace, but a sword. For I have come to turn a man against his father, a daughter against her mother, a daughter-in-law against her mother-in-law—a man's enemies will be the members of his own household (Matthew 10:34-36).

The key to knowing that God's Word is truth is a desire to do what God wants you to do. If you really have a desire to know God's will for your life—if you truly want to do the right thing, God will reveal to you that His Word is true. Jesus promised, "If anyone chooses to do God's will, he will find out whether my teaching comes from God or whether I speak on my own" (John 7:17). Strive to obey what you read in the Bible, and you will discern that it is, indeed, a living book.

Step 4: Realize that with obedience comes blessing and with disobedience comes consequences we often dislike

Once you settle the issue that the Bible is trustworthy and reliable and the counsel it gives comes from the heart of a loving Father who knows what is best for His children, you then confront the reality that God meant what the writers of Scripture penned long ago. But—and this is important—committing to His will and purpose for your life not only relieves you of a great burden but brings His blessing as well.

The first chapter of the book of Psalms begins with the promise of reward, saying, "Blessed is the man who does not walk in the counsel of the wicked or stand in the way of sinners or sit in the seat of mockers." Frankly, some words are difficult to understand in the cultural context of life today. Such is the word "blessed." Check out synonyms for the word and you will find the word "happy," but the Hebrew word that the writer used some 3,000 years ago embraced far more than the state of mind we describe as being "happy." It includes the concepts of wholeness, completeness, and a sense of well-being that is often sought today but seldom found in a world that puts far more importance on what we have than what we are.

Jesus stressed the importance of *doing* as opposed to *hearing and sampling.* "Why do you call me, 'Lord, Lord,'" he asked, "and do not do what I say?" (Luke 6:46).

On another occasion he used the analogy of two individuals who built houses—one on sand, the other on rock (a firm foundation) to contrast those who embrace the truth and those who have no foundation for their lives. Then he went to the bottom line: "The one who hears my words and does not put them into practice is like a man who built a house on the ground without a foundation. The moment the torrent struck that house, it collapsed and its destruction was complete" (Luke 6:49).

James, the half-brother of Jesus, writing one of the first New Testament documents, said, "Do not merely listen to the word, and so deceive yourselves. Do what it says" (James 1:22). He puts the emphasis on commitment and motivation to positive action—not merely "listening" or "hearing" the Word.

This was the same emphasis Paul made in his landmark letter to the Romans. "It is not those who hear the law," he said, "who are righteous in God's sight, but it is those who obey the law who will be declared righteous" (Romans 2:13).

❦

Once you realize Jesus Christ did not come to condemn the world but that the world through Him might be saved (John 3:17), matters embracing the supernatural are no longer stumbling blocks, barricading you from crossing the bridge of confidence to what the Bible says.

The questions confronting us are profound but simple:

- Is there a God?
- What kind of a God is He?
- Has He communicated with us expressing His love, His purpose, and His will through the Bible?

This book specifically deals with the last question, and when you answer that in the affirmative, you have discovered what David did long ago, that God's Word is "a lamp to my feet and a light for my path" (Psalm 119:105). And then you will hear a quiet but powerful voice say, "Whether you turn to the right or to the left, your ears will hear a voice behind you, saying, 'This is the way; walk in it'" (Isaiah 30:21).

What more can you ask for?

Think It Over, Talk It Over

- What possessed so many visitors go to the Louvre Museum to see an empty space on the wall once occupied by a famous painting?

- Describe any encounters with truth that have caused you to make a change in your lifestyle.

- In what ways has postmodern thinking influenced you or your friends?

- The Archbishop of Canterbury once said, "The longest journey in the life of one's belief is from the head to the heart." How has your spiritual journey moved between your head and your heart?

- Charles Farrah grappled with a crisis of faith while he worked on his Ph.D. at the University of Edinburgh. One night he asked himself, *Is there a God who is personal and caring? Is the Bible really true?* How do you answer these questions for yourself?

Where Do I Go from Here?

Getting Started

You have only ten minutes before you head for the kitchen in the morning. After that you're off to work, come home tired at the end of the day, fix supper for your family or think about getting through the file in your briefcase, and then fall exhausted into bed. Your conscience nags at you a bit, and you really want to pick up your Bible and spend a few minutes in the Word. *Can I really get anything out of this in just ten minutes?* you ask yourself as you debate even bothering to pick up your Bible. The following guidelines will help you get started:

Guideline 1: Concentration. As you sit down and let your Bible fall open, your first battle is with your thoughts that flood your mind and wage war with your concentration. Shut out the rest of the day and the tyranny of pressing obligations to the extent that you can and focus on what you are reading. Then, expect God to speak to you. The depth of your encounter with the Word—connecting with God's direction and will for your day—is far more important than how many chapters or pages your eyes quickly scan without comprehending what you are reading.

Guideline 2: Observation. You need to observe what you are reading and understand it to profit from it, right? I am amazed at times that I can read a page, close the book and not remember one thing that I read. Like the seed that falls on the wayside, the vultures of my schedule have plucked it out of my memory. My mind has been racing on to the day's agenda or the problems I'm dealing with instead of concentrating on those moments with the Word.

A one-volume commentary such as Wycliffe's Bible Commentary or *Halley's Bible Handbook* provides concise, focused help. Today there are many study Bibles with reference notes that are helpful and illuminating—well worth the additional cost. If the Bible is new to you, I suggest that you start with the Gospel of John, and then go on to the book of Acts, to get a comprehensive grasp of the whole. No matter what you do, however, do not ignore the Old Testament, which is the cradle of the New, and is all part and parcel of the Book.

Guideline 3: Interpretation. What does it mean? Generally, the clearest, simplest interpretation is the correct one. Some would have you to think that only those with great spiritual insights can interpret the Book. When I hear someone trying to convince an audience that he has "insights" which others have not been spiritual enough to gain, I usually catalog the speaker as a sensationalist. God did not give His Book to Ph.D.s but to common, ordinary people, and common, ordinary meanings are usually right on target.

Guideline 4: Application. How do I apply this great truth to my life? Most of what the Bible says is pretty much "plain vanilla." God's purpose in giving us this magnificent Book is to help us know how to live. Right living, God's plan, His blueprint—all of these are revealed in the Bible. As you apply to your life what you read each day, the Bible will become a living book to you.

Getting the Most
out of Bible Study

Realizing that his death was imminent, William Tyndale, who had been convicted and imprisoned for treason and crimes against the Church of England, wrote a letter to the governor-in-chief. He asked for "a warmer cap, a candle, a piece of cloth to patch my leggings...but above all," he implored, "I beseech and entreat your clemency to be urgent with the Procurer that he may kindly permit me to have my Hebrew Bible, Hebrew grammar and Hebrew Dictionary, that I may spend time with that in study."

Can you believe this? Tyndale was about to be executed, and yet he wanted a Bible and translation resources. He, of course, was no ordinary man. He was a scholar who had excelled at Oxford and Cambridge universities and was determined to give the Bible to common men and women in simple English which they could understand. For that he died!

The fact is, God gave this book for ordinary people, and when you read the text and apply it to your life, God guides, enriches, and challenges you to fulfill His purpose.

The following suggestions may help you get more out of your Bible reading.

Guideline 1: Read with understanding. Simply put, pay attention to what you are reading. If you are losing the battle of concentration, then do what I have done on occasion—read the Book out loud. Notice geographic locations and historical references. Read as much as you can digest, whether it is a few paragraphs or a few chapters, but no more than you can soak up.

Guideline 2: Read with an awareness of other passages of Scripture. That's also where the context comes into the picture. Ask yourself,

"Who wrote this?" and "To whom is it directed?" Important? Yes, just as much as the letter that comes to your residence. Some promises are made to specific individuals. Others are generic; they have your name on them.

Guideline 3: Read with intelligence. Read the Book as you would any other book at the same time you read the Book as you would read no other book. Ask three questions of what you read:

1. What does it say? Rephrase the text in your own words.
2. What does it mean? A rule of thumb is that it means what it says. Remember, God didn't give the text to confuse you but to enlighten you.
3. How can I apply this to my personal life?

Guideline 4: Read with faith. Expect God to speak to you through His Word. Paul told the Romans, "Faith comes by hearing, and hearing by the Word of God" (Romans 10:17 NKJV). In China I have listened to stories of remarkable answers to prayers of very simple individuals. Lacking medicines, scientific technology, and sophistication, these men and women, who have never seen a seminary, read what God says in His Word, believe it, and ask Him to do what He says He will do. God honors their simple faith in ways that I seldom see in the West. Remember John wrote,

> This is the confidence we have in approaching God: that if we ask anything according to his will, he hears us. And if we know that he hears us—whatever we ask—we know that we have what we asked of him (1 John 5:14-15).

Guideline 5: Read with consistency. To the extent that you can, make the reading of Scripture a daily part of your life, whether it is first thing in the morning or the last thing at night. Some people read the Bible through every year. Reading only three chapters every day which takes the average person about 15 minutes, will allow you to read through the Bible in slightly less than 12 months. However, I am more interested in digging until I sense God has touched my heart, rather than just plowing through so many pages or chapters each day. A good rule of thumb is to stay there until God speaks to your heart through the Word—whether it is in the first ten verses or several chapters. Then go do what God has for you to do, but more than that, be what He wants you to be—just for today!

Getting the Word into
Your Heart—Here's How!

The Russian dissident Alexander Solzhenitsyn told how first he was harassed by the Communists, who disliked what he wrote. Then, he said, they came and confiscated what he had written. After that they took his books, his wife and family, and eventually his freedom. Finally, he was imprisoned. Solzhenitsyn, however, said he was never richer than when everything he had was gone except the treasures within his heart that could never be taken away from him.

When I was in the former USSR in 1975, whenever I left the hotel room where I was staying, my bags were rifled. My hotel room was "bugged"—I found the hidden microphone, and for a period of time I had some serious concern about being arrested because of my faith. I was by myself and a long way from a familiar face.

I held three degrees in biblical text. My doctoral program had required knowledge of both text and interpretation for the entire Bible. In the process of my studies, I had memorized a lot of Scripture, but suddenly it hit me: *If I had only the Scripture I have committed to memory, would I be satisfied?* And in that Tashkent hotel room I made a vow to God (the only one that I can remember ever making) that I would continue to memorize God's Word until I met the Author face-to-face.

"Are you still doing that?" you may ask. An honest answer is "yes" with the qualification that it takes longer than it once did (but then everything else does as well!).

First, let's deal with the reason of why you should memorize Scripture. Let's suppose, for example, that you knew a reward had been offered for the arrest of a mass murderer and you are standing on the street corner when you see the individual get into a car, the car in front of yours. You immediately read the license plate, five digits. Could you remember them long enough to write them down or call the police?

If enough money was attached to what you needed to remember, would that improve your ability to concentrate and memorize? It just might make a difference, right? OK, then why not memorize Scripture? After all, you gain benefits from the practice that are far more valuable than getting a reward for helping to capture a felon. The psalmist said that Scripture both keeps us from sin and provides light and guidance for our lives (see Psalm 119:9-11,105).

"I'm too old to memorize anything!" you may say. You can do it! Anyone over age 25 has either said that or thought it at some time or another. It's a proven fact that kids do memorize more quickly and retain better than their parents; but is it true that adults just cannot memorize? Absolutely not! While it is a scientific fact that the average person's ability to memorize does slow down with age, it doesn't stop. With the passing of time your brain doesn't fossilize, and the neurons never cease to record stimuli.

"OK," you may be saying, "tell me how to do it."

The following suggestions will work for you.

First, select a translation with which you are comfortable. I grew up memorizing and quoting the King James Version, and I still think the poetry and majesty—especially of the Psalms—is beautiful and yet unrivaled, but newer, more contemporary versions such as the New International Version and the English Standard Version, as well as the slightly older New American Standard Version, are easier to read, understand, and memorize.

Second, write out the Scripture and focus on it. Make an enlarged copy of what you want to memorize. Put the text on your mirror so you can see it when you shave, or put it over your sink in the kitchen so you will see it several times a day. Print it on a card and put it on the sun visor in your car. The object is to focus on the verses at least five times during the day.

Third, check yourself. Sit down later in the day and write out as much as you possibly can remember, then open your Bible and check the passage to correct your mistakes. Or cover the text you are memorizing in your Bible, say it, uncovering it line by line. When I first awaken in the morning, I try to repeat whatever I'm currently trying to memorize. When you get stuck, pick up your Bible and meditate on the text. Do the same thing the last thing at night before you drift off to sleep. If you waken in the night, ponder the passage you are working on—and besides, that's one of the best ways I know to get the devil to leave you alone so you can fall asleep again!

Take advantage of idle times. Look at a New Testament during the moments your car creeps along in rush hour traffic, the time which is often wasted thumbing through out-of-date magazines in your dentist's office or waiting to pick up your children after school.

Never convince yourself that it can't be done. No matter what your age, you will discover that the benefits and blessings of enriching your life spiritually are worth the hassle to keep your brain from turning to concrete. Begin today. Memorizing Scripture is part of renewing your mind on a daily basis (Romans 12:2) and feeding your soul.

Notes

Coming to Grips with the Bible

1. H.L. Mencken, as quoted by Don Wharton, "The Greatest Bible of Them All," *Reader's Digest*, December 1962, 103.

Chapter 1: Can This Book Be Trusted?

1. Richard E. Byrd, *Alone* (New York: Kodashana International, 1995), 50.

2. Byrd, 118.

3. Geoff Boucher, "Pirating Songs of Praise," *Los Angeles Times*, October 10, 2006, A-1.

4. Dennis Fisher, *The Da Vinci Code: Separating Fact from Fiction* (RCB Ministries, Grand Rapids, MI, 2005), 1.

5. Gary M. Burge, "Jesus Out of Focus," *Christianity Today*, June 2006, 26.

6. Dan Brown, *The Da Vinci Code* (New York: Anchor Books, 2003).

7. *USA Today*, as quoted by Lee Strobel and Gary Poole, *Exploring the Da Vinci Code* (Grand Rapids, MI: Zondervan, 2006), 7.

8. Strobel and Poole, 7.

9. Strobel and Poole, 8.

10. Strobel and Poole, 8.

11. Fisher, 2.

12. Josh McDowell, in an interview with Dr. James Dobson, "Rescuing the Next Generation, part 1," released on Focus on the Family, May 21, 2007. Accessed at http://listen.family.org/daily/A000000454.cfm.

13. Ravi Zacharias, *Can Man Live Without God?* (Dallas: Word Publishing, 1994), ix.

Chapter 2: The Bridge of Uniqueness

1. www.time.com/time/covers/0,16641,19311214,00.html.

2. Neil Lightfoot, *How We Got the Bible* (Grand Rapids, MI: Baker Book House, 2005), 12.

3. Pliny, a first-century Roman historian and educator, said that civilization was dependent upon on the use of papyrus. For a thorough discussion of papyrus and its development see Lightfoot's *How We Got the Bible*, 17-19.

4. The Greek word *biblia,* which gives us the English word *book,* referred to the papyrus manuscripts made from the papyrus reed grown on the banks of the Nile.

5. Much of what was commonly believed in Egypt in the fourteenth century before Christ was in direct conflict with what Moses recorded in the book of Genesis. Moses wrote, "In the beginning God created the heavens and the earth," but common wisdom was that the earth was hatched from an egg and that symbol adorns sarcophagi and monuments of that era. Luke explains: "Moses was educated in all the wisdom of the Egyptians and was powerful in speech and action" (Acts 7:22).

6. Norman L. Geisler and William E. Nix, *From God to Us* (Chicago: Moody Press, 1974), 13.

7. Erwin W. Lutzer, *You Can Trust the Bible* (Chicago: Moody Press, 1998), 38.

8. In 1863 Richard Roethe theorized that *Koine* Greek was a new "language of the Holy Ghost." That premise was widely accepted until Adolf Deissmann, a German pastor and scholar, analyzed the Greek text of various readings in the papyri, comparing it with the Greek text of the New Testament, and discovered that there were many similarities, thus demonstrating that the Greek of the New Testament was only ordinary Greek spoken commonly throughout the world. Norman Geisler and William Nix explain, "Until the late nineteenth century, New Testament Greek was believed to be a special 'Holy Ghost' language, but since that time it has come to be identified as one of the five states of development of Greek itself. This *Koine* Greek was the most widely known language throughout the world of the first century" (Geisler and Nix, 129).

9. Geisler and Nix, 8.

10. W.A. Criswell, *The Bible for Today's World* (Grand Rapids: Zondervan Publishing House, 1965), 32.

11. Philip Yancey, "The Bible Jesus Read," *Christianity Today,* January 11, 1999, 67.

12. While Hebrew Bibles contain 24 books, they consist of the same 39 books found in English Bibles. The Hebrew Scriptures combine some books, generally making three sections: the law, the writings, and the prophets.

13. Ravi Zacharias, *Walking from East to West* (Grand Rapids: Zondervan Publishing House, 2006), 176.

14. J.B. Phillips, as quoted by E. M. Blaiklock, "More and More, Scripture Lives!" in *Christianity Today,* September 28, 1973, 19.

15. According to the German scholar Adolph Deissmann, the oldest use of the Greek word translated "gospel"—*euangelion*—was an inscription on Greek stone telling how two armies had met in combat, one was victorious, and a runner was dispatched to the city with the *euangelion,* or good news, of the victory.

16. The dates that I am providing in this chapter are generally advanced by conservative theologians such as Henry Clarence Thiessen in his benchmark *Introduction to the New Testament* (Peabody, MS: Hendrickson Publishers, 2002).

17. Aramaic was a Semitic language, closely related to Hebrew—a vernacular that was widely spoken by Jews living in Palestine during the time of Christ. It is quite certain that Jesus spoke this language as well.

18. Lightfoot, 203.

19. Lightfoot, 51.

20. Lightfoot, 132.

21. Lightfoot, 88.

22. Paul D. Wegner, *Christianity Today,* September 6, 2006, 9.

23. F.J.A. Hort, as quoted by Howard Vos, *An Introduction to Biblical Archaeology* (Chicago: Moody Press, 1959), 48.

24. Bernard Ramm, as quoted by Chuck Northrop, "Inspiration, Is the Bible From God or Man?" www.kc-cofc.org/39th/ibs/Tracts/Inspiration.htm.

25. Eusebius' writings, VIII, ii, as quoted by the Catholic Encyclopedia, www.newadvent.org/cathen/05007b.htm.

26. Words of a New Faith, 188.

27. Voltaire, as quoted by George Sweeting, *Who Said That?* (Chicago: Moody Press, 1995), 68.

28. George Sweeting, *The Word of God Shall Stand,* June 1978, 1.

29. Ravi Zacharias, *Can Man Live Without God?* (Waco, TX: Word Publishing, 1994), xviii.

30. C.S. Lewis, *Mere Christianity* (New York: The Macmillan Co., 1969), 45.

Chapter 3: The Bridge of Manuscript Evidence

1. Norman L. Geisler, personal correspondence dated December 1, 2006.

2. The Mormon apostle Ballard in an article entitled, "Our Search for Happiness," as quoted in *Christianity Today,* June 14, 1998, 30.

3. *Time,* December 30, 1974.

4. *Time*, December 18, 1995.

5. *U.S. News and World Report*, October 24, 1999.

6. Nigel Gillingham in *Qumran: A Pictorial Guide*, says, "A group of Bedouin from the Ta'amireh tribe were on their way from Transjordan to the black market in Bethlehem. The purpose of the journey was to sell a herd of 'contraband' goats. Normally such a route would not have been used but due to the political scene in Palestine at that time, before the birth of the State of Israel, they needed a route that would avoid both British and Arab patrols. It was on this journey through the Judean Wilderness that the discovery took place" (Herzila, Israel: Palphot Marketing Ltd., n.d.), 4.

7. John Trever was the first to photograph the scroll in its original condition. In their book *The Meaning of the Dead Sea Scrolls* authors James VanderKam and Peter Flint say Trever's *The Untold Story of Qumran* provides the best and most comprehensive account of the initial discovery. In a footnote, they say that Trever refers to numerous tape-recorded interviews with the Bedouins, who responded to 63 questions he put to them. Their answers, of course, comply with the "lost goat" story.

8. Harry Thomas Frank, *Understanding the Dead Sea Scrolls*, ed. Hershel Shanks (New York: Random House, 1992), 5-6.

9. Frank, 6.

10. Eleazar L. Sukenik as quoted by Moshe Pearlman in *The Dead Sea Scrolls in the Shrine of the Book* (Tel Aviv: 1999), 14.

11. Prior to the discovery of the Isaiah manuscripts, the Nash Papyrus, containing among other things the Ten Commandments from Exodus 20 and Deuteronomy 5, dating to the second or first century BC, was considered to be the oldest portion of the Old Testament.

12. Author's personal interview with Mrs. Elizabeth Trever on January 9, 2007, in Lake Forest, California.

13. "The Dead Sea Scrolls," www.crystallinks.com/dss.html.

14. www.jewishvirtuallibrary.org/jsource/History/deadsea.html.

15. Howard F. Vos, *Beginnings in Bible Archaeology* (Chicago: Moody Press, 1971), 54.

16. Frederic Kenyon, *Handbook to the Textual Criticism of the New Testament* (New York: Macmillan, 1912), 5.

17. Frederic Kenyon, *The Bible and Archaeology* (New York: Harper, 1940), 288.

18. C. Tischendorf, *Codex Sinaiticus: The Ancient Biblical Manuscript Now in the British Museum: Tischendorf's Story and Argument Related by Himself*, 8th ed. (London: Lutterworth Press, 1933), 16-17.

19. Tischendorf, 16-17.

20. L. Schneller, *Search on Sinai: The Story of Tischendorf's Life and the Search for a Lost Manuscript*, tr. Dorothee Schroeder (London: Epworth, 1939), 71.

21. Upon the death of Voltaire the Geneva Bible Society purchased his old home and upon his own press printed a complete edition of the Bible.

22. Bruce Metzger, in his seminal *The Text of the New Testament*, says, "[The Sinai Manuscript] is the oldest complete manuscript of the entire Bible…" He says Sinaiticus "once contained the entire Bible…Today parts of the Old Testament have perished, but…the entire New Testament has survived…the only known complete copy of the Greek New Testament in uncial script" (p. 42).

23. While the Vatican dates this manuscript at about AD 325, other scholars, such as Gordon Fee, date the manuscript at about AD 350; however, all are in general agreement that it is dated about the middle of the fourth century. Bruce Metzger says that "the complete absence of ornamentation from Vaticanus has generally been taken as an indication that it is slightly older than Codex Sinaiticus" (Metzger, *The Text of the Old Testament*, 47).

24. Written in Greek, this fragment of papyrus was found in Egypt in 1920. It followed the Alexandrian text and is 3.5 inches long and 2.5 inches wide and contains seven lines of Scripture from John 18:31-33.

25. Howard F. Vos, *An Introduction to Biblical Archaeology* (Chicago: Moody Press, 1959), 51.

26. Evangelical scholars Gordon Fee and D. A. Carson believe O'Callaghan's position does not hold up under careful scrutiny. They believe the unidentified text O'Callaghan thinks is from Mark could have been from the Septuagint…the Apocrypha…or the pseudepigraphical book of 1 Enos. Carson says that his reconstruction "is at best speculative and that it could fit other passages just as well" (D.A. Carson, *The Inclusive-Debate: A Plea for Realism* [Baker Books, 1979], 122).

27. R.C. Sproul, *Renewing Your Mind* (Grand Rapids: Baker Books, 1998), 215.

28. Consider the fact that the average manuscript would consist of about 30 leaves or sheets, and since an animal's hide would provide for about two sheets, the hides of at least 15 animals would be required.

29. A wide-ranging variety of Septuagint readings indicates that multiple copies were distributed throughout the world.

30. Say Norman Geisler and William Nix, "On the whole, the Septuagint closely parallels the Massoretic text and tends to confirm the fidelity of the tenth century A.D. Hebrew text. If no other evidence were available, the case for the fidelity of the Massoretic text could rest with confidence upon the foregoing

lines of evidence alone" (*From God to Us*, [Chicago: Moody Press, 1974], 174).

31. See 1 Corinthians 2:7-13; 14:37; 1 Thessalonians 2:13.

32. Neil Lightfoot, *How We Got the Bible* (Grand Rapids, MI: Baker Book House, 2005) 157.

33. Athanasius is the same one who led the fight against the Arian heresy. He stood alone battling the issue of whether Jesus *was* God or He *became* God. Athanasius stood his ground and was eventually proved right.

34. www.bible-researcher.com/bruce1.html (downloaded July 3, 2006). In his book *The Books and the Parchments*, F.F. Bruce says, "What is particularly important to notice is that the New Testament canon was not demarcated by the arbitrary decree of any Church Council" (Westwood, NJ: Fleming H. Revell, 1963), 113.

35. Bruce, 260-261.

36. Lightfoot, 169.

37. Andrew Cockburn, "The Judas Gospel," *National Geographic*, May 2006, 78-95.

38. See the Gospel of Bartholomew and the Gospel of Peter in the Apocrypha.

39. D. James Kennedy, televised sermon dated December 12, 2006.

40. Ravi Zacharias, *Can Man Live Without God?* (Word Publications, Dallas, TX: 1994), 162.

Chapter 4: The Bridge of Archaeology

1. Nelson Glueck, *Rivers in the Desert*, as quoted by Richard De Haan in *The Book You Can Trust* (Grand Rapids, MI: RBC Publications, n.d.) 7.

2. Twenty-two references to the Hittites are found in the Bible, beginning with Genesis 15:20, where God made land promises to Abraham.

3. Wikipedia, an online dictionary, defines pure science as "the exact science of the development of scientific theories…Pure science is sometimes used to refer specifically to physics and pure mathematics, but chemistry and biology may also be considered as examples." Archaeology lacks the specificity of other scientific disciplines because it is less precise and often more subjective.

4. Jefferey Sheler, "Where history is all too alive today," *U.S. News and World Report*, December 24, 2001, 42.

5. Sheler, "Where history," 62.

6. In one of his books on Christian evidences, Harry Rimmer called attention to the fact that the historical books of the Old Testament record the names of 47

kings in addition to those kings who reigned in Israel and Judah. As great as some of these men were, they were completely forgotten by posterity, and for some 2,300 years their names were unknown to secular scholars. Most secular historians relegated their existence to mythology and considered their exploits as myths. "Now," says Guy P. Duffield, "all 47 of them have been transferred from the columns of mythology to the accepted records of established history."

7. Jeffery Sheler, "Mysteries of the Bible," *U.S. News and World Report*, April 17, 1995, 64.

8. "Geographica," *National Geographic*, January 1992, 20.

9. Following Garstang's work the British archaeologist Kathleen Kenyon broke with Garstang's findings holding to a later date for the destruction of Jericho. At this point the ruins have been so sacked that it is impossible to determine exactly what happened and when it took place.

10. Mark 10:47 agrees with the Matthew account—seemingly in contradiction to what Luke wrote.

11. Thomas Maugh II, "Biblical Pool Uncovered in Jerusalem," the *Los Angeles Times*, August 9, 2005, A-8.

12. Sheler, "Mysteries of the Bible," 60-68.

13. A complete discussion and evaluation of the evidence can be found in two issues of the magazine *Biblical Archaeological Review*, November-December 2002 and January-February 2003.

14. Michael Specter, "Tomb of Caiaphas," *Orange County Register*, August 14, 1992, 1.

15. Leonard David, "Satellite Sleuth Closes in on Noah's Ark Mystery," www.space.com/news/060309_ark_update.html, October 27, 2006.

16. www.noahsarksearch.com/ararat.htm (as of March 15, 2006).

17. Boyce Rensberger, quoted in the *Los Angeles Herald Examiner*, January 21, 1979, A-9.

18. *The Jerusalem Post International Edition*, "The Ebla Tablets," Friday, November 30, 1976, 11.

19. George Alexander and John Dart, the *Los Angeles Times*, "Tablet Sheds New Light on the Bible," May 7, 1976, vol. xcv, 1.

20. Rensberger.

21. It is of interest that many secular historians denied the literal existence of both Sodom and Gomorrah, considering them to be mythical or legendary names.

22. Many if not most contemporary Jewish scholars have viewed their ancestors as being "composite" individuals, not real persons. Typical is Dr. David Noel Freedman, then director of the Albright Institute for Archaeological Research in Jerusalem, who expressed surprise at the Mara finds saying, "We always thought of our ancestors...as symbolic. Nobody ever regarded them as historic."

23. Abraham Rabinovich, the *Jerusalem Post*, 76.

24. Hayim Tadmor, the *Jerusalem Post*, 76.

25. W.F. Albright, "Archaeological Discovery and the Scriptures," *Christianity Today*, June 21, 1968, 3.

26. Millar Burrows, *What Mean These Stones?* as quoted by Howard Vos, *Beginnings in Bible Archaeology* (Chicago: Moody Press, 1973), 106.

Chapter 5: The Bridge of Fulfilled Prophecy

1. Carl Henry, as quoted in *Living Quotations for Christians*, ed. by Sherwood Eliot Wirt and Kersten Beckstrom (New York: Harper & Row Publishers, 1974), 191.

2. *Antiquities of the Jews* XI, chapter viii, paragraphs 3-5.

3. Alexander's only heir was a baby boy who had not yet been born at the time of his death.

4. D. James Kennedy, *Why I Believe* (Waco, TX: Word Publishing, 1981), 16.

5. Brian Johnston, "Future Tense—The Predictions of Nostradamus," *Mabuhay*, published by Philippine Airlines, January 1998, 35, 36.

6. www.danceage.com/biography/sdmc_Criswell, Oct. 3, 2006.

7. There is a category of individuals who have unusual insights to the future coming from neither Satan nor divine revelation.

8. George Ladd, writing the critical notes for *The Wycliffe Bible Commentary*, says, "The priestess of Apollo at Delphi was called *pithon*, and the word was extended to soothsayers. A person having a python spirit was thought to be inspired by Apollo, who was associated with oracles. This girl was demon-possessed, and her uncontrolled utterances were regarded as the utterance of a God" (Chicago: Moody Press, 1962), 443.

9. Phillip Myers, *General History for Colleges and High Schools* (Boston: Ginn & Co.), 55.

10. William Foxwell Albright, *Living Quotations*.

11. Jack Fellman, "Eliezer Ben-Yehuda and the Revival of Hebrew," www.jewishvirtuallibrary.org/jsource/biography/ben_yehuda.html.

12. Harry Rimmer, *Palestine: The Coming Storm Center* (Grand Rapids: Eerdmans Publishing Co., 1941).

13. "If a prophet, or one who foretells by dreams, appears among you and announces to you a miraculous sign or wonder, and if the sign or wonder of which he has spoken takes place, and he says, 'Let us follow other gods' (gods you have not known) 'and let us worship them,' you must not listen to the words of that prophet or dreamer. The Lord your God is testing you to find out whether you love him with all your heart and with all your soul" (Deuteronomy 13:1-3).

14. Fulfilled prophecy and mathematical probabilities are from Peter W. Stoner's *Science Speaks Out* (Chicago: Moody Press, 1963).

15. J. Edward Barrett, "Can Scholars Take the Virgin Birth Seriously?" *Bible Review*, October, 1998, 11.

Chapter 6: The Bridge to a Truce with Science

1. Lee Strobel, *The Case for a Creator* (Grand Rapids: Zondervan, 2004), 346.

2. Henry M. Morris, "Games Some People Play," *Foundation for Family and Nation*, (El Cajon, CA: Institute for Creation Research, March, 1964), 1.

3. Morris, 2.

4. Richard C. Lewontin, *The Inferiority Complex*, as quoted by Morris, 3.

5. Richard Dawkins as quoted by Brad Holland, "God vs. Science," *Time*, November 13, 2006, 52.

6. Francis Collins, as quoted by Holland, 53.

7. Charles Townes, *Think* (published by IBM, volume 32, March-April, 1966), 2, used by permission of the author.

8. Strobel, 357.

9. Charles Darwin in *Origin,* as quoted by Ray Bohlin, "Darwin's Black Box," www.leaderu.com/orgs/probe/docs/darwinbx.html, October 10, 2006.

10. Strobel, 248.

11. David Roach, "Famed atheist admits evidence for God," *Christian Examiner* (Orange County edition: January, 2005), 5.

12. http://biola-edu/news/articles/060327_flew.cfm, October 4, 2006.

13. Townes.

14. John Horgan, *National Geographic,* "Francis Collins—The Scientist as Believer," February, 2007, 33.

15. Erwin W. Lutzer, *Seven Reasons Why You Can Trust the Bible* (Chicago: Moody Press, 1998), 141.

16. For a refutation of the Miller experiment, see Strobel, 42-44.

17. Strobel, 22-24.

18. Genesis 1:1, 1:21, and 1:27.

19. There is no consensus among Christians and neither does the Bible state precisely that the six days of creation are literal 24-hour periods, creative periods of time, or whether an indefinite period of time elapsed between Genesis 1:1 and 2.

20. www.aboutdarwin.com/timeline/time_06.html#0070. October 15, 2006.

21. Rick Cornish, *5 Minute Apologist* (Colorado Springs, CO: NavPress, 2005), 223.

22. Charles Darwin as quoted by Phillip Johnson, *Darwin on Trial* (Downers Grove, IL: InterVarsity, 1993), 46.

23. Darwin as quoted by Cornish, 213.

24. Walter Brown, *In the Beginning: Compelling Evidence for Creation and the Flood*, www.creationscience.com/onlinebook/LifeSciences27.html, October 15, 2006.

25. Malcolm Muggeridge, *The End of Christendom* (Grand Rapids: Eerdmans Publishing, 1980), 59.

26. Samuel J. Alibrando, *Nature Never Stops Talking* (Reedley, CA: Tsaba House, 2005), 124; and Jennifer Kahn, *National Geographic*, "Mending Broken Hearts," February, 2007, 46.

27. www.emc.maricopa.edu/faculty/farabee/BIOBK/BioBookNERV.html, November 1, 2006.

28. Strobel, 352.

29. Paul Brand and Philip Yancey, *Fearfully and Wonderfully Made* (Grand Rapids: Zondervan Publishing House, 1980), 45-46.

30. Alibrando, 39.

31. Genesis 1:27.

32. Paul Brand and Philip Yancey, *In His Image* (Grand Rapids: Zondervan Publishing House, 1984), 32.

33. "Amish Victim..." *Los Angeles Times*, October 7, 2006, A-12.

34. Robert J. Schadewald, *Science Digest*, 1980, as quoted at www.lhup.edu/DSI-MANEK/fe-scidi.html.

35. www.firstbaptisthenderson.org/10reasons.html.

36. CNN, Wednesday, July 23, 2003; posted at www.cnn.com at 12:29 a.m. EDT.

37. While some of the most reliable Greek manuscripts do not contain the word blood *(haimatos)*, other manuscripts have that word including those used by the King James translators of the seventeenth century and the use of that word flies in the face of racial prejudice held in their day, that various races of people have different blood.

38. Nigel Brush, *The Limitations of Scientific Truth* (Grand Rapids: Kregel, 2005), 13.

39. For a discussion of Wernher von Braun's religious beliefs see "Plain Talk From von Braun," *Life*, vol. 34, No. 21, Nov. 18, 1957, 136, and *Time*, June 27, 1977, 71.

40. Robert Jastrow, "Have Astronomers found God?" *Reader's Digest*, July, 1980, 53.

Chapter 7: The Living Book That Changes Lives

1. Soren Kierkegaard as quoted by George Sweeting, *Who Said That?* (Chicago: Moody Press, 1995), 65.

2. Presently open churches are known as Three-Self Patriotic Churches and are recognized by the government. Many of these have small bookstores where Bibles and a very limited assortment of Christian books can be purchased. A very large percentage of Chinese Christians, however, worship in house churches that may or may not be registered with the government.

3. Brother Andrew in an interview on *Guidelines—A Five Minute Commentary on Living*, broadcast on March 2, 2005.

4. Carl Lawrence, *The Church in China* (Minneapolis: Bethany House, 1985) 122.

5. Sir William Ramsey as quoted in www.maranatha-bpc.com/MESSENGER/ MM-99-07-18.htm, (July 17, 2006).

6. Ramsey.

7. Viggo Olsen, *The Agnostic Who Dared to Search* (Chicago: Moody Press, 1990), 13.

8. Olsen, 62, 63.

9. C.S. Lewis, *A Grief Observed* (New York: Harper Collins, 1961), 8.

10. Philip Yancey, *The Bible Jesus Read* (Grand Rapids, MI: Zondervan Publishing House, 1999), 18.

11. E.M. Blaiklock, "More and More, Scripture Lives!" *Christianity Today*, September 28, 1973, 19.

12. Alexander Solzhenitsyn, *One Day in the Life of Ivan Denisovich* (New York: Dutton, 1953), tr. Ralph Parker, as quoted by Malcolm Muggeridge, *The End of Christendom*, (Grand Rapids: William B. Eerdmans, 1980), 44.

13. Ravi Zacharias, *Walking from East to West* (Grand Rapids: Zondervan, 2006), 219.

14. The *Orange County Register*, December 12, 1999, Commentary, 4.

Chapter 8: The Implications of Uncertainty

1. Isaac Taylor as quoted by Warren Wiersbe, *With the Word* (Nashville: Thomas Nelson, 1991), 521.

2. "The Bible in Moscow," *Los Angeles Herald Examiner*, September 20, 1966, C-2.

3. As quoted by Ravi Zacharias, *Walking from East to West* (Grand Rapids: Zondervan, 2006), 173.

4. Malcolm Muggeridge, *The End of Christendom* (Grand Rapids: William Eerdmans Publishing, 1980), 28.

5. Billy Graham, *Just As I Am* (San Francisco: HarperCollins, 1997), 139, used by permission.

6. W.H. Murray understood the importance of commitment. Taken prisoner by the Nazis in World War 2, for three years he was moved from one POW camp to another, but during that time he began writing a draft of a book on mountaineering on the only paper that was available—rough toilet paper. The Gestapo found the draft and destroyed it. Undaunted he began the task again in spite of the fact he was living on a starvation diet and so weak he was quite certain he would never climb again. His rewritten manuscript was eventually published in 1947.

7. www.gurteen.com/gurteen/gurteen.nsf/id/X00006CB6/, October 16, 2006.

8. www.en.wikipedia.org/wki/Post_Christian, February 10, 2007.

9. Charles Darwin, as quoted by Philip Yancey, "Nietzsche Was Right," *Books & Culture*, January/February 1998, 15.

10. Brian D. McLaren, *A New Kind of Christian* (San Francisco: Jossey-Bass, 2001), 159.

11. Muggeridge, 43.

More Resources for Study...Why You Can Have Confidence in the Bible

DR. HAROLD SALA has designed this book so it can be used as a basic textbook in a classroom, Bible study, or home-school setting. For chapter-by-chapter review questions as well as other resources, please go to **www.guidelines.org.**

About Guidelines International Ministries

In 1963 God placed a burden on the hearts of Harold and Darlene Sala to reach the world for Christ using the media—especially in restricted countries. In prayerful partnership with God, they formed Guidelines, a nonprofit Christian organization devoted to reaching people, teaching people, and touching them with the compassionate heart of Christ.

Dr. Sala began using radio because it can not be stopped by political barriers or illiteracy. His radio program, *Guidelines—A Five-Minute Commentary on Living,* is the longest running program of its type on Christian radio. Internet is also a vital part of the ministry, and the Web site at **www. guidelines.org** features available resources and allows the broadcasts to be distributed in a variety of forms. Publications by Harold and Darlene are continually being translated into other languages, including Burmese, Korean, Spanish, Russian, Ukrainian, Thai, Chinese, and more! Their books have been an encouragement and wonderful source for spiritual growth for many. A bookstore offering the books is available at Guidelines' Web site.

Harold and Darlene are personally involved in teaching biblical principles of family living and training future

Christian leaders all over the world. Frequent destinations include China, Africa, the Philippines, Russia, and Ukraine.

You may reach the author at this address:

Dr. Harold Sala
Guidelines International
26076 Getty Drive
Laguna Niguel, CA 92677
E-mail: guidelines@guidelines.org
Web site: www.guidelines.org
Phone: 949.582.5001

About the Author

DR. HAROLD J. SALA is an internationally known radio personality, author, Bible teacher, lecturer, husband, and grandfather. His radio program, *Guidelines—A Five Minute Commentary on Living*, is heard on more than 600 stations in 17 languages, reaching more than 100 countries. It has been the recipient of the Catholic media Award for Moral Excellence in Broadcasting.

Dr. Sala holds a Ph.D. in English Bible from Bob Jones University with proficiencies in Hebrew and Greek. His further graduate studies have been at the University of Southern California, California Baptist Seminary, Fuller Theological Seminary, and the Conservative Baptist Seminary in Denver, Colorado.

More than 40 books and hundred of publications have been authored by Dr. Sala, focusing on marriage, parenting, singles, counseling, and daily devotionals. His latest devotional, *Today Counts!* was released in 2006. His book *Heroes—People Who Have Changed the World* received the prestigious Angel Award for moral excellence in the media in the US. Dr. Sala has also been honored by CASA with the Heritage of Faithfulness Award.

His warm, personal style of sharing wisdom and insight from God's Word has brought hope to many. Dr. Sala is a frequent guest lecturer and teacher at many churches, schools, and international conferences, such as the Asian Theological Seminary in Manila and Donetsk Christian University in Ukraine, and the Ukrainian Institute for Artificial Intelligence.

His hobbies include golf, photography, and people—the driving focus of his life and ministry. Residing in California, Dr. Sala and his wife, Darlene, have three adult children and eight well-loved grandchildren.

More Harvest House Resources to Help You with
God's Message to You

HOW TO STUDY THE BIBLE FOR YOURSELF
Tim LaHaye

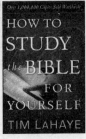

Many Christians think they can't understand the Bible without the help of theologians or ministers. But the Bible was written to *all* people—including you—and anyone can understand its message!

With easy-to-understand charts, flexible study options, and practical suggestions, *How to Study the Bible for Yourself* (nearly 1 million sold) will help you develop the skills to make your time in God's Word rich and meaningful. You'll learn how to...

- find the Bible's major themes, principles, and promises
- understand key teachings and verses
- cultivate strong Bible study habits
- keep a spiritual diary
- talk about the Bible with others

SEARCHING FOR THE ORIGINAL BIBLE
Who Wrote It and Why? • *Is It Reliable?* • *Has the Text Changed over Time?*
Randall Price

Lost...destroyed...hidden...forgotten. For many centuries, no one has seen any of the original biblical documents. How can you know whether today's Bible is true to them?

Researcher and archaeologist Randall Price brings his expert knowledge of the Bible to tackle crucial questions:

- What happened to the original Bible text? If we don't have it, what *do* we have?
- How was the text handed down to our time? Can you trust that process?
- What about the Bible's claim to be inspired and inerrant?

Current evidence upholds the Bible's claim to be the authoritative record of God's revelation—a Book you can build your life and faith on.

THE POPULAR BIBLE PROPHECY COMMENTARY
Understanding the Meaning of Every Prophetic Passage
Tim LaHaye and Ed Hindson

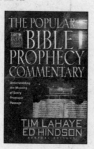

It's all here—clear and concise explanations for key prophetic passages from Genesis to Revelation. Written by Bible scholars but created for everyday students of the Bible, this resource makes it possible for you to enrich and expand your knowledge of prophecy in ways unmatched by other books. Among the notable features are...

- More than 500 easy-to-read pages of prophetic commentary
- Useful charts, diagrams, and time lines that enhance clarity
- Simple format for easy referencing
- Helpful word definitions for greater understanding
- Special attention to passages that are particularly difficult or important

Assembled by bestselling prophecy teachers Tim LaHaye and Ed Hindson and associate editor Wayne A. Brindle, this volume brings together many decades of highly qualified expertise on Bible prophecy.

KNOWING AND LOVING THE BIBLE
Face-to-Face with God in His Word
Catherine Martin

Is it time for you to step out of the routine and enter an exciting new romance with God through His love letter to you? Join Catherine Martin on a 30-day journey to a heart-to-heart relationship with God in the Bible. As you walk with her through these interactive, devotional chapters, you will...

- refresh your passion for Christ through exciting quiet times with God
- realize the Bible's reliability as truth, authority for your belief, and secure foundation for your life
- renew your mission as God's Word works in your own life and through you to touch others

You'll enjoy a deeper, life-changing relationship with God and His Word as you are *Knowing and Loving the Bible.*

To read a sample chapters of these and other Harvest House books,
go to ***www.harvesthousepublishers.com***

Growing in the Christian Faith

CLASSIC CHRISTIANITY
Life's Too Short to Miss the Real Thing
Bob George

If you're feeling bogged down, tied up, or burnt out, maybe you're missing part of the picture. Bob George cuts straight to the heart of the issues that cause so many believers to start out in excited enthusiasm only to end up merely going through the motions of their life as Christians.

Drawing on his own struggles and years of teaching and counseling experience, Bob shows you the way back to the life Jesus provided for you when He set you free from the bondage of the law and points you to the newness of life lived in His Spirit.

> *"Classic Christianity is a real challenge for the believer to return to biblical Christianity. I have underlined paragraph after paragraph which were especially meaningful to me."*

> BILL BRIGHT
> Founder, Campus Crusade for Christ

BECOMING WHO GOD INTENDED
A New Picture for Your Past • A Healthy Way of Managing Your Emotions • A Fresh Perspective on Relationships
David Eckman

Whether you realize it or not, your imagination is filled with *pictures* of reality. The Bible indicates these pictures reveal your true "heart beliefs"—the beliefs that actually shape your everyday feelings and reactions.

David Eckman compassionately shows you how to allow God's Spirit to build new, *biblical* pictures in your heart and imagination. As you do this, you will be able to experience the life God the Father has always intended for you.

> *"I strongly urge you to get Becoming Who God Intended and put it to work in your life."*

> JOSH McDOWELL

To read a sample chapters of these and other Harvest House books,
go to **www.harvesthousepublishers.com**